BOOKKEEPING

THIRD EDITION

Wallace W. Kravitz
Former Business Education Chairman
Mineola High School
Mineola, New York

BARRON'S

All inquiries should be addressed to:
Barron's Educational Series, Inc.
250 Wireless Boulevard
Hauppauge, NY 11788
http://www.barronseduc.com

Library of Congress Catalog Card No. 99-17245

ISBN-13: 978-0-7641-1079-5
ISBN-10: 0-7641-1079-9

Library of Congress Cataloging-in-Publication Data
    Kravitz, Wallace W.
        Bookkeeping the easy way / Wallace W. Kravitz. — 3rd ed.
            p.   cm.
        ISBN 0-7641-1079-9
        1. Bookkeeping.   I. Title.
    HF5635.K87   1999
    657'.2—dc21   99-17245
                                                    CIP

PRINTED IN THE UNITED STATES OF AMERICA
19 18 17 16 15 14 13 12 11

CONTENTS

Preface   vii

CYCLE ONE   A PERSONAL/SERVICE-TYPE BUSINESS

Chapter 1 Assets, Liabilities, and Owner's Equity   3
Definition of Assets   3
Examples of Assets—Personal and Business   3
Definition of Liabilities   4
Examples of Liabilities—Personal and Business   4
Definition of Owner's Equity   5
Examples of Owner's Equity   5
The Fundamental Bookkeeping Equation:
   Assets = Liabilities + Owner's Equity   5
Variations of the Fundamental Equation   6

Chapter 2 Business Transactions and Changes in the
             Fundamental Bookkeeping Equation   9
Transactions Increasing Accounts   10
Transactions Decreasing Accounts   10
Transactions That Increase and Decrease Accounts   11

Chapter 3 The Balance Sheet   15
Purpose, Form, and Content   15
Fundamental Bookkeeping Equation   16
Changes in Owner's Equity   17

Chapter 4 The Ledger   23
"T" Form of Accounts—Ruled Forms, Debit and Credit   23
Opening Account Balances   24
Rules for Increases/Decreases in Assets, Liabilities, and Owner's Equity   24
Proving the Equality of Debits and Credits   25

Chapter 5 Owner's Equity Accounts   31
Revenue Accounts for Income Earned   31
Expenses   31
Net Income/Net Loss   31
Effect of Revenue/Expenses on Owner's Equity   32
Owner's Drawing Account   32
Effect of Withdrawal on Owner's Equity   33

Chapter 6 Two-Column General Journal   **39**
   Book of Original Entry   39
   Source Documents   40
   Journalizing   42

Chapter 7 Posting the General Journal   **45**
   Posting Procedure   45
      Journal to Ledger   46
      Cross Referencing   47
   Trial Balance   47

Chapter 8 The Trial Balance and Work Sheet   **55**
   Locating Errors   55
   Errors That the Trial Balance Does Not Reveal   56
   The Six-Column Work Sheet   56

Chapter 9 Financial Statements   **63**
   Income Statement—Form and Content   63
   Capital Statement   64
   Balance Sheet—Form and Content   66

Chapter 10 Closing the Ledger   **73**
   Revenue and Expense Summary   73
   Accounts Closed/Accounts Open—Ruling, Balancing   76

Chapter 11 Cash Systems, Checking Accounts   **91**
   Opening a Checking Account   91
   Endorsing Checks   91
   Making Deposits   92
   Drawing Checks   93
   The Bank Statement   94
   Reconciling Check Stub Balance and Bank Statement   94
   Two-Column Cashbook   95

Chapter 12 The Petty Cash Fund   **101**
   Purpose of the Fund   101
   Establishing the Fund   101
   Making Disbursements   102
   Proving Petty Cash   103
   Replenishing the Fund   103

Cycle One Examination   **109**

CYCLE TWO   A MERCHANDISING BUSINESS

Chapter 13   Purchases of Merchandise   **119**
Purchasing on Account—Accounts Payable   119
Purchases Journal   119
Posting Creditors' Accounts   120
Summarizing the Purchases Journal   120
Schedule of Accounts Payable   122

Chapter 14   Cash Disbursements Journal   **129**
Columnar Journal—Special Columns   129
Summarizing the Journal   130
Schedule of Accounts Payable   132
Source Document for Cash Disbursement   133

Chapter 15   Sales of Merchandise   **137**
Sales on Account   137
Sales Journal and Accounts Receivable Ledger   137
Source Documents for Sales Journal Entries   138
Posting and Summarizing the Sales Journal   138
Schedule of Accounts Receivable   140

Chapter 16   Cash Receipts Journal   **147**
Purpose of Cash Receipts Journal   147
Posting to Accounts   148
Summarizing the Cash Receipts Journal   148
Schedule of Accounts Receivable   151
Expanding the Journal   151
Source Documents for Cash Receipts   152

Chapter 17   General Journal, Four-Column Format   **159**
Sales Returns and Allowances, and Purchases Returns and Allowances   159
Source Documents   160
Correcting Errors in Ledger Postings   161
Statement of Account   162

Chapter 18   Eight-Column Work Sheet   **171**
Trial Balance   171
Adjusting Entries   171
  Merchandise Inventory   172
  Supplies   172
  Other Prepaid Expenses   172
Extending Updated Balances   172
Determining Net Income or Net Loss   172

Chapter 19   Financial Statements   **183**
Income Statement   184
Capital Statement   185
Balance Sheet   187

Chapter 20   Adjusting and Closing the General Ledger   **197**
Adjusting Accounts   197
Closing Accounts   199
Post-Closing Trial Balance   201

Chapter 21   Using a Combination Journal   **207**
Combination Journal for Personal Use   207
Combination Journal for Business Use   208
Computer Spreadsheets   210

Cycle Two Examination   **217**

Answers   **231**
Index   **326**

PREFACE

Bookkeeping the Easy Way presents a simplified step-by-step approach to learning bookkeeping/accounting principles and practices. In the late 1990s, the Ohio Business Institute studied the effects of a knowledge of bookkeeping on 5,000 firms. It found that 70 percent of successful owners understood bookkeeping procedures, while only 10 percent of failed business owners shared that understanding. This indicates that a knowledge of the fundamentals of bookkeeping is essential to the success of small businesses.

Understanding basic bookkeeping procedures is vital to developing an understanding of more advanced accounting theory and practice. Therefore, mastering the concepts of double-entry bookkeeping is a prerequisite to any further study.

This text is designed to be used in a variety of ways, depending on the need of the learner.

(1) Those who wish to study independently, at their own pace, will find this presentation clear and concise, without distractions.

(2) Those enrolled in adult education or continuing education courses will find that this text is designed for a relaxed, successful learning experience.

(3) Those who wish to study this subject in a one-semester course will find this work ideally arranged to coincide with most school half-year time schedules.

(4) Those who are having difficulty in grasping the fundamentals in a traditional introductory course in bookkeeping or accounting will find the text ideal for review or for remedial study.

Bookkeeping the Easy Way presents basic material for the individual, family, or sole proprietorship—a business owned by one person, typical of many business organizations. With improved bookkeeping skills, each individual, family, or business will gain a better command of available resources and help in planning a more profitable future.

Each chapter introduces one or two basic concepts of bookkeeping/accounting. Succeeding chapters build on the work that is covered in the preceding chapters. None can be omitted, nor should the order be changed. At the end of each chapter, students will find questions and problems, as well as analytical situations designed to explain not only the "how" but also—and equally important—the "why" of bookkeeping practices. These situations relate book learning to the business world. Including this work will result in a better understanding of legal obligations, a greater awareness of the private enterprise system, and, for learners, a career exploration experience.

I would like to acknowledge the invaluable and inspirational aid of my wife, Mollie S. Kravitz, in helping with editorial work, as well as the typing of the original manuscript.

WALLACE W. KRAVITZ

CYCLE ONE
A Personal/Service-Type Business

CHAPTER 1

ASSETS, LIABILITIES, AND OWNER'S EQUITY

The fundamental elements of all bookkeeping systems deal with keeping records for changes that occur in ASSETS, LIABILITIES, and OWNER'S EQUITY.

Definition of Assets

ASSETS are all things of value owned by an individual or business. Personal assets may include cash on hand, as well as savings and checking accounts, an automobile, and a home. Business assets may include similar items, as well as amounts due from customers—ACCOUNTS RECEIVABLE—and a building owned, not rented.

Examples of Assets—Personal and Business

A high school student's personal assets might include the following:

> Cash on hand and in a savings account
> Clothing
> Sporting equipment
> Jewelry
> Bicycle

A family's personal assets might include the following:

Cash on hand, savings, and checking account
Home owned, not rented
Furniture and furnishings
Investments in stocks, bonds, and/or land

The assets of a small service-type business might include the following:

Cash on hand and in checking accounts
Building owned, not rented
Equipment
Supplies
Delivery truck

Consider the following list of assets used by the Evergreen Landscaping Service, a company owned by Thomas Morales, the proprietor:

Cash	$ 1,450
Truck	11,000
Haulaway Trailer	1,500
Customers' Accounts	3,600
Equipment	3,320
Office Furniture	750
Supplies	645
Total Assets	$22,265

Customers' accounts, the amounts due to be collected in a short time, are assets because they represent amounts that will be turned into cash as they are received. These are ACCOUNTS RECEIVABLE, and will be referred to by that term in this text.

Definition of Liabilities

LIABILITIES are the debts owed by an individual or business. Personal liabilities may include unpaid charge account balances, as well as amounts owed on a home and/or automobile loan. Business liabilities may include similar items: amounts owed, or ACCOUNTS PAYABLE.

Examples of Liabilities—Personal and Business

A high school student's personal liabilities might include the following:

Loan from parents to purchase car
Balance owed on school yearbook or class ring

A family's personal liabilities might include the following:

Balance owed on home mortgage
Balance owed on installment purchases
Unpaid household bills—gas, electric, telephone

Consider the following list of liabilities owed by the Evergreen Landscaping Service:

Truck Loan, Island National Bank	$6,200
Supplies Bought on Account	345
Equipment Bought on Account	1,000
Total Liabilities	$7,545

Definition of Owner's Equity

OWNER'S EQUITY is the net worth or capital of an individual or business. It is the amount of assets remaining after all liabilities are paid. To determine an individual's or family's owner's equity, total all assets, then deduct all liabilities. The difference is the owner's equity.

Examples of Owner's Equity

If a high school student's assets total $2,675, and liabilities total $450, the student's owner's equity equals $2,225:

Total Assets	$2,675
Less Total Liabilities	450
Owner's Equity, Net Worth, or Capital	$2,225

If a family's assets total $105,700, and liabilities total $44,960, the family's owner's equity equals $60,740:

Total Assets	$105,700
Less Total Liabilities	44,960
Owner's Equity, Net Worth, or Capital	$ 60,740

To determine Thomas Morales's owner's equity in the Evergreen Landscaping Service, follow the same calculation:

Total Assets	$22,265
Less Total Liabilities	7,545
Owner's Equity, Net Worth, or Capital	$14,720

Owner's equity is frequently referred to as NET WORTH, CAPITAL, or PROPRIETORSHIP. Individuals, however, usually refer to their owner's equity as "net worth" or "capital." A business might use all of these terms; however, this text will use most frequently OWNER'S EQUITY and CAPITAL.

The Fundamental Bookkeeping Equation

The relationship among the three elements of bookkeeping—assets, liabilities, and owner's equity—may be stated as follows:

ASSETS	=	LIABILITIES	+	OWNER'S EQUITY

Consider these in the following way:

ASSETS (everything of value *owned*)	LIABILITIES (all debts *owed*) plus OWNER'S EQUITY

An example of these three elements as they apply to Thomas Morales's truck is:

Truck

Original cost	$11,000	Balance owed to bank and	$ 6,200
		Morales's equity in truck	4,800
Total	$11,000	Total	$11,000

These three elements of bookkeeping may be stated as an equation:

$$\text{Assets} = \text{Liabilities} + \text{Owner's Equity}$$
$$\$11,000 = \$6,200 + \$4,800$$

or, simply,

$$A = L + OE$$

If owner's equity is referred to as capital, the equation is restated as

$$A = L + C$$

Variations of the Fundamental Equation

When any two of the fundamental elements are known, the third can be found. If assets total $10,000 and liabilities total $4,000, owner's equity equals $6,000. Assets minus liabilities equal owner's equity, or

$$A - L = OE$$

If assets total $12,835 and owner's equity totals $7,000, liabilities equal $5,835. It is also true that assets minus owner's equity equal liabilities, or

$$A - OE = L$$

If liabilities total $16,000 and owner's equity totals $22,900, assets equal $38,900. It is also true that liabilities plus owner's equity equal assets. This reverses the sides of the fundamental bookkeeping equation:

$$L + OE = A$$

These examples illustrate the variations of the fundamental bookkeeping/accounting equation: $A = L + OE$. All of these are true statements, whether for an individual, a family, or a business.

YOU SHOULD REMEMBER

All assets are subject to *two* claims—those to whom debts are owed, and those of the owner(s).

In listing claims against assets, claims of those to whom debts are owed *always* come before claims of the owner(s).

KNOW YOUR VOCABULARY

Use each of the following words or terms in a statement relating to bookkeeping/accounting:

Accounts payable	Liabilities
Accounts receivable	Net worth
Asset(s)	Owner's equity
Capital	Proprietorship

QUESTIONS

Classify each of the following items by writing *Asset*, *Liability*, or *Owner's Equity* in the column at the right:

Item	Classification
Example: Cash on hand	Asset
1. Automobile	1. Asset
2. Balance owed on loan	2. Liability
3. Gerald Smith's capital	3. O.E.
4. Supplies on hand	4.
5. Personal clothes	5.
6. Charge account balances	6.
7. One's net worth	7.
8. Bank loan	8.
9. Allison Paris, account receivable	9.
10. Panos & George, account payable	10.

PROBLEMS

1-1 Complete each of the fundamental bookkeeping equations so that each will be a true statement.

	Assets	= Liabilities	+ Owner's Equity
Example:	$ 10,500	$ 4,000	?($6,500)
1.	$ 15,750	$ 4,250	?
2.	24,900	?	$ 21,200
3.	?	5,000	12,500
4.	24,742.50	8,655.40	?
5.	31,070.92	?	22,501.85
6.	175,882.35	68,951.39	?
7.	?	58,042.78	152,775.56
8.	229,953.11	?	189,638.63
9.	686,020.49	114,362.74	?
10.	?	330,172.41	786,570.87

THINK IT OVER

Jack Calhoun's assets total $22,500; his liabilities total $7,500.

Mary Winslow's assets total $30,000; her owner's equity totals $25,000.

Which of these two individuals has a stronger "financial situation" or is better able to pay all debts owed? What other information might be needed in order to give a more definite answer?

WORDS TO REMEMBER
Account   *each specific item* listed as either an asset, a liability, or an owner's equity
Business Transaction   something that occurs, causing at least *two changes in accounts*
Investment   a transaction made by an owner that *directly increases capital*, owner's equity

CHAPTER

BUSINESS TRANSACTIONS AND CHANGES IN THE FUNDAMENTAL BOOKKEEPING EQUATION

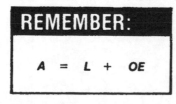

A BUSINESS TRANSACTION always results in at least two changes in the fundamental bookkeeping equation. Since both sides of this equation must be equal, a transaction that changes total assets must also change either total liabilities or total owner's equity.

Each item listed as either an asset, a liability, or an owner's equity is referred to as an ACCOUNT and is given a title—the Cash account, Truck account, Island National Bank account, Thomas Morales's Capital account, and so on.

9

Transactions Increasing Accounts

Assume that Morales, the owner of the Evergreen Landscaping Service, borrows $2,500 cash from the Island National Bank. The original bookkeeping equation showed:

$$\text{Assets} = \text{Liabilities} + \text{Owner's Equity}$$
$$\$22,265 = \$7,545 + \$14,720$$

With the cash borrowed, the equation changes because the asset account, Cash, increases and the liability account, Island National Bank, increases:

Assets	=	Liabilities	+	Owner's Equity
$22,265		$ 7,545		$14,720
+ 2,500		+ 2,500		---
$24,765 =		$10,045	+	$14,720

     This transaction resulted in two account increases; total assets increased and total liabilities increased.

     Assume that Morales takes $5,000 of his personal cash to make an additional INVESTMENT in this business. The equation now shows an increase in the Cash account and an increase in Thomas Morales's Capital account:

Assets	=	Liabilities	+	Owner's Equity
$24,765		$10,045		$14,720
+ 5,000		---		+ 5,000
$29,765 =		$10,045	+	$19,720

     This transaction also resulted in two account increases; total assets increased and total owner's equity increased.

Transactions Decreasing Accounts

Assume that Morales pays $1,000 cash to the Island National Bank as part payment on the truck loan. The equation now shows a decrease in the Cash account and a decrease in the Island National Bank account:

Assets	=	Liabilities	+	Owner's Equity
$29,765		$10,045		$19,720
− 1,000		− 1,000		---
$28,765 =		$ 9,045	+	$19,720

     This transaction resulted in two account decreases; total assets decreased and total liabilities decreased.

Transactions That Increase and Decrease Accounts

Some transactions may change two accounts on the *same side* of the equation without changing any totals. Assume that Morales bought $100 worth of supplies, paying cash for them. His Cash account decreased by $100, while his Supplies account increased by $100, with no change in total assets.

All transactions cause two (or more, as will be shown later) changes in accounts. These changes may result in

(1) two increases,
(2) two decreases, or
(3) one increase and one decrease.

When transactions result in two account increases or two account decreases, totals on both sides of the fundamental equation change:

	A	=	L	+ OE	
(1)	$10,000		$2,000	$8,000	
	+ 1,500		+ 1,500	---	(two increases)
	$11,500	=	$3,500	+ $8,000	
(2)	- 500		- 500	---	(two decreases)
	$11,000	=	$3,000	+ $8,000	
(3)	+ 350				(one increase,
	$11,350				
	- 350				one decrease)
	$11,000	=	$3,000	+ $8,000	

YOU SHOULD REMEMBER

All transactions cause at least two changes in accounts. Either:
—two accounts increase, or
—two accounts decrease, or
—one account increases, as one account decreases.

KNOW YOUR VOCABULARY

Use each of the following words or terms in a statement relating to bookkeeping/accounting:

Account   Investment

Business transaction

QUESTIONS

Classify each of the following accounts as an asset, liability, or owner's equity. Indicate on which side of the fundamental equation—left or right—each account would appear.

	Account	Classification	Side
Example:	Cash (checking account)	Asset	Left
1.	Delivery truck	1.	
2.	Account payable, J. Glover	2.	
3.	Paul Jacob, Capital	3.	
4.	Account receivable, K. Day	4.	
5.	Balance due J. C. Woolco	5.	
6.	Customer's account balance	6.	
7.	Equipment	7.	
8.	Balance owed on truck	8.	
9.	Stamp collection	9.	
10.	Proprietor's claim	10.	

PROBLEMS

2–1   Write the words *Increase* or *Decrease*, or both words, or *None*, to show any change(s) in TOTAL assets, liabilities, and owner's equity for each of the following transactions:

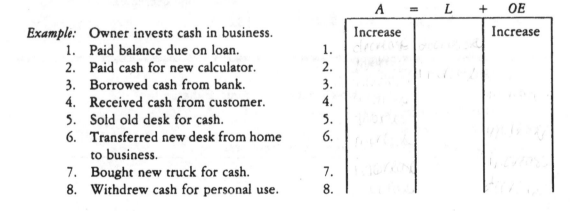

		A =	L +	OE
Example:	Owner invests cash in business.	Increase		Increase
1.	Paid balance due on loan.	1.		
2.	Paid cash for new calculator.	2.		
3.	Borrowed cash from bank.	3.		
4.	Received cash from customer.	4.		
5.	Sold old desk for cash.	5.		
6.	Transferred new desk from home to business.	6.		
7.	Bought new truck for cash.	7.		
8.	Withdrew cash for personal use.	8.		

2–2   For each of the following business transactions, add or subtract the amounts to update total assets, liabilities, and owner's equity:

Example: Karen Glaser, owner, invested $15,000 in a dry-cleaning business.

1. Bought $2,000 worth of <u>equipment</u>, paying <u>cash</u>.
2. Borrowed $7,500 from River National Bank.
3. Bought $450 worth of supplies, paying cash.
4. Bought a truck for $12,000, paying cash.
5. Made a $1,500 payment on loan to River National Bank.

	A	=	L	+	OE
Start with	$14,250		$4,250		$10,000
Example:	+ 15,000		---		+ 15,000
	$29,250		$4,250		$25,000
1.					
2.					
3.					
4.					
5.					

THINK IT OVER

Kenneth Lee operates a computer software business. He has a $16,000 cash balance. New equipment needed to develop the latest type of programs for his clients will cost $20,000. This will require some borrowing in order to pay for it. Lee wants to use $6,000 of cash from his business, arranging a bank loan for the balance.

What will be the amount of the loan? What changes will occur in the fundamental bookkeeping equation? Does Lee have any other choice in deciding how to buy this equipment?

CHAPTER 3

THE BALANCE SHEET

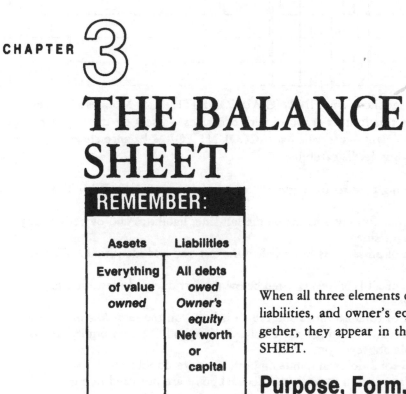

REMEMBER:

Assets	Liabilities
Everything of value owned	All debts owed Owner's equity Net worth or capital

When all three elements of bookkeeping—assets, liabilities, and owner's equity—are examined together, they appear in the form of a BALANCE SHEET.

Purpose, Form, and Content

A balance sheet is a financial statement or business form that lists, as of a certain date, all assets owned and all claims against these assets. These claims are held by CREDITORS, to whom money is owed, and the owners themselves, in the form of their owner's equity. When arranged in this way, it is easy to see that the fundamental bookkeeping equation again holds true:

$$A = L + OE$$

A bookkeeper or accounting clerk prepared a balance sheet for Thomas Morales's business on September 30 of the current year.

Evergreen Landscaping Service
Balance Sheet
September 30, 200—

Assets			Liabilities		
Cash	7850	00	Gardners Supply Co.	345	00
Truck	11000	00	Equipment Mfg. Corp.	1000	00
Haulaway Trailer	1500	00	Island National Bank	7700	00
Accounts Receivable	3600	00	Total Liabilities	9045	00
Equipment	3320	00	Owner's Equity		
Office Furniture	750	00	Thomas Morales, Capital	19720	00
Supplies	745	00	Total Liabilities &		
Total Assets	28765	00	Owner's Equity	28765	00

This balance sheet shows the FINANCIAL CONDITION of Morales's business on the specified date. When this form is arranged with two sides—assets on the left, liabilities and owner's equity on the right—it is called an ACCOUNT FORM balance sheet.

Note the following details carefully:

(1) The heading consists of "answers" to the questions WHO, WHAT, and WHEN.

(2) The account form lists assets on the left side, liabilities and owner's equity on the right side.

(3) The sum of all assets is listed below the last one and identified as "Total Assets."

(4) The sum of all liabilities is listed below the last one and identified as "Total Liabilities."

(5) The sum of total liabilities and capital is listed on the *same line level* as the total assets and identified as "Total Liabilities and Owner's Equity" or with acceptable abbreviations.

(6) The final total dollar amounts on both sides are double ruled.

(7) The dollar symbol, comma, and decimal point are not used in any bookkeeping form or statement.

(Single ruled lines indicate an addition or subtraction. Double ruled lines indicate the end of the work.)

Fundamental Bookkeeping Equation

The fundamental bookkeeping equation is clearly seen on each balance sheet. The dollar value of total assets on the left side equals the dollar value of the creditors' claims (liabilities) plus capital (owner's equity) on the right side.

As shown earlier, each business transaction changes the dollar values of two items listed on the balance sheet. Therefore, a balance sheet showing a new financial condition, or picture, could be developed after each transaction. However, hundreds of transactions may occur daily, weekly, or monthly, making it impractical to do this so often. Usually financial statements are prepared at the end of a definite period of time—the FISCAL PERIOD. This can be monthly, quarterly, semimonthly, or annually. A 12-month fiscal period, however, need not coincide with the 12 calendar months of the year. A fiscal year could run from July 1 to the following June 30, or from April 1 to the following March 31.

Changes in Owner's Equity

Many of the transactions that occur during a fiscal period result in changes in owner's equity. These changes will eventually show up as increases or decreases in the owner's capital account. The exact amount of change can be determined by completing the fundamental bookkeeping equation. In completing the balance sheet for the Evergreen Landscaping Service, Morales's capital could have been calculated by subtracting total liabilities from total assets:

$$\$28,765 - \$9,045 = \$19,720 \quad \text{or} \quad A - L = OE$$

YOU SHOULD REMEMBER

Three items in a statement heading explain WHO, WHAT, and WHEN.
Assets *equal liabilities plus owner's equity*, or
Assets *minus liabilities equal owner's equity*.

KNOW YOUR VOCABULARY

Use each of the following words or terms in a statement relating to bookkeeping/accounting:

Account form	Creditor
Balance sheet	Financial condition
Claims against assets	Fiscal period

QUESTIONS

1. What three questions are answered in the heading of a balance sheet?
2. How many days are there in each month?
3. What is the last day of a quarterly fiscal period beginning on July 1? On January 1? On October 1?
4. What determines that a balance sheet is "in balance"?
5. How can owner's equity be found if total assets and total liabilities are known?
6. Write the following amounts in a ruled form, arranged for addition, and find the total: $7,650; $19,560; $835; $2,750; $182.

PROBLEMS

3–1 Identify each of the following items by writing *Asset*, *Liability*, or *Owner's Equity* in the column at the right:

Item	Classification
Example: Cash on hand	Asset
1. Automobile	1.
2. Balance owed on time purchase	2.
3. Cash in bank	3.
4. Owner's claim against assets	4.
5. Supplies for business use	5.
6. Personal clothing	6.
7. Unpaid balance on charge account	7.
8. Creditor's claim against assets	8.
9. Net worth	9.
10. Money borrowed	10.

3–2 Name the section of a balance sheet—Assets, Liabilities, or Owner's Equity—in which each of the following items should be located:

	Balance Sheet	
	Left Side	Right Side
Example: Machinery	Asset	
1. Supplies	1.	
2. Amounts owed to creditors	2.	
3. Tools	3.	
4. Bank loan	4.	
5. Office equipment	5.	
6. Checking account balance	6.	
7. Amount due from customer	7.	
8. Owner's financial claim	8.	
9. Furniture	9.	
10. Capital	10.	

3–3 On August 31 of the current year, the following assets and liabilities were listed by Maria Lopez, owner of Maria's Beauty Salon:

Assets:	Cash	$1,750
	Furniture and Fixtures	8,900
	Beauty Supplies	600
Liabilities:	Regal Laundry	275
	Marvelle Corp.	2,500

Prepare a balance sheet for Maria's Beauty Salon on the date indicated. Use the form in this chapter (page 16) for your model.

3–4 Paul Whitefeather, an accountant, has the following business assets and liabilities:

Assets:	Cash	$ 750
	Office Machines	3,500
	Furniture and Fixtures	3,150
	Office Supplies	285
Liabilities:	Kearney Evans Co.	650
	Cal's Stationery Co.	175

Prepare a balance sheet for Paul Whitefeather, dated September 30 of the current year.

3–5 The Dramatic Society of your local school has the following assets and liabilities on October 31 of the current year:

Assets:	Cash	$ 60.00
	Scenery	750.00
	Costumes	480.00
	Make-up Supplies	64.50
	Scripts	35.00
Liabilities:	E. Exter (seamstress)	75.00
	Field Lumber Co.	100.00
	Rex Drugstore	22.75

Prepare a balance sheet for the Dramatic Society on the date indicated. Indicate the owner's equity as Dramatic Society, Capital.

3–6 Lady Cake Bake Shoppe reports the following assets and liabilities on July 31 of the current year:

Assets:	Cash	$ 1,250.00
	Building	68,500.00
	Bakery Equipment	26,200.00
	Furniture and Fixtures	6,300.00
	Supplies	1,800.00
Liabilities:	Mortgage Loan Owed to Madison Bank	23,575.00
	Bakery Supplies Co.	350.00
	Baking Equipment Co.	5,000.00

Prepare a balance sheet for the Lady Cake Bake Shoppe on the date indicated. Gustave Mueller is the owner.

THINK IT OVER

Consider your own personal financial position. Prepare a list of all the assets you own. Place an estimated (or known) value on each. Do you owe any debts? What is your net worth or capital? Prepare your own balance sheet, complete with heading.

Do the same for your family as a whole. Ask other members of the family for estimated values to place on all assets owned and all debts owed, if you are not certain of the amounts.

CHAPTER

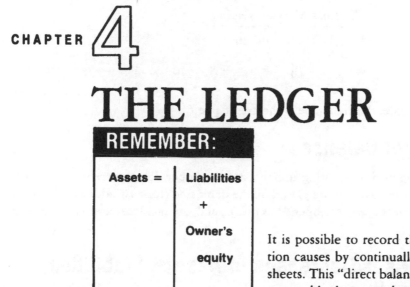

THE LEDGER

REMEMBER:

Assets =	Liabilities
	+
	Owner's
	equity

It is possible to record the changes each transaction causes by continually preparing new balance sheets. This "direct balance sheet" approach is not reasonable, however, because of the frequency of transactions and the amount of bookkeeping work involved. Furthermore, this does not provide a record that shows *how* each account changes; all that is shown is the final total in each account.

"T" Form of Accounts—Ruled Forms, Debit and Credit

To keep track of transactions and changes as they occur, a system of ACCOUNTS is used. The account form is used to record the changes that result in increases and decreases. Each item listed on a balance sheet is recorded in a separate account form. All accounts, taken together as one group, are called a LEDGER. The ruling for an account originates from the account form of a balance sheet: assets listed on the left side, liabilities and owner's equity on the right side.

Examine the Evergreen Landscaping Service's cash account, starting with an opening BALANCE of $1,450. (See page 4.) This account has a title: Cash. The left side of an account is the DEBIT side; the right side of an account is the CREDIT side.

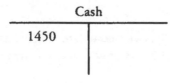

Cash

1450

Each of the *assets* listed on page 4 would appear in the same way—as *debit balances*. Notice that they are in the form of an enlarged "T" and therefore are called T-ACCOUNTS.

Examine the T-account for Evergreen Landscaping Service's liability owed to Island National Bank. (See page 5.) This account has a title: Island National Bank. The left side is the debit side; the right side is the credit side.

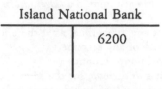

Island National Bank

	6200

Each of the *liabilities* listed on page 5 would appear in the same way—as a *credit balance*.

Examine Morales's owner's equity account: Thomas Morales, Capital. The account has a title: Thomas Morales, Capital.

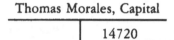

Thomas Morales, Capital

	14720

The left side is the debit side; the right side is the credit side.

Opening Account Balances

Each account balance is opened by entering amounts on the proper debit or credit side. *Assets* are opened as *debits*, and any increases are placed on the debit side (for easy addition to obtain a total). *Liabilities* and *owner's equity* are opened as *credits*, and any increases are placed on the credit side.

Rules for Increases/Decreases in Assets, Liabilities, and Owner's Equity

The accepted bookkeeping/accounting abbreviations for debit and credit are Dr. and Cr., or dr. and cr. These are used in various business forms. Written statements will, however, use the complete words. Note carefully the following statements:

(1) *Assets* are accounts that appear on the left-hand side of a balance sheet and will show *increases* by *debits*.
(2) *Liabilities* are accounts that appear on the right-hand side of a balance sheet and will show *increases* by *credits*.
(3) *Owner's equity* (*capital*) appears on the right-hand side of a balance sheet and will show *increases* by *credits*.

Assets		Liabilities		Owner's Equity	
Dr.	Cr.	Dr.	Cr.	Dr.	Cr.
+			+		+

Evergreen Landscaping Service's complete ledger has been opened from the account information listed on pages 4 and 5. Asset accounts are arranged first, followed by liabilities and owner's equity accounts.

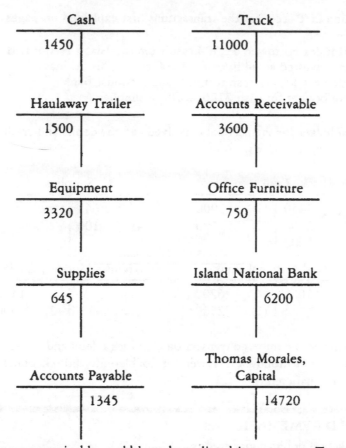

Cash		Truck	
1450		11000	

Haulaway Trailer		Accounts Receivable	
1500		3600	

Equipment		Office Furniture	
3320		750	

Supplies		Island National Bank	
645			6200

Accounts Payable		Thomas Morales, Capital	
	1345		14720

Each account receivable could have been listed in a separate T-account to show the individual amount *due from each customer*. In the same way, each account payable could have been listed in a separate T-account to show the individual amount *owed to each creditor*. One creditor was listed in a separate account—Island National Bank. It could have been combined with the other accounts payable for one total amount owed—$7,545.

Because assets increase by debits, it follows that any *asset decreases* are recorded as *credits*. Because liabilities and owner's equity increase by credits, it follows that any *liability* and *owner's equity decreases* are recorded as *debits*. The three T-accounts shown on page 24 can now be completed to illustrate the RULES OF DEBITS AND CREDITS:

(1) Assets increase by debits and decrease by credits.
(2) Liabilities increase by credits and decrease by debits.
(3) Owner's equity increases by a credit and decreases by a debit.

Assets		Liabilities		Owner's Equity	
Dr.	Cr.	Dr.	Cr.	Dr.	Cr.
+	−	−	+	−	+

Proving the Equality of Debits and Credits

As transactions occur, changes are recorded in accounts. For every transaction, at least one account will be debited and one will be credited. Even though each transaction changes two or more account balances, the fundamental bookkeeping/accounting equation will always be in balance: $A = L + OE$. This is the explanation of the theory of DOUBLE-ENTRY BOOKKEEPING: for every transaction **debits always equal credits.**

Reexamine in T-accounts the transactions first explained on pages 10 and 11:

   (1) Morales borrowed $2,500 cash from the Island National Bank.
   (2) He invested an additional $5,000 cash in his business.
   (3) He paid $1,000 cash to the Island National Bank.
   (4) He bought for cash $100 worth of supplies.

A *partial* ledger for the accounts involved and the debits and credits for (1), (2), (3), and (4) above is shown as follows:

Cash					Supplies	
	1450	(3)	1000		645	
(1)	2500	(4)	100	(4)	100	
(2)	5000					

Island National Bank					Thomas Morales, Capital	
(3)	1000		6200			14720
		(1)	2500		(2)	5000

Notice that each numbered transaction identifies a debit and a credit of equal amount. This is helpful in order to follow the system of double-entry bookkeeping. For every transaction, debits must equal credits.

YOU SHOULD REMEMBER
In every transaction debits equal credits.
Assets increase by debits and decrease by credits.
Liabilities increase by credits and decrease by debits.
Owner's equity increases by credits and decreases by debits.

KNOW YOUR VOCABULARY

Use each of the following words or terms in a statement relating to bookkeeping/accounting:

Account form	Double-entry bookkeeping
Balance	Ledger
Credit (cr.)	Rules of debits and credits
Debit (dr.)	T-account

QUESTIONS

1. Which of the following statements is true?
  a) For *every* transaction, the account(s) debited equal the account(s) credited.
  b) For *every* transaction, the account(s) increased equal the account(s) decreased.
2. Explain why the incorrect statement in Question 1 is not true.
3. What would be the normal balance of any asset account?
4. On which side—debit or credit—do accounts decrease?

PROBLEMS

4-1 Emilee Suzanne listed the following account balances:

Cash	$1,245
Equipment	3,670
Supplies	430
Accounts Payable:	
L. D. Brown	400
J. C. Tucker	175

(1) Open a ledger of T-accounts for each of these accounts, including one for each creditor.

(2) Open a T-account to record Emilee Suzanne's capital, net worth, or owner's equity. Remember: $A - L = OE$.

4-2 Paul Jacobs listed the following account balances:

Cash on Hand and in Bank	$1,305
Accounts Receivable:	
D. R. Able	150
M. O. Jackson	225
V. L. Witten	85
Truck	5,750
Supplies	395
Accounts Payable:	
City Trust Company	1,250
H. & H. Manufacturing Co.	800

(1) Open a ledger of T-accounts for each account, including Jacobs's owner's equity.

(2) Prove that Assets = Liabilities + Owner's Equity.

(empty T-accounts)

4–3   Kimberley Travis completed the following transactions last week:

Example: Paid Regal Bank, $150.
(1)   Bought $75 worth of supplies for cash.
(2)   Borrowed $1,000 from Regal Bank.
(3)   Invested $2,500 cash in her business.
(4)   Bought $500 worth of equipment from Bixby Company, agreeing to pay in 30 days.

Record the debits and credits for each of the above transactions in the following partial ledger. Beginning account balances are indicated. Identify each debit and each credit by the number of the transaction.

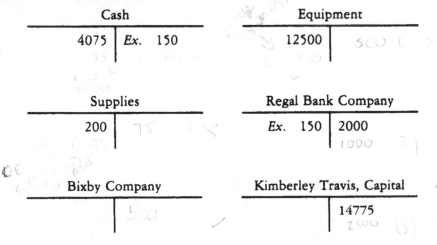

Cash		Equipment	
4075	*Ex.* 150	12500	

Supplies		Regal Bank Company	
200		*Ex.* 150	2000

Bixby Company		Kimberley Travis, Capital	
			14775

4–4   Using the transactions in Problem 4–3, indicate any increases or decreases in *total* assets, liabilities, and owner's equity.

Trans. No.	Assets	Liabilities	Owner's Equity
Example	Decrease	Decrease	
(1)			
(2)			
(3)			
(4)			

4–5 (1) Open T-accounts for Lori Luing, the owner of Luing's Answering Service, for the following balances, including her owner's equity:

Cash	$ 437.50
Accounts Receivable:	
H. L. Rhodes, MD	50.00
Mary Turner, MD	50.00
T. W. Vine, DDS	35.00
Equipment	2,650.00
Supplies	25.00
Accounts Payable:	
State Telephone Co.	215.00
Ace Electricians	65.00
Lori Luing, Capital	———— ?

(2) Complete each of the following transactions, indicating by letter the debits and credits:

    a) Received $50, the amount due, from H. L. Rhodes, MD.

    b) Paid $65, the amount owed, to Ace Electricians.

    c) Bought $75 worth of supplies, paying cash.

    d) Invested $500 cash in the business.

    e) Received $25 on account from Mary Turner, MD.

(3) Prove that Assets = Liabilities + Owner's Equity.

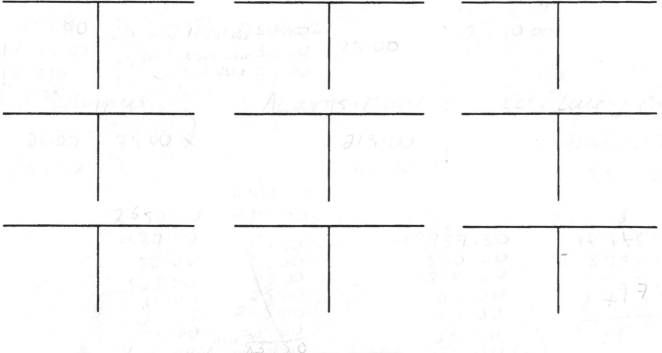

THINK IT OVER

Select any service-type business and consider the many different kinds of transactions that are carried on in any typical day. Think about the reason(s) why the owner is in business. What is his/her goal? What is the "profit motive" that keeps the owner going?

CHAPTER 5

OWNER'S EQUITY ACCOUNTS

REMEMBER:

$$A = L + OE$$

Owner's

Equity

| − | + |

Revenue Accounts for Income Earned

A business earns its income (or REVENUE) by selling merchandise and/or services. In this section of this text, all revenue will be earned by charging fees for services performed by the business. The Evergreen Landscaping Service charges each customer a fee for the work performed on a regular basis—weekly or monthly. Special jobs, such as tree removals, are also a source of revenue. The term "revenue" will refer to various fees that are earned by services rendered to the customers of a business. In each case they will be identified by the account title, including the word "income."

Expenses

Any payments made in connection with the earning of revenue are called EXPENSES. These include such items as advertising, rent, employees' salaries, and utilities (heat, light, telephone).

Net Income/Net Loss

If, during a fiscal period, the revenue earned is greater than the total expenses, the business will have a PROFIT or NET INCOME:

Revenue > Total Expenses = Net Income

If, however, expenses are greater than revenue, a NET LOSS will result:

$$\boxed{\text{Expenses} > \text{Revenue} = \text{Net Loss}}$$

(In these equations the symbol ">" means "is greater than.")

Effect of Revenue/Expenses on Owner's Equity

Whenever *revenue* is received, owner's equity is *increased*. Whenever *expenses* are paid, owner's equity is *decreased*. At the end of a fiscal period, if all revenue exceeds all expenses, the resulting net income belongs to the owner. Owner's equity will, therefore, be increased by that amount. If expenses exceed revenue, the resulting net loss is suffered by the owner. Owner's equity will, therefore, be decreased by that amount.

Assume that the Evergreen Landscaping Service earned $2,500 in fees last month, and expenses totaled $1,500 for the same period:

Revenue: Fees Income	$2,500
Expenses	1,500
Net Income	$1,000

Revenue and expense transactions will change account balances. The accounts listed on page 26 will change as follows: for the revenue earned (*a*), and for the expenses paid (*b*).

Additional accounts will be opened to record the revenue and expenses rather than recording these transactions directly in the owner's equity account. Because *revenue* increases owner's equity, it will be recorded as a *credit*. Because *expenses* decrease owner's equity, they will be recorded as a *debit*. (Expenses are combined in one T-account for this example.)

```
                Cash
         1450    |    1000
         2500    |     100
         5000    | (b) 1500
     (a) 2500    |

              Fees income
                 | (a) 2500

               Expenses
     (b) 1500    |
```

By the end of the fiscal period, the fundamental bookkeeping/accounting equation will have changed:

All Assets,	29765	Liabilities,		9045
		Owner's Equity,	19720	
		+ Net Income	1000	20720
Total Assets	29765	= Total Liab. + OE		29765

Owner's Drawing Account

At any time the owner of a business may withdraw cash for personal use, very much like a salary. WITHDRAWALS by the owner, however, are not included with other expenses. Instead, a separate account is opened for the owner's DRAWING ACCOUNT.

Effect of Withdrawal on Owner's Equity

Any *withdrawal* by the owner *decreases owner's equity*; therefore it must be recorded as a *debit*. Note the transaction to record Morales's withdrawal of $500 cash: transaction (*c*).

This transaction changes the fundamental bookkeeping equation: $500 less cash (assets) and $500 less capital (owner's equity).

Cash	
1450	1000
2500	100
5000	1500
2500	(c) 500

Thomas Morales, Drawing	
(c) 500	

Assets,	29765	Liab.,		9045
	− 500	OE,	20720	
		−	500	20220
A	29265	= L	+ OE	29265

Revenue and expenses are temporary owner's equity accounts. They change—increase and decrease—owner's equity. Compare a capital account with revenue and expense accounts:

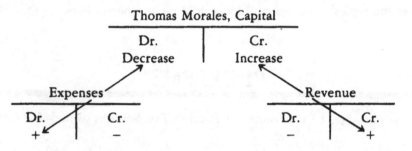

As *expenses increase* by *debits*, owner's equity decreases.
As *revenue increases* by *credits*, owner's equity increases.

When the owner has made a withdrawal during the fiscal period as well as earned a net income, owner's equity is determined as follows:

Owner's Equity		
Ruth Brown, Capital, October 1,		12 000
Net Income	800	
Less Withdrawals	650	
Net Increase in capital		150
Ruth Brown, Capital, October 31,		12 150

YOU SHOULD REMEMBER

Income *increases owner's equity*; therefore, *income accounts increase by credits*.
Expenses *decrease owner's equity*; therefore, *expense accounts increase by debits*.

KNOW YOUR VOCABULARY

Use each of the following words or terms in a statement relating to bookkeeping/accounting:

Drawing account	Profit
Expenses	Revenue
Net income	Withdrawals
Net loss	

QUESTIONS

1. What are the sources of revenue received by each of the following service businesses?
    a) A tailor   d) A lawyer
    b) A beauty salon   e) A dentist
    c) An architect   f) An accountant
2. What are the typical expenses paid by each of the businesses listed in Question 1?

PROBLEMS

5–1 (1) Open a ledger of T-accounts for Puccio's Taxi Service, owned by Frank Puccio:

Assets:	Cash	$ 562
	Taxis (2)	28,000
	Supplies	150
Liabilities:	Landia National Bank	6,400
	Wilson Garage	75
OE:	Frank Puccio, Capital	?

Open T-accounts for each of these accounts, as well:
  Frank Puccio, Drawing
  Fare Income
  Gas and Oil Expense
  Repairs Expense
  Salary Expense

(2) Record the following transactions, indicating by letter each of the debits and credits:
  a) Collected $250 in fares.
  b) Paid Landia National Bank, $100.
  c) Paid driver's salary, $200.
  d) Withdrew cash for personal use, $300.
  e) Collected $325 in fares.
  f) Paid for gasoline, $45.
  g) Paid Wilson Garage, $75.
  h) Paid for taxi repairs, $40.

(3) List the debit and credit balance of each account.
  Prove the total debits equal the total credits.

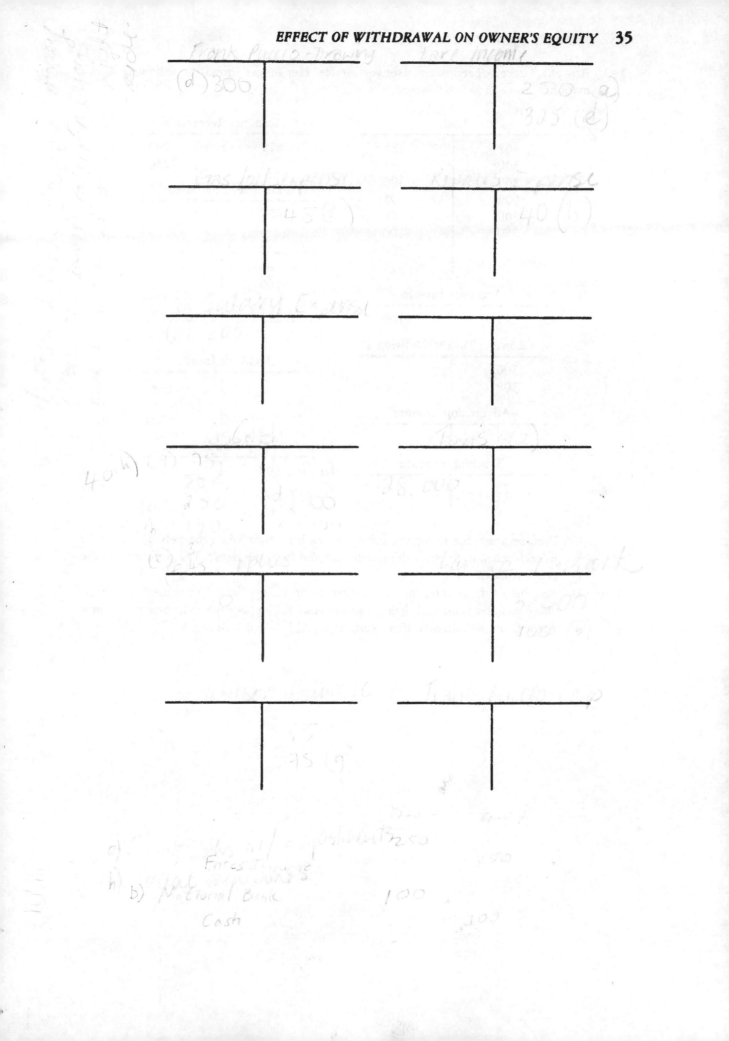

5–2 Rowena Tucker operates a messenger service. Her ledger shows the following information:

Cash			Accounts Receivable	
462	75		875	200
300	75			250
200	300		**Delivery Equipment**	
600	95		12000	
200	140			
250	100		**Supplies**	
	300		60	
	25		100	

Accounts Payable			Rowena Tucker, Capital	
25	1100			12297

Rowena Tucker, Drawing			Delivery Income	
300				300
300				600
				200

Advertising Expense			Telephone Expense	
95			140	

Trucking Expense	
75	
75	

(1) Prepare a list that shows the balance of each account. (Add the debits and credits in each account. Subtract the smaller amount from the larger. The difference is the account balance.)

(2) Prepare a balance sheet for Ms. Tucker, using today's date. Remember: A balance sheet includes assets, liabilities, and owner's equity plus any net income or less any net loss and withdrawals. (See illustration p. 33 for Ruth Brown.)

(1)

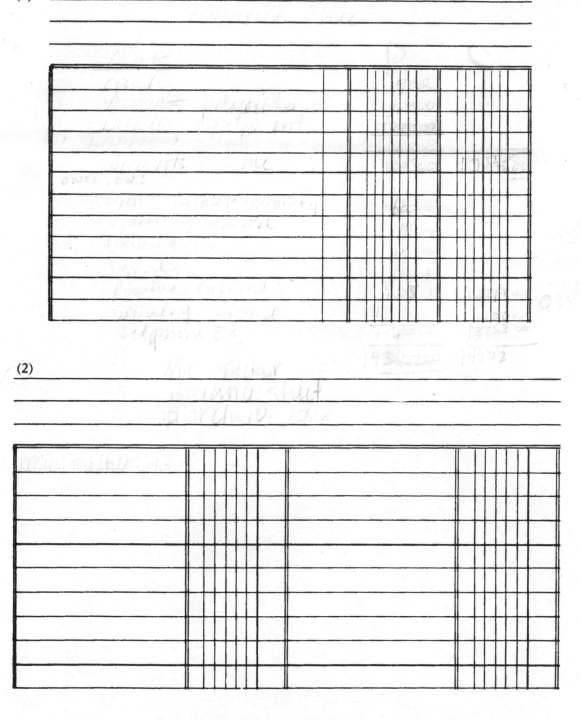

(2)

THINK IT OVER

James Lightfoot owns three sporting goods stores, each located in a suburban center near a large midwestern city. For several years he has had a net income. Last year, however, he had a small net loss. He is anxious to find the reason for this loss. Lightfoot maintains one ledger for his business. What would you recommend that he do differently, and why?

CHAPTER **6**

TWO-COLUMN GENERAL JOURNAL

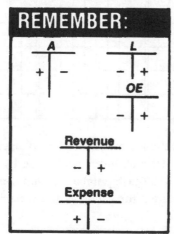

Records of business transactions can be entered directly into ledger accounts. However, DIRECT LEDGER bookkeeping can be a difficult and complicated procedure. Since each transaction involves at least one debit equal to one credit, examining one account gives only one half of the information about a transaction. If amounts are similar, finding the other half, even when numbered or lettered, may require a great deal of time. In order to tie together the debits and the credits of the same transaction, every account would have to be examined to find the matching amount.

Bookkeeping/accounting should be orderly. The direct ledger system does not give an orderly running record of all transactions day by day. If an error is made in recording—entering two debits or two credits instead of one of each, or reversing the accounts to be debited and credited, or changing the amount of a debit or credit—locating that error can become a very difficult, time-consuming process. Because there may be hundreds or more entries in a single day, week, or month, the bookkeeping clerk will have to examine each account to find the offsetting amounts in tracing an entry.

Book of Original Entry

To solve this problem, a system of JOURNALS can be used. A journal is a book of ORIGINAL ENTRY, where complete information about a transaction is first recorded. Each page is numbered; columns provide space for a complete date—year, month, day; names of accounts debited and credited; posting references (to be discussed in Chapter 7); and amount columns for debits and for credits. All entries are recorded in CHRONOLOGICAL order as they occur. All information—the date of the transaction, the accounts involved, the amount of each debit and each credit—and any needed explanation are included in this book, a general journal. It becomes the diary of the business for which it is kept.

	JOURNAL			Page 12

Date	Account Title	PR	Debit	Credit
200– Sept 4	Cash		1500 00	
	George Corbo, Capital			1500 00
	Investment			
7	Supplies		100 00	
	Cash			100 00
	Check No. 418			
10	Cash		2000 00	
	Landia National Bank			2000 00
	30-day Loan, Note No. 25			

This general journal illustrates several transactions entered in chronological order on page 12. The first one, dated September 4, is for a $1,500 cash investment made by the owner, George Corbo. The second, dated September 7, is for a $100 cash purchase of supplies. The third, dated September 10, is for a $2,000 cash loan received from the Landia National Bank. Note that *zeros* are used, rather than a dash, to indicate *no cents*.

Source Documents

As transactions occur, SOURCE DOCUMENTS are prepared as evidence of these transactions. In some cases the source document may be referred to in the short explanation. A source document is any prepared form or VOUCHER, such as a check or check stub, a numbered bill for services, or a memorandum of a transaction. These will be discussed in more detail in Chapters 14, 15, and 16.

The bookkeeping clerk records additional entries on the next page of the journal, starting again with a complete date:

Date	Account Title	PR	Debit	Credit
200- *Sept.* 15	Cash		50 00	
	Accounts Receivable (John Smith)		100 00	
	Fees Income			150 00
	Sales Slip No. 284			
20	Equipment		800 00	
	Regional Supply Company			800 00
	Voucher No. 31			

JOURNAL   Page *13*

On September 15, services were performed for a customer, John Smith, who was charged $150. We received $50 and he charged the balance, $100. This transaction illustrates a COMPOUND ENTRY, where two accounts are debited and one account is credited. Notice, however, that the debit amounts equal the credit. The other entries illustrated are SIMPLE entries—one debit equal to one credit.

The entry on September 20 is for $800 worth of equipment purchased on account from the Regional Supply Company. This is called a CHARGE purchase, as opposed to a cash purchase. (Accounts Payable could have been credited in this entry; however, it is preferable to show the creditor's balance in an account with an identifiable name.)

Notice that the debit account is always listed first in each journal entry. The account to be credited is indented. The amounts of the debit and credit line up with the account titles. Any explanation is listed below the last account title. The name of the month, with the year, is entered once and is not repeated until the next page. Only the day number is used unless the month changes.

Journalizing

Journalizing *begins with the source document.* The information on it tells the bookkeeping clerk all that is needed for the entry—the date, the names of the accounts to debit and credit, the amount, and, if needed, a brief explanation. Here, for example, is a check stub:

NO. *173*	*Oct. 1.* 200=			
TO *Ace Realty*				
FOR *Oct. Rent*				
AMOUNT *500.00*				
BAL.		6	253	15
THIS CK.			500	00
BAL.		5	753	15

The entry to record this transaction in a general journal is:

JOURNAL   Page 8

Date	Account Title	PR	Debit	Credit
200– Oct. 1	Rent Expense		500 00	
	Cash			500 00
	Check No. 173			

Learn the rules of how accounts increase and decrease in order to properly debit and credit accounts. Knowing these rules simplifies the entire journalizing procedure.

YOU SHOULD REMEMBER

Journal entries are listed *chronologically*.

Debit accounts and amounts are always *listed first* in journal entries.

Credit accounts and amounts *are indented following debits*.

A brief explanation ends a journal entry.

In every entry *debits equal credits*.

KNOW YOUR VOCABULARY

Use each of the following words or terms in a statement relating to bookkeeping/accounting:

Book of original entry	Journal
Chronological order	Simple entry
Compound entry	Voucher

QUESTIONS

1. If there are 250 transactions in one month, at least how many entries will there probably be in a *ledger* that month?
2. Why would a numbering or lettering system not be practical in recording entries directly in a ledger?
3. Why is a journal similar to a diary?
4. How does the journal entry identify the debit(s) part of any entry compared to the credit(s) part?

PROBLEMS

6–1   Using a general journal, page 7, record each of these transactions for Rose Klein, owner of a dress designing business:

October 2,   Paid employee's salary, $175

7,   Received $600 cash for a design (design income)

14,   Paid $200 cash for supplies and material

16,   Borrowed $1,000 cash from the Veron Trust Co.

21,   Received $500 cash for a design

23,   Bought a new $360 drawing table (equipment) from the Textile Equipment Company. Paid $160 cash and charged the balance, $200.

30,   Withdrew $400 cash for personal use

31,   Received $100 cash from Mary Wu, a customer (who bought a design last month for $350 and was charged that amount then)

GENERAL JOURNAL   Page

Date	Account Title	PR	Debit	Credit

6–2   What would be a typical source document for each of the transactions listed in Problem 6–1?

THINK IT OVER

Simon Bredhoff has been using the direct ledger method in his bookkeeping records. His business activity has been increasing in recent months. Exactly what should Bredhoff do in order to maintain better control, giving him a more immediate and continuous set of information, and allowing him to follow his business activities day by day?

Ethel Cosmos keeps a ledger and a general journal for her professional consulting business. As each transaction occurs, she wonders which would be the wiser action:

(1) to enter debits and credits in accounts to keep account balances up to date, or

(2) to journalize each transaction first, to keep a running record.

What help can you offer Cosmos in making a decision that will help her follow her business in a more logical way? Which logically comes first: the journal or the ledger?

CHAPTER 7

POSTING THE GENERAL JOURNAL

The system of recording transactions in a general journal does not replace the use of ledger accounts. At some point, each *amount* debited or credited in the journal must be transferred to the ledger account named in the journal entry. This step is called POSTING. Posting should be done on a regular—daily, weekly, or monthly—basis, depending on the frequency of transactions.

Posting Procedure

Every ledger account must be numbered. Each one appears on a separate page or card with a number that identifies the type of account:

Classification	Account Number
Assets	11–19
Liabilities	21–29
Owner's Equity	31–39
Revenue	41–49
Expenses	51–59

If more accounts are needed in any classification, the entire ledger must be renumbered in the hundreds: 111–199; 211–299; 311–399; 411–499; 511–599.

JOURNAL TO LEDGER

The steps in posting a journal entry are as follows:

(A) Enter, for the account debited, the *amount* on the debit side of that account.

(B) Enter the date—year, month, and day (thereafter, do not repeat the year and month).

(C) Enter the *journal* page number in the Posting Reference (PR) column of the account.

(D) Enter the *account number* in the Posting Reference (PR) column of the journal.

Repeat the posting procedure for the next account listed in the journal. Continue with each journal entry, posting debits and credits to each of the accounts listed. If the work of posting is interrupted, the bookkeeping clerk will always know exactly where to resume work—after the last posting reference *account number* in the journal PR column.

Just as debits must equal credits in each journal entry, debits must equal credits when posted to ledger accounts. The following journal entry will be posted to the accounts involved. (Assume that cash has an $800 debit balance (√) from the preceding month.)

GENERAL JOURNAL   Page 8

Date	Account Title	PR	Debit	Credit
200- Oct. 4	Rent Expense	53	500 00	
	Cash	11		500 00
	Check No. 173			

GENERAL LEDGER

Cash   No. 11

200- Oct.	1	Balance	√	800 00	200- Oct.	4		8	500 00

Rent Expense   No. 53

200- Oct.	4		8	500 00			

CROSS REFERENCING

It is now possible to tie together quickly the debit and credit for each transaction. Posting references refer to each other—the journal to the account number, the account to the journal page number. This is called CROSS REFERENCING. It makes the work of checking the records much simpler.

The bookkeeping process starts with the source document for a transaction. A journal entry is then recorded. The entry is posted to ledger accounts:

```
┌─────────────┐        ┌─────────────┐        ┌─────────────┐
│  Source     │ ─────▶ │  Journal    │ ─────▶ │  Ledger     │
│  Document   │        │  Entry      │        │  Accounts   │
└─────────────┘        └─────────────┘        └─────────────┘
```

Trial Balance

When all journalizing and posting have been completed at the end of a fiscal period, or at the end of a month, the bookkeeping clerk makes a check on the accuracy of that work. A listing is made of all ledger accounts and their balances; this is called a TRIAL BALANCE.

In preparing a trial balance, the following steps are taken:

(1) Find the balance of each account, using pencil. Total all debits and credits; these are written below the last figure on each side. This is called FOOTING the ledger, and the totals are called *pencil footings*.

(2) Subtract the smaller footing from the larger (on scrap paper). In pencil, write the difference, or BALANCE of the account, on the *larger side* in the item column. Accounts will normally have balances (debit or credit) on their *increase* sides—assets are debits, liabilities are credits, owner's equity (capital) is a credit, revenue is a credit, and expenses are debits.

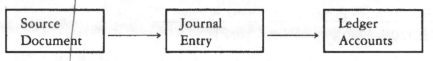

Supplies   No. *16*

200-Oct.	2		5	100 00	200-Oct.	28		9	20 00
	14		7	50 00					
	30	165.00	10	35 00					
				185 00					

Above is a typical account that has pencil footings and a balance. Since only one credit is posted, there is no need to total that side of the account. This account, an asset, has a debit balance of $165.00.

(3) Start the trial balance with a heading to answer the questions WHO, WHAT, and WHEN.

(4) List all accounts by name in their numerical order. Each account balance is placed in either the first (debit) or second (credit) money column (see page 48).

(5) Finally, total each column. If all work is done correctly, the totals should be equal. Once again debits equal credits. The trial balance is said to be IN BALANCE. Double-rule the totals to show that the work has been completed and no further adding or subtracting will be done.

Following is a ledger of simple T-account balances:

Cash	Equipment	Supplies
2500	5000	300

Accounts Payable	De Van Loc, Capital	Rent Income
1200	5150	2000

Advertising Expense	Salary Expense
150	400

At the end of the fiscal period (October 31) the bookkeeping clerk will prepare a trial balance of the general ledger, following the five steps listed above.

De Van Loc Company
Trial Balance
October 31, 200—

Account Title	Acct. No.	Debit	Credit
Cash		2500 00	
Equipment		5000 00	
Supplies		300 00	
Accounts Payable			1200 00
De Van Loc, Capital			5150 00
Rent Income			2000 00
Advertising Expense		150 00	
Salary Expense		400 00	
		8350 00	8350 00

YOU SHOULD REMEMBER

Account *balances* normally appear on the debit or credit side on which *the account increases.* A trial balance *proves* the *equality of debits and credits in the ledger.*

KNOW YOUR VOCABULARY

Balance   In balance

Cross referencing   Posting

Footings   Trial balance

QUESTIONS

1. What steps are followed in posting journal entries?
2. On which side of accounts are balances normally found?
3. a) What does the journal posting refer to?
   b) What does the account posting refer to?
4. A bookkeeping clerk resumes his/her posting work after returning from lunch. How will he/she know where to resume?
5. What does a trial balance "in balance" prove?

PROBLEMS

7-1   After each account is posted, enter the account number in the posting reference column.

	GENERAL JOURNAL			Page 6	
200- Oct	1	Equipment		1000 00	
		Landers Mfg. Co.			1000 00
		5 Motors, Voucher No. 31			
	10	Cash		2500 00	
		Service Income			2500 00
		Receipts Nos. 1-35, to date			
	18	L. D. Berger, Drawing		500 00	
		Cash			500 00
		Withdrawal, Personal Use,			
		Check No. 57			
	25	Landers Mfg. Company		250 00	
		Cash			250 00
		Partial Payment, Check No. 58			

(A partial ledger is shown here.)

Cash   No. 11

| 200-
Oct. | 1 | Balance | ✓ | 1750 00 | | | | | | |

Equipment   No. 12

| 200-
Oct. | 1 | Balance | ✓ | 3000 00 | | | | | | |

Landers Mfg. Company   No. 21

| | | | | | | | | | | |

L. D. Berger, Drawing   No. 32

| | | | | | | | | | | |

Service Income   41

| | | | | | | | | | | |

7-2 Below, in T-account form, is the general ledger for Alan Korn, who operates a computer consulting firm:

```
          Cash        No. 11              Equipment      No. 12
    1500 | 00    100 | 00           3500 | 00 ‖
     750 | 00     50 | 00            465 | 00 ‖
     495 | 00     75 | 00
              500 | 00                  Supplies       No. 13
                                     60 | 00 ‖
   Hi-Tech Company  No. 21
     75 | 00 ‖  2000 | 00        Comp-Software Company No. 22
                                         ‖  465 | 00
   Alan Korn, Capital  No. 31
          ‖  3060 | 00            Alan Korn, Drawing  No. 32
                                  500 | 00 ‖
   Services Income   No. 41
          ‖   750 | 00            Advertising Expense  No. 51
          ‖   495 | 00            100 | 00 ‖

                                  Utilities Expense   No. 52
                                   50 | 00 ‖
```

(1) Pencil-foot the ledger to find the balance of each account.
(2) Prepare a trial balance, using today's date.

7–3 Anita Schaffer runs knitting and sewing classes from her home. Last month she completed the following transactions:

October 2, Bought class supplies for cash, $125
7, Received class fees, $200
11, Made a $50 payment to Jessup Bank due on loan
21, Received class fees, $240
27, Paid $65 for miscellaneous expenses
31, Withdrew for personal use, $300

(1) Record the transactions above in Schaffer's journal.
(2) Post the journal entries to Schaffer's ledger accounts.
(3) Foot the ledger accounts, indicating the balances at the end of the month.
(4) Prepare a trial balance, dated October 31, 200—.

(1)   **GENERAL JOURNAL**   **Page 3**

Date	Account Title	PR	Debit	Credit

(2) and (3)

Cash   No. 11

Date		Item	PR	Debit	Date	Item	PR	Credit
200- Oct.	1	Balance	✓	1375 00				

Equipment   No. 12

Date		Item	PR	Debit	Date	Item	PR	Credit
200- Oct.	1	Balance	✓	1642 50				

Supplies   No. 13

Date		Item	PR	Debit	Date	Item	PR	Credit
200- Oct.	1	Balance	✓	230 00				

Jessup Bank   No. 21

Date	Item	PR	Debit	Date		Item	PR	Credit
				200- Oct.	1	Balance	✓	875 00

Anita Schaffer, Capital   No. 31

Date	Item	PR	Debit	Date		Item	PR	Credit
				200- Oct.	1	Balance	✓	2372 50

Anita Schaffer, Drawing   No. 32

Date	Item	PR	Debit	Date	Item	PR	Credit

Fee Income   No. 41

Date	Item	PR	Debit	Date	Item	PR	Credit

Miscellaneous Expense   No. 51

Date	Item	PR	Debit	Date	Item	PR	Credit

(4) _____

_____

_____

THINK IT OVER

Dina Fowler has prepared a trial balance for her business. It is not in balance. She asks you where she should review her bookkeeping work, in order to find the reason. What suggestions will you make?

Ira Jacobs has prepared a trial balance that is in balance. On reviewing one entry, however, he discovers that he omitted another entry for a payment of $50 for an expense. Why did this error, or omission, not affect the equality of debits and credits in his ledger?

Can you suggest any other kinds of errors that might not cause a trial balance to be "out of balance"?

CHAPTER

THE TRIAL BALANCE AND WORK SHEET

Locating Errors

A trial balance taken at the time interval desired—end of month, fiscal period, year—is a test of the equality of the debit and credit account balances in the ledger. If, however, a trial balance is OUT OF BALANCE, the following steps—in reverse order—should be taken to determine the reason(s):

(1)   Re-add the columns of the trial balance; perhaps they were totaled incorrectly.
(2)   Examine each account balance in the trial balance, and compare these account balances to the ledger account balances. Perhaps they were carried forward incorrectly, or perhaps an account was omitted, listed twice, or placed in the wrong amount column of the trial balance (reversing a debit or a credit).
(3)   Re-foot the ledger accounts to verify each account balance.
(4)   If an error is not located at this point, compare each entry in the account with the original debit and credit recorded in the journal entry.

When an error is discovered in the ledger, neatly cross out the incorrect entry and write the correction above it. Never erase ink amounts or mark through an error in any way that causes the first figure to be altered. This could cause legal problems, inasmuch as book-keeping/accounting records are legal documents.

Errors That the Trial Balance Does Not Reveal

Not all errors show up in a trial balance. The following errors do not affect the equality of debits and credits in the ledger:

(1)   Omitting an entire entry.
(2)   Posting to an incorrect account—a debit to another debit, a credit to another credit.
(3)   Using an incorrect amount in a journal entry and posting that amount to ledger accounts.
(4)   Recording a transaction twice.

The Six-Column Work Sheet

By the end of a fiscal period, the owner of a business wants the answer to a very important question: What was the net income or net loss for that period? To answer that question, a WORK SHEET is prepared. A work sheet is a ruled form of analysis paper with several columns. Because it is not part of the permanent records, however, it can be completed in pencil. The steps taken to complete a work sheet are as follows:

(1)   Write a heading that answers the questions WHO, WHAT, and WHEN. The "when" part indicates the fiscal period *ending date.*
(2)   List all ledger accounts in the Account title column and their balances in the first pair of money columns, arranged as they would be in a trial balance.
(3)   Extend the balance of each account to one of the remaining columns by determining whether the account is a BALANCE SHEET account—assets, liabilities, and owner's equity—and a debit or credit, or an INCOME STATEMENT account—revenue, expenses—and a debit or credit.
(4)   Total all remaining columns; the difference between the Income Statement columns and the difference between the Balance Sheet columns should be equal.
(5)   Determine whether there was a net income or a net loss. In the Income Statement *column totals*, if the credit (revenue) is greater than the debit (expenses), there has been a net income; if the reverse is true, there has been a net loss.
(6)   Identify the net income or net loss in the Account Title column; the amount is entered in the smaller of the two Income Statement and Balance Sheet columns; totals (which must be equal) are then entered in each pair of columns and they are double ruled.

Examine carefully the completed work sheet on page 57. It begins with the trial balance completed for the De Van Loc Company, illustrated in Chapter 7, page 48. Note the heading (1), the trial balance (2), extending the account balances (3), totaling the last four columns and finding the difference (4), determining the amount of net income (5), and adding it to the lesser amount in both the income statement and balance sheet totals to make them equal, then double ruling (6).

De Van Loc Company
Work Sheet
For the Month Ended October 31, 200–

Account Title	Acc No	Trial Balance Debit	Trial Balance Credit	Income Statement Debit	Income Statement Credit	Balance Sheet Debit	Balance Sheet Credit
Cash	11	250000				250000	
Equipment	12	500000				500000	
Supplies	13	30000				30000	
Accounts Payable	21		120000				120000
De Van Loc, Capital	31		515000				515000
Rent Income	41		200000		200000		
Advertising Expense	51	15000		15000			
Salary Expense	52	40000		40000			
		835000	835000	55000	200000	780000	635000
Net Income				145000			145000
				200000	200000	780000	780000

(Deductions from employees' salaries are not covered in this text.)

YOU SHOULD REMEMBER

Clear up all errors revealed in a trial that is out of balance *before extending* items on a work sheet.

Differences in column totals in each statement (income statement and balance sheet) on the work sheet *should be equal*.

KNOW YOUR VOCABULARY

Balance sheet	Net loss
Income statement	Out of balance
Net income	Work sheet

QUESTIONS

1. What is the order in which work will be checked to find an error in the trial balance?
2. What errors will cause a trial balance to be out of balance?
3. What errors can be made that will not cause a trial balance to be out of balance?
4. How is the net income or net loss for the fiscal period determined on the work sheet?

PROBLEMS

8–1 T. R. Price is a carpenter who receives a commission for odd jobs in his neighborhood. His bookkeeping records indicate the following balances (shown in T-account form):

Cash 11		Equipment 12		Truck 13	
2645		1500		7500	

County Mfg. Co. 21		T. R. Price, Capital 31		T. R. Price, Drawing 32	
	550		10570	500	

Commissions Income 41		Advertising Expense 51		Miscellaneous Expense 52	
	1650	100		50	

Rent Expense 53		Salary Expense 54	
175		300	

Complete a six-column work sheet for the month ended November 30, 200—.(Save your work for future problems.)

Account Title	A. N.	Trial Balance		Income Statement		Balance Sheet	
		Debit	Credit	Debit	Credit	Debit	Credit

8–2 Below is a trial balance for Ann Danziger; however, it contains an error.

Danziger Designs
Trial Balance
September 30, 200–

Cash	11	1 7 6 2 50	
Accounts Receivable	12	7 3 8 90	
Equipment	13	2 6 0 5 00	
Supplies	14	3 9 5 00	
Accounts Payable	21	6 0 0 00	
Ann Danziger, Capital	31		4 2 5 1 40
Ann Danziger, Drawing	32	8 0 0 00	
Fees Income	41		2 4 0 0 00
Advertising Expense	51	1 6 0 00	
Insurance Expense	52	4 0 00	
Materials Expense	53	1 0 0 00	
Rent Expense	54	2 5 0 00	
Salary Expense	55	4 0 0 00	

(1) Find the error and move the amounts from one column to the other, thus correcting the trial balance.
(2) Total the trial balance.
(3) What is Danziger's net income for this period?
    (Complete the worksheet on the next page.)

(3) Complete the work sheet for the quarter year ended September 30. (Save your work for future problems.)

Account Title	A. N.	Trial Balance		Income Statement		Balance Sheet	
		Debit	Credit	Debit	Credit	Debit	Credit

8–3 Rebecca Gayle operates a message delivery service. Her trial balance for the month ended October 31, 200–, is shown below:

Gayle's Reliable Service
Trial Balance
October 31, 200–

Cash	11	760 00	
Accounts Receivable	12	142 50	
Automobile	13	9200 00	
Supplies	14	350 00	
County Bank & Trust Co.	21		360 00
Rebecca Gayle, Capital	31		6302 00
Rebecca Gayle, Drawing	32	600 00	
Service Income	41	1875 50	
Advertising Expense	51	200 00	
Auto Expense	52	400 00	
Miscellaneous Expense	53	50 00	
Telephone Expense	54	75 00	

(1) Find the error and move the amounts from one column to the other, thus correcting the trial balance.

(2) Complete the work sheet. (Save your work for future problems.)

Account Title	A.N.	Trial Balance		Income Statement		Balance Sheet	
		Debit	Credit	Debit	Credit	Debit	Credit

THINK IT OVER

Damien Spyridon's trial balance is not in balance. He checks his work and finds two errors. An expense account with a $100 balance was listed on the trial balance as a credit. The other error is found when he checks his posting. A journal entry amount was $54; he posted the debit as $45. Why did the trial balance columns differ by $209?

CHAPTER 9

FINANCIAL STATEMENTS

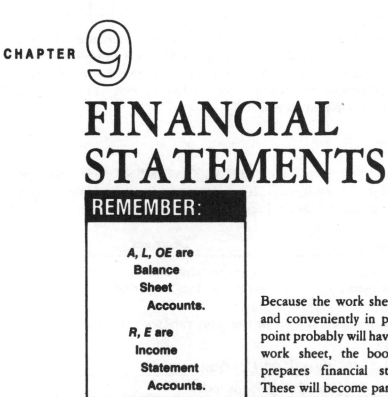

REMEMBER:

A, L, OE are
Balance
Sheet
Accounts.

R, E are
Income
Statement
Accounts.

Because the work sheet can be completed easily and conveniently in pencil, all errors up to that point probably will have been corrected. Using the work sheet, the bookkeeping/accounting clerk prepares financial statements more formally. These will become part of the permanent records of a business.

Income Statement—Form and Content

An INCOME STATEMENT is prepared first, using the information in the Income Statement columns of the work sheet. The heading will answer the questions WHO, WHAT, and WHEN. All revenue is listed first, and totaled. Expenses are then listed, totaled, and subtracted from total revenue. The difference is the same net income (or net loss) as shown on the work sheet. (Account numbers are not listed on financial statements.)

Revenue − Expenses = Net Income or Net Loss

Follow this illustration (based on the work sheet on page 57).

De Van Loc Company
Income Statement
For the Month Ended October 31, 200-

Revenue:			
Rent Income			2000 00
Expenses:			
Advertising Expense		150 00	
Salary Expense		400 00	
Total Expenses			550 00
Net Income			1450 00

If expenses are greater than revenue, the difference (revenue subtracted from expenses) is identified as a net loss. Note that the first money column is used to list more than one item; the second money column is for totals (or a single item) and the results of the business operations for the fiscal period—net income or net loss. Double lines are ruled through both money columns to show a completed statement.

Capital Statement

The next financial statement to be prepared is a CAPITAL STATEMENT. This shows how owner's equity has changed during a fiscal period. It starts with the *beginning* capital account balance. Any changes that occur are then listed. Possible changes in owner's equity are:

Increases	Decreases
(1) additional investments	(1) withdrawals
(2) net income for period	(2) net loss for period

De Van Loc's capital statement is a simple one; only two items are involved.

De Van Loc Company
Capital Statement
For the Month Ended October 31, 200-

Beginning Balance, Oct. 1, 200-			5150 00
Plus: Net Income			1450 00
Ending Balance, Oct. 31, 200-			6600 00

Following are illustrations of capital statements with more changes (headings are omitted here):

Beginning Balance, Sept. 1, 200—			750000
Plus: Additional Investment		100000	
Net Income		250000	
		350000	
Less: Withdrawals		150000	
Net Increase in Capital			200000
Ending Balance, Sept. 30, 200—			950000

With decreases less than increases, there is a *net increase* in capital. Always verify whichever one there is before writing the words "Net Increase" or "Net Decrease." (If withdrawals are greater than any additional investment, there may still be a net decrease—assuming a net income that does not make up the difference.)

Beginning Balance, Nov. 1, 200—			1250000
Plus: Additional Investment		300000	
Less: Withdrawals	1,500 00		
Net Loss	2,000 00	350000	
Net Decrease in Capital			50000
Ending Balance, Nov. 30, 200—			1200000

Balance Sheet—Form and Content

The next financial statement to be prepared is one that was discussed in Chapter 3—a balance sheet. The information is found in the Balance Sheet columns of the work sheet, *except for owner's equity*. The capital *at the end of the fiscal period* is the ending balance found on the capital statement.

De Van Loc Company
Balance Sheet
October 31, 200—

Assets			Liabilities		
Cash	2500	00	Accounts Payable	1200	00
Equipment	5000	00	Owner's Equity		
Supplies	300	00	De Van Loc, Cap, Oct 31	6600	00
Total Assets	7800	00	Total Liab + O.E.	7800	00

Compare De Van Loc's capital with the amount listed on his capital statement, page 64. These two items will always agree.

YOU SHOULD REMEMBER

When *revenue is greater than expenses* there is a *net income*.

When *expenses are greater than revenue* there is a net loss.

Owner's equity is *increased* by:
— additional investments and
— net income.

Owner's equity is *decreased* by:
— withdrawals by the owner and
— net loss.

KNOW YOUR VOCABULARY

Balance sheet	Income statement
Capital statement	

QUESTIONS

1. From which source of information are financial statements prepared?
2. In what order should statements be prepared?
3. What are the causes for an increase in owner's equity?
4. What are the causes for a decrease in owner's equity?
5. Why is the work sheet capital balance not used in completing a balance sheet?
6. How are the dates indicated in the "when" part of each statement's heading?

PROBLEMS

9–1 Using the completed work sheet in Problem 8–1 for T. R. Price, complete the following:
    a)   An incomplete statement.
    b)   A capital statement.
    c)   A balance sheet. (Enter the liabilities and owner's equity total on the same line level with the assets total before double ruling.)

a)

b)

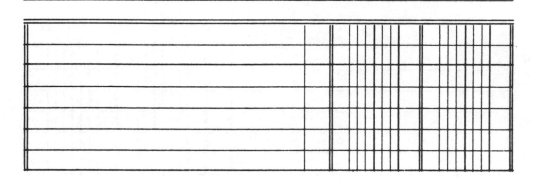

c)

9–2 Using the completed work sheet in Problem 8–2 for Danziger Designs, complete the following:

    a)   An income statement.

    b)   A capital statement.

    c)   A balance sheet. (Enter the liabilities and owner's equity total on the same line level with the assets total before double ruling.)

a)

b)

c)

9–3 Using the completed work sheet in Problem 8–3 for Rebecca Gayle, complete the following:

    a) An income statement.

    b) A capital statement.

    c) A balance sheet. (Enter the liabilities and owner's equity total on the same line level with the assets total before double ruling.)

a)

b)

c)

9–4   Below is the T-account ledger for Walter Finnegan Associates, an architectural consulting firm: (Note account numbers are not listed.)

Cash		Accounts Receivable	
5648		2655	

Equipment		Truck	
10400		15000	

Supplies		Accounts Payable	
420			8600

Walter Finnegan, Capital		Walter Finnegan, Drawing	
	28243	2500	

Fees Income		Advertising Expense	
	3680	800	

Miscellaneous Expense		Rent Expense	
400		1200	

Salary Expense	
1500	

(1) Complete a work sheet for the month ended November 30, 200—
(2) Complete the following:
   a) An income statement.
   b) A capital statement. Assume that Finnegan's beginning capital was $25,243, and an additional $3,000 was invested during the fiscal period.
   c) A balance sheet.

(1)

Account Title	A. N.	Trial Balance		Income Statement		Balance Sheet	
		Debit	Credit	Debit	Credit	Debit	Credit

2a) _____

2b) _____

2c) _____

THINK IT OVER

A balance sheet has been compared to a photograph. An income statement has been compared to a moving picture. What might be the explanation for such comparisons?

CHAPTER **10**

CLOSING THE LEDGER

REMEMBER:

Investments and Revenue Increase Capital.

Withdrawals and Expenses Decrease Capital.

At the end of each fiscal period, all revenue and expense accounts and the owner's drawing account are closed. These accounts list information for a fiscal period and should not carry over to succeeding fiscal periods. Since these accounts show the changes that take place in owner's equity, their balances should be transferred to the permanent capital account in order to bring that account up to date. After being closed, these accounts can be used again, starting at a zero balance, for recording revenue, expenses, and withdrawals for the next fiscal period.

Revenue and Expense Summary

To close an account, an entry must be made which will result in posting on the opposite side of that account an amount equal to its balance. The CLOSING ENTRY procedure will reduce the balance of all revenue, expense, and drawing accounts to zero.

Revenue accounts are closed first. Since they have credit balances, they must be debited in order to ZERO OUT their balances. The account credited is REVENUE AND EXPENSE SUMMARY, an owner's equity account used for special entries, including this closing procedure. This account is used to summarize the changes caused by income and expenses each fiscal period.

The second closing entry will ZERO OUT expense accounts. Since they have debit balances, they must be credited in order to have zero balances. The account debited is Revenue and Expense Summary.

The third closing entry will ZERO OUT the balance of the Revenue and Expense Summary account. The amount will always be equal to the *net income* or *net loss* for the fiscal period. If there is a net income, the summary account has a credit balance; if there is a net loss, the summary account has a debit balance. This closing entry *increases capital* for the amount of the *net income,* or *decreases capital* for the amount of the *net loss,* whichever has occurred during the fiscal period.

The following are the closing entries for the De Van Loc Company (see work sheet, page 57, Income Statement columns). These entries have been posted to the ledger accounts, which follow below.

GENERAL JOURNAL   Page 4

Date	Account Title	PR	Debit	Credit
	Closing Entries			
Oct. 31	Rent Income	41	200000	
	Revenue and Expense Summary	33		200000
	to close income acct.			
31	Revenue and Expense Summary	33	55000	
	Advertising Expense	51		15000
	Salary Expense	52		40000
	to close expense accts.			
31	Revenue and Expense Summary	33	145000	
	De Van Loc, Capital	31		145000
	to close net income			

LEDGER

De Van Loc, Capital   No. 31

				Oct. 1	Balance	✓	515000
				31		4	145000

Revenue and Expense Summary   No. 33

Oct. 31		4	55000	Oct. 31		4	200000
31		4	145000				

Rent Income   No. 41

Date		Item	PR	Debit	Date		Item	PR	Credit
200- Oct.	31		4	2000 00	200- Oct.	15		2	1000 00
						30		3	1000 00
									2000 00

Advertising Expense   No. 51

Date		Item	PR	Debit	Date		Item	PR	Credit
200- Oct.	5		1	150 00	200- Oct.	31		4	150 00

Salary Expense   No. 52

Date		Item	PR	Debit	Date		Item	PR	Credit
200- Oct.	7		1	100 00	200- Oct.	31		4	400 00
	14		2	100 00					
	21		2	100 00					
	28		3	100 00					
				400 00					

A fourth closing entry is needed if the owner has made withdrawals during the fiscal period. Assume that John Wade's capital balance on November 30 is $12,750. His drawing account indicates withdrawals of $1,200. His net loss for the fiscal period is $500. The following are his third and fourth closing entries, which have been posted to the accounts affected.

GENERAL JOURNAL   Page 8

Date		Account	PR	Debit	Credit
200- Nov.	30	John Wade, Capital	31	500 00	
		Revenue and Expense Summary	33		500 00
		to close net loss			
	30	John Wade, Capital	31	1200 00	
		John Wade, Drawing	32		1200 00
		to close withdrawals			

LEDGER

John Wade, Capital   No. 31

200- Nov.	30		8	500 00	200- Nov.	1	Balance	✓	17500 00
	30		8	1200 00					
							(Closing Entry No. 3)		
							(Closing Entry No. 4)		

John Wade, Drawing   No. 32

200- Nov.	15		6	600 00	200- Nov.	30		8	1200 00
	30		7	600 00					
							(Closing Entry No. 4)		

Revenue and Expense Summary   No. 33

200- Nov.	30		8	3000 00	200- Nov.	30		8	2500 00
						30		8	500 00
							(Closing Entry No. 3)		

Accounts Closed/Accounts Open—Ruling, Balancing

Accounts that are closed have zero balances—all revenue, expenses, the summary account, and the drawing account. To show this clearly, they are totaled on both sides and ruled with double lines. An account that is closed and ruled is illustrated as follows.

Salary Expense   No. 517

200- Dec.	20		19	300 00	200- Dec.	31		22	600 00
	30		21	300 00					
				600 00					600 00

All ledger accounts, starting with the drawing account, would be ruled in this way. They have no balances; they are closed at the end of the fiscal period.

Balance sheet accounts, on the other hand, have balances that carry over to the next fiscal period. These accounts are BALANCED AND RULED. The following steps are taken:

(1) Pencil-foot the ledger—already done to take a trial balance; see page 47, steps (1) and (2).
(2) Enter in ink on the *smaller side* the amount of the account balance (√) so that both sides are equal.
(3) Write total amounts on the same line level on both debit and credit sides; double-rule the account through the date and money columns.
(4) Enter the account balance on the *larger side* as of the first day of the next fiscal period, with the word "Balance" and check mark (√) in the posting reference column.

The following are two typical accounts that have been balanced and ruled.

Cash — No. 111

Date		Item	PR	Debit	Date		Item	PR	Credit
200– Dec.	1	Balance	√	1520 00	200– Dec.	20		19	300 00
	15		17	390 00		30		21	300 00
	30		21	860 00		31	Balance	√	2170 00
		2170.00		2770 00					2770 00
200– Jan.	1	Balance	√	2170 00					

Eleanor Smith, Capital — No. 311

Date		Item	PR	Debit	Date		Item	PR	Credit
200– Dec.	31		22	800 00	200– Dec.	1	Balance	√	15000 00
	31	Balance	√	16200 00		22		22	2000 00
				17000 00		31	16200.00		17000 00
					200– Jan.	1	Balance	√	16200 00

If an account has entries on one side only, it does not have to be formally balanced and ruled. Either the pencil footing or the single-entry amount stands out clearly as the balance.

Supplies — No. 115

Date		Item	PR	Debit					
200– Dec.	5		14	35 00					
	19		16	110 00					
				145 00					

To prove the equality of ledger debits and credits after the balancing and ruling procedure, the bookkeeping/accounting clerk prepares another trial balance—a POST-CLOSING TRIAL BALANCE. All debit account balances must equal all credit account balances. These accounts will list the same balances that are reported on the balance sheet. However, the capital account will now be updated for any net increases or net decreases that may have occurred during the fiscal period.

Compare the post-closing trial balance for De Van Loc Company with the trial balance prepared earlier (see page 48).

De Van Loc Company
Post-closing Trial Balance
October 31, 200—

Cash	250000	
Equipment	500000	
Supplies	30000	
Accounts Payable		120000
De Van Loc, Capital		660000
	780000	780000

A complete BOOKKEEPING/ACCOUNTING CYCLE has been illustrated in the work done to date. To complete such a cycle follow these steps carefully:

(1) Journalize transactions.
(2) Post to ledger accounts.
(3) Prepare a trial balance.
(4) Prepare a work sheet and financial statements.
(5) Make closing entries and post to accounts.
(6) Balance and rule ledger.
(7) Prepare the post-closing trial balance.

YOU SHOULD REMEMBER

The Revenue and Expense Summary account is used in closing entries *to zero out revenue and expense account balances*.

The *balance of the Revenue and Expense Summary Account* after zeroing out revenue and expense account balances *equals the net income or net loss* for the fiscal period.

After all closing entries are posted, *the Capital account* balance *equals* the amount of *owner's equity* as indicated on the capital statement and the balance sheet

KNOW YOUR VOCABULARY

Balance and rule   Post-closing trial balance

Bookkeeping/accounting cycle   Revenue and expense summary

Closing entry   Zero out

QUESTIONS

1. How are net increases and/or decreases transferred to the owner's capital account?
2. What are the four closing entries in correct order?
3. What does a credit balance in the Revenue and Expense Summary account represent?
4. What closing entry is made when the Revenue and Expense Summary account has a debit balance?
5. How is a revenue account closed?
6. How are expense accounts and the drawing account closed?
7. Which accounts remain open at the end of each fiscal period?

PROBLEMS

10-1   The following is the *partial work sheet* for Gwen Vreeland, a publishers' consultant and editor. Journalize her four closing entries at the end of the annual fiscal period *after determining the amount of her net income or net loss.* (Note that her withdrawals for the period were $1,800. This would appear in the Balance Sheet columns of the work sheet.) Explanations are not needed for these entries, inasmuch as the words "Closing Entries" are written before the first one is recorded.

Account Title	A.N.	Trial Balance Debit	Trial Balance Credit	Income Statement Debit	Income Statement Credit
Cash		2000 00			
Furniture and Fixtures		5000 00			
Supplies		350 00			
Accounts Payable			1000 00		
Gwen Vreeland, Capital			4800 00		
Gwen Vreeland, Drawing		1800 00			
Consulting Fees Income			3750 00		3750 00
Royalty Income			500 00		500 00
Advertising Expense		100 00		100 00	
Miscellaneous Expense		60 00		60 00	
Rent Expense		250 00		250 00	
Salary Expense		400 00		400 00	
Telephone Expense		90 00		90 00	
		10050 00	10050 00	900 00	4250 00

GENERAL JOURNAL   Page *18*

10–2 Below is a listing of the ledger accounts and their balances for the Allen Insurance Agency.

Cash	$ 2,800.00
Accounts Receivable	3,895.00
Equipment	4,000.00
Automobile	12,500.00
Supplies	750.00
Accounts Payable	6,000.00
Elliot Allen, Capital	12,920.00
Elliot Allen, Drawing	1,500.00
Commissions Income	8,500.00
Automobile Expense	600.00
Office Expense	175.00
Rent Expense	300.00
Salary Expense	900.00

(1) Complete a work sheet for the month ended November 30.

(2) Journalize the four closing entries.

(1)

Account Title	A. N.	Trial Balance		Income Statement		Balance Sheet	
		Debit	Credit	Debit	Credit	Debit	Credit

(2)

10–3 Earl Alpert, an attorney, has asked you to complete the work indicated:

(1) Complete the work sheet below.

Earl Alpert, Esquire
Work Sheet
For 3 Months Ended June 30, 200 –

Account Title	A.N.	Trial Balance Debit	Trial Balance Credit	Income Statement Debit	Income Statement Credit	Balance Sheet Debit	Balance Sheet Credit
Cash	11	1 60500					
Accounts Receivable	12	1 45800					
Office Equipment	13	3 86000					
Furniture	14	5 25000					
Supplies	15	83075					
Accounts Payable	21		1 87500				
Earl Alpert, Capital	31		24300 75				
Earl Alpert, Drawing	32	4 80000					
Legal Fees Income	41		9500 00				
Miscellaneous Expense	51	15000					
Office Expense	52	22500					
Rent Expense	53	1 00000					
Salary Expense	54	3 00000					
Travel Expense	55	7500					

(2) Complete the following financial statements:

a) An income statement.

b) A capital statement. Assume that Alpert's capital was $23,300.75 at the beginning of the fiscal period; he made an additional investment of $1,000 during the fiscal period.

c) A balance sheet.

(3) Journalize the closing entries.

2a)

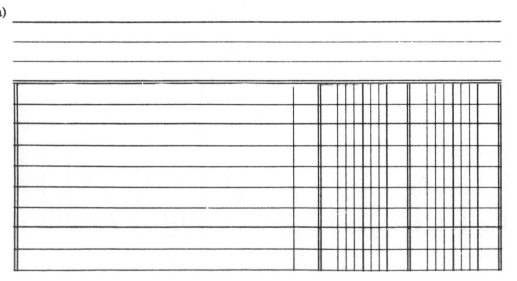

2b)

2c)

(3)

10–4 Pamela Washington is a recent college graduate who has started her own private accounting practice. Her journal and ledger indicate that all transactions have been posted, and she is about to complete the work of the bookkeeping/accounting cycle.

(1) Pencil-foot the ledger and take a trial balance, using the work sheet form.

(2) Complete the work sheet, and prepare the following:
   a) An income statement.
   b) A capital statement.
   c) A balance sheet.

(3) Journalize and post the closing entries.

(4) Balance and rule the ledger.

(5) Take a post-closing trial balance.

Cash   No. 11

200-Dec.	1	Balance	✓	1000 00	200-Dec.	20		5	250 00
	10		4	500 00		30		5	175 00
	22		5	750 00		31		6	100 00
			6	1350 00		31		6	90 00
						31		6	800 00

Accounts Receivable   No. 12

200-Dec.	1	Balance	✓	200 00	200-Dec.	22		5	750 00

Equipment   No. 13

200-Dec.	1	Balance	✓	3500 00					
	15		4	1500 00					

Supplies   No. 14

200-Dec.	1	Balance	✓	580 00					

Accounts Payable   No. 21

Date		Item	PR	Amount	Date		Item	PR	Amount
200– Dec.	20		5	250 00	200– Dec.	1	Balance	✓	450 00
						15		4	1500 00

Pamela Washington, Capital   No. 31

Date		Item	PR	Amount	Date		Item	PR	Amount
					200– Dec.	1	Balance	✓	6630 00

Pamela Washington, Drawing   No. 32

Date		Item	PR	Amount	Date		Item	PR	Amount
200– Dec.	31		6	800 00					

Revenue and Expense Summary   No. 33

Date		Item	PR	Amount	Date		Item	PR	Amount

Fees Income   No. 41

Date		Item	PR	Amount	Date		Item	PR	Amount
					200– Dec.	10		4	500 00
						31		6	1350 00

Automobile Expense   No. 51

200-					
Dec.	31		6	90 00	

Office Expense   No. 52

200-					
Dec.	31		6	100 00	

Rent Expense   No. 53

200-					
Dec.	30		5	175 00	

Account Title	A. N.	Trial Balance		Income Statement		Balance Sheet	
		Debit	Credit	Debit	Credit	Debit	Credit

Pamela Washington
Income Statement
For the Month Ended December 31, 200-

Pamela Washington
Capital Statement
For the Month Ended December 31, 200-

Pamela Washington
Balance Sheet
December 31, 200—

GENERAL JOURNAL   Page **7**

Date	Account Title	PR	Debit	Credit

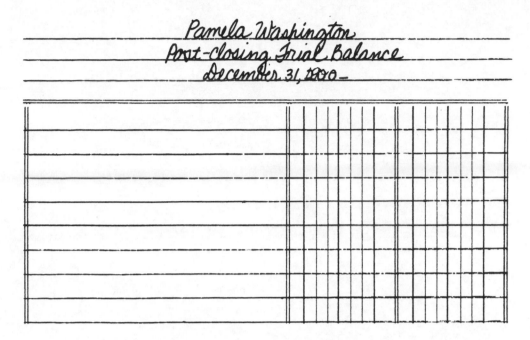

Pamela Washington
Post-closing Trial Balance
December 31, 1900

THINK IT OVER

Len Green says he does not make closing entries, nor does he ever prepare a post-closing trial balance. He claims these steps are not needed because he uses only ten to twelve accounts. What difficulties will he encounter two or three fiscal periods from now, if he wishes to prepare financial statements? Do you think the Internal Revenue Service would approve of a tax return based on statements that confuse information from one fiscal period to the next?

CHAPTER **11**

CASH SYSTEMS, CHECKING ACCOUNTS

Most businesses make payments by checks drawn on local commercial banks. Many individuals now use checking accounts drawing on funds in savings banks and/or in money funds. A check is a written order directing the DRAWEE (the bank) to make payment to the PAYEE (the party indicated by the words "Pay to the order of") from the account balance of the DRAWER (the party who signs the order or check).

Opening a Checking Account

When a checking account is opened, each person authorized to sign checks completes a signature card. A deposit slip is used to list items to be added to the account, including checks received from others—paychecks, amounts collected from customers, and so on.

Endorsing Checks

Each check deposited must be endorsed, that is, signed on the back by the payee. There are several types of endorsements.

(1)   An ENDORSEMENT IN BLANK. This is a simple signature of the payee.

(2) A SPECIAL (or FULL) ENDORSEMENT. This states to whom a check is to be paid.

> *Pay to the order of*
> *Wilma Higgins*
> *Gordon J. Barnes*

(3) A RESTRICTIVE ENDORSEMENT. This limits the further purpose or use of the check.

> *For deposit only*
> *Acct. no. 831456*
> *Gordon J. Barnes*

(4) A QUALIFIED ENDORSEMENT. The endorser (payee) assumes no legal responsibility for payment, should the drawer have insufficient funds to honor his/her own check.

> *Without recourse*
> *Gordon J. Barnes*

The restrictive endorsement should be used on checks to be deposited. The blank endorsement should be used only when presenting a check for *immediate* payment, for example, when cashing one's paycheck.

Making Deposits

Assume that Gordon Barnes opens a checking account and completes the following deposit slip:

FOR DEPOSIT TO THE ACCOUNT OF		DOLLARS	CENTS
NAME *Gordon J. Barnes*	BILLS	250	00
ADDRESS *125 Main St. Bolton*	COINS	—	
DATE *Jan. 2* 20___	CHECKS AS FOLLOWS, PROPERLY ENDORSED	150	00
		500	00
BOLTON NATIONAL BANK		375	00
New York, NY			
CHECKS AND OTHER ITEMS ARE RECEIVED FOR DEPOSIT SUBJECT TO THE TERMS AND CONDITIONS OF THIS BANK'S COLLECTION AGREEMENT	TOTAL DEPOSIT	1,275	00

⑆0860⑈0830⑆1243⑈676⑈

His account balance will be $1,275, and that amount will be entered on his check stub record on the balance brought forward (Bal. Bro't For'd) line. As future deposits are made, he will add to find the total; as checks are drawn, he will subtract to find the balance carried forward (Bal. Car'd For'd).

Drawing Checks

Follow these stubs and checks completed by Barnes for each of these cash payment transactions:

January 2, 200–, Paid Ace Realty $250 for month's rent; check No. 101
5, 200–, Paid Security National Bank $300 on loan balance; check No. 102

(Be sure stubs are completed first, showing all information; then complete each check, using pen and ink.)

	DOLLARS	CENTS
NO. 101 $250.00		
DATE Jan. 2 20		
TO Ace Realty		
FOR January rent		
BAL. BRO'T FOR'D	1275	00
AMT. DEPOSITED		
TOTAL	1275	00
AMT. THIS CHECK	250	00
BAL. CAR'D FOR'D	1025	00

No. 101
1-830 / 860

January 2   20 ____

Pay to the order of Ace Realty $250 00

Two hundred fifty + 00/100 ————— Dollars

BOLTON NATIONAL BANK
of New York, NY

Gordon J. Barnes

⑆0860⑈0830⑆ 1243⑈671⑈

	DOLLARS	CENTS
NO. 102 $300.00		
DATE Jan. 5 20		
TO Security National Bank		
FOR loan payment		
BAL. BRO'T FOR'D	1025	00
AMT. DEPOSITED		
TOTAL	1025	00
AMT. THIS CHECK	300	00
BAL. CAR'D FOR'D	725	00

No. 102
1-830 / 860

January 5   20 ____

Pay to the order of Security National Bank $300 00

Three hundred + 00/100 ————— Dollars

BOLTON NATIONAL BANK
of New York, NY

Gordon J. Barnes

⑆0860⑈0830⑆ 1243⑈671⑈

Notice that the balance carried forward from stub No. 101 is brought forward to stub No. 102. In this way, Barnes will always have a running balance in his checking account.

Each check stub will serve as the source document for making a journal entry. The two entries for stubs No. 101 and No. 102 are illustrated as follows.

200–					
Jan. 2	Rent Expense		250	00	
	Cash				250 00
	Check No. 101				
5	Security National Bank		300	00	
	Cash				300 00
	Check No. 102				

The Bank Statement

At the end of the month, or at a set date during each month, the bank sends each depositor a BANK STATEMENT. This is the bank's record of the deposits made, and the checks drawn *and presented for payment*. These checks are CANCELED—marked paid—and returned to the depositor with the bank statement. If any charges have been made by the bank for handling this account, they are identified as "SC" ("service charge") and deducted from the balance. The depositor makes a similar deduction on the next check stub.

Here is the entry Barnes makes in his journal for the service charge made on his statement at the end of the month:

31	Miscellaneous Expense		3 75	
	Cash			3 75
	Bank Service Charge, Jan.			

Reconciling Check Stub Balance and Bank Statement

Frequently, the depositor's check stub balance and the checking account bank statement balance do not agree by the end of each month. There are several reasons for these differences.

(1) A late deposit, or a DEPOSIT IN TRANSIT, is added into the *check stub balance* but does not reach the bank in time to be recorded on the bank statement—*add any late or omitted deposits to the bank balance.*
(2) Some checks drawn and sent to distant points have not cleared back to the depositor's bank in time to be recorded on the bank statement—*subtract the amount of OUTSTANDING CHECKS from the bank balance.*
(3) If the bank made any service charges, they are deducted on the bank statement—*subtract the service charge on the check stub record.*

At this point, Barnes prepares a BANK RECONCILIATION STATEMENT to determine his correct, available checkbook and bank balance. This amount must be the same for both balances at any given time.

Gordon I. Barnes
Bank Reconciliation Statement
January 31, 200-

Checkbook Balance	675.00	Bank Balance	895.00
Deduct: Service		Add: Deposit in	
Charge	3.75	Transit	200.00
			1095.00
		Deduct: Outstanding	
		Checks	
		No. 119, 100.00	
		No. 120, 200.00	
		No. 121, 123.75	
			423.75
Correct Check Stub		Available Bank	
Balance	671.25	Balance	671.25

The amount of cash that Barnes has in his checking account, against which he can draw future checks, is $671.25. If he had not prepared this reconciliation, he might have OVERDRAWN his account. One or more of his checks might have been dishonored because of insufficient funds.

Two-Column Cashbook

A convenient recordkeeping form may be used to keep a two-column record of all cash received and paid, assuming all cash is deposited and drawn out by check. This is a single-entry procedure, not requiring a debit and credit for each transaction. It *should not,* however, be used as a substitute for a double-entry bookkeeping system.

The following is an illustration of a cashbook used by Christine Ghent for her household records:

Date	Explanation	Ck. No.	Cash Payment	Cash Received
200- aug. 1	Checkbook balance	✓		1562 50
10	Personal use	35	275 00	
15	2 weeks salary check	✓		976 40
28	Atlantic-Bell Phone bill	36	62 50	
30	Stern-Taylor Dept. Store	37	148 95	
31	Personal use	38	300 00	
			786 45	2538 90
Sept 1	Checkbook balance	✓		1752 45

At the end of the month, the cashbook is totaled and double ruled. The checkbook balance should equal the difference between the column totals. This balance is then entered on the next line as the September 1 checkbook balance.

> **YOU SHOULD REMEMBER**
> Outstanding checks *reduce* a bank statement balance.
> A bank reconciliation is necessary to avoid *overdrawing* one's checking account.

KNOW YOUR VOCABULARY

Bank reconciliation

Bank statement

Canceled

Deposit in transit

Drawee; drawer

Endorsement in blank

Full endorsement (special)

Outstanding checks

Overdrawn

Payee

Qualified endorsement

Restrictive endorsement

QUESTIONS

1. Why is a check referred to as a "three-party instrument"?
2. How is a signature card used by the bank teller?
3. What entry is recorded for a bank service charge?
4. Why is a reconciliation statement necessary?

PROBLEMS

11-1   Complete Aliza Michele's deposit slip for the following items:

23 twenty-dollar bills
48 ten-dollar bills
16 five-dollar bills
29 one-dollar bills
Checks: $148.65 and $79.15

18 quarters
31 dimes
14 nickels
42 pennies

FOR DEPOSIT TO THE ACCOUNT OF		DOLLARS	CENTS
NAME	BILLS		
	COINS		
ADDRESS	CHECKS AS FOLLOWS, PROPERLY ENDORSED		
DATE 20			
BOLTON NATIONAL BANK New York, NY			
CHECKS AND OTHER ITEMS ARE RECEIVED FOR DEPOSIT SUBJECT TO THE TERMS AND CONDITIONS OF THIS BANK'S COLLECTION AGREEMENT	TOTAL DEPOSIT		

⑈0860⑈0830⑈1843⑈671⑈

11-2 Jordan Glaser, owner of a home cleaning service, completed the following checkbook transactions:

January 15, Paid for cleaning supplies, $40; check No. 118
     19, Paid for taxi service, $15; check No. 119
     22, Deposited $75 in bills and checks for $60 and $40
     22, Withdrew $50 for personal use; check No. 120

(1) Complete each stub and check, signing each check as Glaser would.
(2) Complete the deposit slip and enter the amount on the deposit line of the last check stub.

(1)

	DOLLARS	CENTS
BAL. BRO'T FOR'D	136	50
AMT. DEPOSITED		
TOTAL		
AMT. THIS CHECK		
BAL. CAR'D FOR'D		

NO. _____ $ _____
DATE _____ 20 ___
TO _____
FOR _____

No. _____
1-830 / 860
_____ 20 _____

Pay to the order of _____ $ _____
_____ Dollars

BOLTON NATIONAL BANK
of New York, NY
⑆0860⑈0830⑆ 1848⑈671⑈

	DOLLARS	CENTS
BAL. BRO'T FOR'D		
AMT. DEPOSITED		
TOTAL		
AMT. THIS CHECK		
BAL. CAR'D FOR'D		

NO. _____ $ _____
DATE _____ 20 ___
TO _____
FOR _____

No. _____
1-830 / 860
_____ 20 _____

Pay to the order of _____ $ _____
_____ Dollars

BOLTON NATIONAL BANK
of New York, NY
⑆0860⑈0830⑆ 1848⑈671⑈

(See next page to continue with check No. 120.)

(2)

FOR DEPOSIT TO THE ACCOUNT OF

NAME _____
ADDRESS _____
DATE _____ 20 ___

BOLTON NATIONAL BANK
New York, NY
CHECKS AND OTHER ITEMS ARE RECEIVED FOR DEPOSIT SUBJECT TO THE TERMS AND CONDITIONS OF THIS BANK'S COLLECTION AGREEMENT.

	DOLLARS	CENTS
BILLS		
COINS		
CHECKS AS FOLLOWS, PROPERLY ENDORSED		
TOTAL DEPOSIT		

⑆0860⑈0830⑆ 1848⑈671⑈

(1)

```
NO._____  $_____
DATE_____ 20 ____
TO_____
FOR_____
_____
_____
                    | DOLLARS | CENTS |
BAL. BRO'T FOR'D    |         |       |
AMT. DEPOSITED      |         |       |
                    |         |       |
TOTAL               |         |       |
AMT. THIS CHECK     |         |       |
BAL. CAR'D FOR'D    |         |       |
```

No._____

$\dfrac{1\text{-}830}{860}$

_____ 20 _____

Pay to the
order of _____ $ _____

_____ **Dollars**

BOLTON NATIONAL BANK
of New York, NY

⑆0860⑈0830⑆ 1848⑈671⑈

11-3 Helen Spiro's last check stub balance was $420.90. Her bank statement balance dated November 30 was $397.40. A $250 deposit was in transit on that date. Outstanding checks were as follows: No. 217, $75.00; No. 219, $105.50; No. 220, $50.00. The bank service charge for the month was $4.00. Prepare a reconciliation statement, indicating the correct checkbook balance and available bank balance on November 30.

Checkbook Balance	Bank Balance

11-4 Yoshi Kawahara, a landscape engineer, received his January bank statement on February 2. The balance was $626.66. His last check stub balance was $708.92. On comparing the two, he noted that a deposit of $375 made on January 31 was not included on the statement; also, a bank service charge of $3.60 was deducted. Outstanding checks were as follows: No. 641, $92.50; No. 644, $107.25; No. 646, $37.80; and No. 647, $58.79.

(1) Complete a reconciliation statement, indicating Kawahara's correct, available bank balance.

(2) Record the service charge in Kawahara's general journal.

(1)

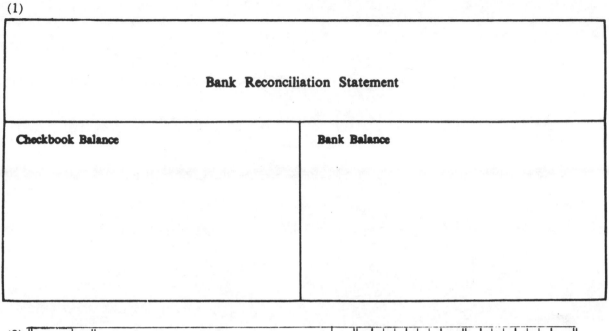

Bank Reconciliation Statement

Checkbook Balance	Bank Balance

(2)

THINK IT OVER

Timothy Hankins used a qualified endorsement in depositing a check that subsequently was dishonored because of insufficient funds. What rights does the bank cashing the check have? Who is liable for payment?

CHAPTER

12

THE PETTY CASH FUND

Purpose of the Fund

All cash received by a business should be deposited promptly in a checking account. Also, withdrawals are usually made by issuing checks signed by an authorized officer of the business. In that way there is a record of all funds coming in (cash debit) and all funds paid out (cash credit). However, there are times when small amounts must be paid out, perhaps for postage stamps, a collect telegram, or a package delivered collect on delivery, for which drawing a check would not be practical.

A special PETTY CASH fund is maintained for these small payments. This fund requires strict control because of the danger of missing cash. The following procedures are recommended to safeguard the petty cash fund:

(1) Petty cash should be kept separately from any other cash on hand.
(2) One person only should be held responsible for the petty cash fund.
(3) A record of each payment from petty cash should be kept, showing the person to whom it was paid, the reason, the date, the amount, and, if possible, the signature of the person to whom it was given.

Establishing the Fund

To establish a petty cash fund, a check is drawn *payable to Petty Cash*, a new ledger account, directly following the Cash account.

NO. 376	$40 00		
DATE August 2 20			
TO Petty Cash			
FOR to Establish fund			

	DOLLARS	CENTS
BAL. BRO'T FOR'D	581	36
AMT. DEPOSITED	400	00
TOTAL	981	36
AMT. THIS CHECK	40	00
BAL. CAR'D FOR'D	941	36

ACE TRAVEL SERVICE No. 376

1-830 / 860

August 2 20

Pay to the order of _Petty Cash_ $40 00

Forty & 00/100 ———————————— Dollars

BOLTON NATIONAL BANK of New York, NY

Hans Petersen

⑆0860⑈0830⑆ 1243⑈671⑈

The preceding check is endorsed by Hans Petersen and cashed. The amount is turned over to the person in charge of the fund, to be placed in a drawer or cash box, under lock and key. The check stub becomes the source document for the following journal entry:

200-					
aug.	2	Petty Cash		40 00	
		Cash			40 00
		To Establish Fund, Check No. 376			

Making Disbursements

Petty cash DISBURSEMENTS are made now whenever small amounts must be paid. The person requesting the amount may be required to fill out a numbered PETTY CASH VOUCHER, giving all required information and signing the voucher. The authorized signature is then obtained to make the disbursement from the fund. The voucher is filed or kept in a separate compartment of the fund box. The following is a typical petty cash voucher:

No. _____

ACE TRAVEL SERVICE
Petty Cash Voucher

Date _____ 20____

Pay to _____

For _____

Amount $ _____

Payment Received   Authorized

As the amount of petty cash remaining in the fund decreases, the dollar amount of the vouchers increases. At any time, the two taken together will total the *original amount in the fund*. When the petty cash fund balance gets low, it will be REPLENISHED by drawing another check payable to petty cash. The amount of this check will be exactly *equal to the total of the vouchers*. The check is cashed, and the money is placed in the petty cash drawer or box. Once again, the petty cash fund equals the total amount for which the fund was established originally.

Assume that petty cash vouchers indicate that payments were made over a period of time for many items. These vouchers are sorted out as follows:

Office expenses	$17.50	
Delivery expenses	9.60	
Miscellaneous expenses	5.95	$33.05

Proving Petty Cash

To *prove petty cash* at this point, the remaining cash is counted. Since the fund started with $40, there should be $6.95 remaining in the petty cash fund. This proves correct:

$40.00	(original balance)
− 33.05	(disbursements)
$ 6.95	(cash fund count)

The replenishing check stub and check are shown below:

Replenishing the Fund

The replenishing entry prepared from the check stub will result in a debit to the various items for which petty cash has been disbursed. In that way *the only debit to the petty cash account is from the entry to establish the fund*; that will remain the account balance, unless the fund is changed. The items for which petty cash was spent will be posted to the specific accounts for which petty cash was disbursed.

	31	Delivery Expense			9 60		
		Miscellaneous Expense			5 95		
		Office Expense			17 50		
		Cash					33 05
		To Replenish Petty Cash,					
		Check No. 387					

Petty cash should be replenished at least once each month, usually at the end of the month, or the end of a fiscal period, and whenever the fund runs low.

YOU SHOULD REMEMBER

Only *one person* should be *responsible for a petty cash fund*.

The *sum of all vouchers* (for which disbursements have been made) *plus cash* in the petty cash fund must *equal the original amount* of the fund.

The *replenishing entry* debits the *accounts* for which petty cash was disbursed.

Only *one amount* appears as a *debit in the petty cash account—the amount* for which it was *established*.

KNOW YOUR VOCABULARY

Disbursements	Petty cash voucher
Petty cash	Replenish

QUESTIONS

1. Why is it recommended procedure to have one person in charge of the petty cash fund?
2. What is the source document for the *entry* to establish petty cash? To replenish petty cash?
3. What is the journal entry to establish petty cash?
4. What is the journal entry to replenish petty cash?
5. How is petty cash proved?

PROBLEMS

12–1 Hilda Marcello, owner of Space Travel Services, has decided to establish a petty cash fund because of frequent, small disbursements.

(1) Draw a check for $35 to establish the fund.

(2) As the authorized person, complete petty cash vouchers for each of the following disbursements:

April 2, $2.75 to messenger who delivered a package (delivery expense)
9, $8.00 for postage (office expense)
16, $10.00 gasoline for auto (auto expense)
23, $7.50 for printing business cards (miscellaneous expense)
30, $4.00 for postage

(3) Sort these vouchers; prove petty cash; complete a check stub and check to replenish the petty cash fund on the last day of the month.

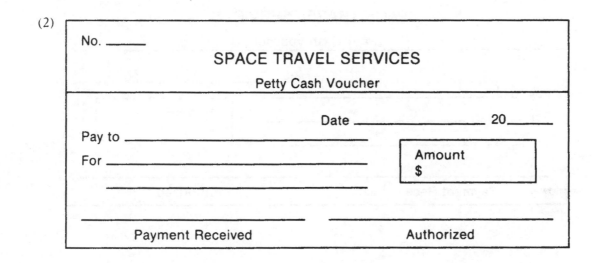

	DOLLARS	CENTS
NO. *138* $_____		
DATE_____ 20____		
TO_____		
FOR_____		
BAL. BRO'T FOR'D	*1406*	*92*
AMT. DEPOSITED		
TOTAL		
AMT. THIS CHECK		
BAL. CAR'D FOR'D		

SPACE TRAVEL SERVICES

No._____
1-830
860

_____ 20____

Pay to the
order of _____ $_____

_____ **Dollars**

BOLTON NATIONAL BANK
of New York, NY

⑆0860⑈0830⑆ 1243⑈671⑊

(2)

SPACE TRAVEL SERVICES

Petty Cash Voucher

No. _____

Date _____ 20_____

Pay to _____

For _____

_____

Amount
$

_____   _____
Payment Received   Authorized

SPACE TRAVEL SERVICES

Petty Cash Voucher

No. _____

Date _____ 20_____

Pay to _____

For _____

_____

Amount
$

_____   _____
Payment Received   Authorized

No. _____

SPACE TRAVEL SERVICES

Petty Cash Voucher

Date _____ 20_____

Pay to _____

For _____

     _____

Amount
$

_____   _____

Payment Received   Authorized

No. _____

SPACE TRAVEL SERVICES

Petty Cash Voucher

Date _____ 20_____

Pay to _____

For _____

     _____

Amount
$

_____   _____

Payment Received   Authorized

No. ____

SPACE TRAVEL SERVICES
Petty Cash Voucher

Date _____ 20____

Pay to _____

For _____

_____

Amount
$

_____   _____
Payment Received   Authorized

3)

NO. *156* ____ $____

DATE ____ 20____

TO ____

FOR ____

____

____

	DOLLARS	CENTS
BAL. BRO'T FOR'D	1091	37
AMT. DEPOSITED	500	00
TOTAL	1591	37
AMT. THIS CHECK		
BAL. CAR'D FOR'D		

SPACE TRAVEL SERVICES

No. ____

1-315
860

_____ 20____

Pay to the
order of _____ $____

_____ Dollars

BOLTON NATIONAL BANK
of Long Island, NY

⑇0860⑇0830⑇ 1243⑇671⑇

12-2   Using the information in Problem 12-1 (1) and (3), complete the journal entries to establish the petty cash fund and to replenish it.

	GENERAL JOURNAL				Page *15*

Date	Account Title	PR	Debit	Credit

THINK IT OVER

Connie's Interior Designs has a $50 petty cash fund. The owner's assistant, Jim Landers, is authorized to draw checks from the regular checking account and is also in charge of the petty cash fund. Last month, disbursements from the fund increased, and the fund had to be replenished several times. What recommendations might be made to the owner regarding the control factor, as well as the amount in the fund?

CYCLE ONE
EXAMINATION

Part I   Indicate by a check (√) in the column at the right whether each statement is TRUE or FALSE.

		T	F
Example:	All accounts increase by debits.		√
1.	Liabilities and owner's equity increase by credits.		
2.	For every transaction, increases equal decreases.		
3.	For every transaction, debits equal credits.		
4.	A debit to the Cash account results in an increase.		
5.	A debit to J. Smith, Capital, results in an increase.		
6.	A journal entry is posted to ledger accounts.		
7.	The ledger account PR column indicates the journal page number.		
8.	A balance sheet describes the financial operations over a period of time.		
9.	An income statement is a picture of the financial condition of a business.		
10.	The omission of a transaction will cause a trial balance to be out of balance.		
11.	A $100 debit posted as a credit will cause Trial Balance columns to differ by $200.		
12.	A work sheet aids in the preparation of financial statements.		
13.	A capital statement starts with owner's equity at the end of the fiscal period.		
14.	Closing entries result in zero balances in revenue and expense accounts.		
15.	A net loss for the fiscal period is closed into the capital account by a debit to Revenue and Expense Summary and a credit to the capital account.		
16.	Balance sheet accounts normally have balances that carry over to succeeding fiscal periods.		
17.	A check stub should be completed before writing the check.		
18.	A bank statement balance will identify the checks that are outstanding.		
19.	Each petty cash voucher is the source document for a journal entry.		
20.	The petty cash fund replenishing entry results in debits to the various accounts for which petty cash was spent.		

Part II   Match the definition with the term by writing the appropriate *letter* in the column at the right (A term is used once only.)

Terms	Definitions	Letter
	Example: The value in an account	C
A. Accounts receivable	1. A simple signature on the back of a check	1.
B. Asset	2. All accounts arranged by number	2.
C. Balance	3. Transferring entries from the journal to accounts	3.
D. Bank statement	4. A listing of all accounts with debit or credit balances for a work sheet	4.
E. Closing entry		
F. Creditor	5. The one to whom a debt is owed	5.
G. Disbursement	6. Payments made from the petty cash fund	6.
H. Drawee	7. A statement prepared to find the correct checkbook and bank balance	7.
I. Endorsement in blank		
J. Income statement	8. Income earned	8.
K. Journal	9. Any form used as a source document for a transaction	9.
L. Ledger	10. A journal entry that zeros out an account balance	10.
M. Liabilities	11. Anything of value owned	11.
N. Owner's equity	12. Net worth or capital	12.
O. Payee	13. Customers' accounts	13.
P. Post-closing trial balance	14. A chronological list of transactions, as a diary	14.
Q. Posting		
R. Reconciliation statement	15. The bank on which a check is drawn	15.
S. Restrictive endorsement	16. Two-column record-keeping form	16.
T. Revenue		
U. Single-entry procedure		
V. Trial balance		
W. Voucher		

Part III For each of the following transactions, indicate the accounts to be debited and credited. Use the account titles listed at the left.

Account Titles	Transactions		Account Dr.	Account Cr.
	Example: Received $100 fee from customer.		A	G
A. Cash	1. Paid employee salary, $200.	1.		
B. Supplies	2. Bought $30 worth of supplies for cash.	2.		
C. Accounts Payable	3. Invested $1,000 cash.	3.		
D. J. Owner, Capital	4. Closed the revenue account.	4.		
E. J. Owner, Drawing	5. Bought $500 worth of supplies, paying $100 down, and balance on account.	5.		
F. Revenue and Expense Summary	6. Withdrew $150 cash for personal use.	6.		
G. Commissions Income	7. Closed the expense accounts	7.		
H. Auto Expense	8. Closed net income to owner's equity.	8.		
I. Miscellaneous Expense	9. Closed net loss to owner's equity.	9.		
J. Salary Expense	10. Closed the drawing account	10.		

Part IV (1) Complete Chet Gorski's work sheet.

(2) Complete a capital statement; assume that Gorski's capital includes a $5,000 investment during the year. His capital Jan. 1 is $9,685.00.

(3) Complete a balance sheet.

(4) Journalize the closing entries.

County-Wide Plumbing
Work Sheet
For the Year Ended December 31, 200—

Account Title	A. N.	Trial Balance Debit	Trial Balance Credit	Income Statement Debit	Income Statement Credit	Balance Sheet Debit	Balance Sheet Credit
Cash	111	1472 50					
Petty Cash	112	25 00					
Accounts Receivable	113	385 00					
Supplies	114	242 50					
Truck	115	4650 00					
Accounts Payable	211		97 00				
Chet Gorski, Capital	311		14685 00				
Chet Gorski, Drawing	312	950 00					
Fees Income	411		1862 00				
Advertising Expense	511	980 00					
Automobile Expense	512	240 00					
Miscellaneous Expense	513	120 00					
Rent Expense	514	340 00					
Telephone Expense	515	120 00					

(2) _____

(3) _____

Part V   (1)   Complete the following check stub and check:

NO. 207	$ 35.50		
DATE January 7 20			
TO Wilson Supply Co			
FOR Smoke alarm			
(Equipment)			
		DOLLARS	CENTS
BAL. BRO'T FOR'D		382	47
AMT. DEPOSITED		225	00
TOTAL			
AMT. THIS CHECK			
BAL. CAR'D FOR'D			

No.____

1-315
860

_____ 20 ____

Pay to the
order of _____ $ ____

_____ Dollars

BOLTON NATIONAL BANK
of Long Island, NY

_____

⑆0860⑆08 30⑈ 1 248⑈ 6 7 1⑆

(2)   Record the journal entry for the above payment to Wilson Supply Company for the purchase of equipment.

JOURNAL

CYCLE TWO
A Merchandising Business

CHAPTER **13**

PURCHASES OF MERCHANDISE

Purchasing on Account—Accounts Payable

A merchandising business buys goods for resale to its customers; these goods are its MERCHANDISE. The usual procedure for most businesses is to buy ON ACCOUNT, rather than for cash. The balance is paid sometime in the future, perhaps within 30 to 60 days. As a result of such purchases, debts, called ACCOUNTS PAYABLE, are owed to creditors.

Purchases Journal

When many such purchases on account occur, it is preferred practice to record these transactions in a separate, special journal—a PURCHASES JOURNAL. This journal is used exclusively for recording one type of transaction—a *purchase of merchandise on account*.

   This expense or *cost of merchandise* creates a new account, Purchases. Like expenses, *cost accounts increase by debits and decrease by credits*. If this entry appeared in *general journal* form, it would look as follows:

200- Feb	2	Purchases		500	00		
		Accounts Payable / B Winslow ✓				500	00
		Purchases Invoice No. 152					

If there are many purchases of merchandise on account during a fiscal period, this entry will be repeated, and each entry posted to the Purchases account as well as the Accounts Payable account. (Purchases will be numbered 51; Accounts Payable will be numbered 21; all expenses will be *renumbered,* starting with 61.)

Posting Creditors' Accounts

To eliminate this repetitive posting to both Purchases and Accounts Payable, a PURCHASES JOURNAL is used. Creditors' accounts are posted for all entries so that up-to-date balances will be available. These accounts are located in a seperate payable ledger—a SUBSIDIARY LEDGER— where they are arranged alphabetically, or by special account number. Examine the following purchases journal entries:

PURCHASES JOURNAL   Page **6**

Date	From Whom Purchased - Account Credited		Invoice No.	PR	Purchases Dr. Accts. Pay. Cr.	
200- apr. 2	Tri-Royal Sales Company		4834		3096	00
7	Thomas Gregorius + Sons		045		375	00
19	Vincent Morock, Inc.		380		400	00
26	Thomas Gregorius + Sons		061		250	00

Each of these entries originated with a source document, an INVOICE, a statement or bill completed by the seller of merchandise. As can be seen from the following invoice, this form contains a complete description of the transaction. When received, it is checked against the merchandise that was shipped. Then it is recorded in the special purchases journal. Tri-Royal *sold* merchandise to Best-West and prepared the following invoice. Best-West *bought* merchandise from Tri-Royal and received a copy of that invoice, from which the purchases journal entry is made.

TRI-ROYAL SALES COMPANY
2158 Chambers Street
Trenton, NJ 08609

Sold to
Best-West Sewing Machine Corp   **Invoice No. 4834**
296 South Street   **Date** *April 2, 200—*
Newark, NJ 07114   **Our Order No. 7985**
                                          Customer's Order No. 924
Terms *30 days*   **Shipped via** *Truck*

Quantity	Description	Unit Price		Total Amount	
18	*EZ Sewing Machines #A15*	145	75	2623	50
75	*Hooks #H107*	6	30	472	50
				3096	00

Summarizing the Purchases Journal

The purchases journal is posted on a regular basis to creditors' accounts in the subsidiary ledger. At the end of the month, this journal is SUMMARIZED—totaled and ruled, and the total is posted to the accounts named in the column headed "Purchases Dr. and Accounts Payable Cr." These accounts are in the GENERAL LEDGER. In this way, the general ledger maintains debits equal to credits.

Review the purchases journal below, which has now been posted to both subsidiary and general ledger accounts. Note the 3-column arrangement of the creditors' accounts and the 4-column arrangement of the general ledger accounts. These provide for a balance *on the same line* as the entry—thus avoiding any pencil footings. To determine new balances, remember:

(1) Debit entries are added to prior debit balances.
(2) Credit entries are added to prior credit balances.
(3) Debit entries are deducted from prior credit balances.
(4) Credit entries are deducted from prior debit balances.

PURCHASES JOURNAL — Page 6

Date	From Whom Purchased - Account Credited	Invoice No.	PR	Purchases Dr. Accts. Pay. Cr.
200- Apr. 2	Tri-Royal Sales Company	4834	✓	3096 00
7	Thomas Gregorius + Sons	045	✓	375 00
19	Vincent Nurock, Inc.	380	✓	400 00
26	Thomas Gregorius + Sons	061	✓	250 00
30	Total			4121 00
				(51) (21)

ACCOUNTS PAYABLE LEDGER

Thomas Gregorius + Sons
515 Capital Avenue, Trenton, NJ 07114

Date		PR	Dr.	Cr.	Cr. Bal.
200- Apr. 7		P6		375 00	375 00
26		P6		250 00	625 00

Vincent Nurock, Inc.
170 Underhill Boulevard, Syosset, NY 11791

Date		PR	Dr.	Cr.	Cr. Bal.
200- Mar. 4		P5		150 00	150 00
Apr. 19		P6		400 00	550 00

Tri-Royal Sales Company
2158 Chambers Street, Trenton, NJ 08609

Date		PR	Dr.	Cr.	Cr. Bal.
200- Feb. 28		P4		100 00	100 00
Mar. 18		P5		200 00	300 00
Apr. 2		P6		3096 00	3396 00

GENERAL LEDGER

Accounts Payable   No. 21

Date			PR	Dr.	Cr.	Balance Dr.	Balance Cr.
200- Feb. 28			P4		100 00		100 00
Mar. 31			P5		350 00		450 00
Apr. 30			P6		4121 00		4571 00

Purchases   No. 51

				Dr.	Cr.	Balance Dr.	Balance Cr.
200- Apr. 30			P6	4121 00		4121 00	

    The creditors' postings are indicated by check marks (√) in the purchases journal because these accounts have no numbers—they are arranged alphabetically. The journal total was posted to ledger accounts No. 51 and No. 21 (Purchases and Accounts Payable).

    In the accounts payable ledger, note carefully the three-column arrangement of creditors' accounts, some of which have balances carried over from prior months. A credit posting increases an account with a credit balance. We will see in Chapter 14 that posting debits to these accounts decreases their balances.

    As stated above, posting references to creditors' accounts are indicated by check marks in the purchases journal because they have no account numbers. The journal total is posted to general ledger accounts No. 51 and No. 21. This same technique for posting will be used whenever special journals are involved.

Schedule of Accounts Payable

At the end of the month, the accuracy of postings can be proved by preparing a SCHEDULE OF ACCOUNTS PAYABLE. This is a listing of creditors' accounts and the balance owed to each creditor. The total of the schedule should be equal to the balance in the CONTROLLING ACCOUNT—Accounts Payable—which shows the *total* balance of the sum of the individual subsidiary account balances. A creditor with a zero balance may or may not be included in the schedule of accounts payable. If it is, list the name with zeros in the amount column.

Best-West Sewing Machine Company
Schedule of Accounts Payable
April 30, 200-

Thomas Gregorius & Sons	625 00
Vincent Nurock, Inc.	550 00
Tri-Royal Sales Company	3396 00
Total Accounts Payable	4571 00

KNOW YOUR VOCABULARY

Accounts Payable	Purchases journal
Controlling account	Schedule of accounts payable
General ledger	Subsidiary ledger
Merchandise	Summarize (summary entry)
On account	

QUESTIONS

1. How does one distinguish between a service-type business and a merchandising business?
2. What type of transaction is recorded in a purchases journal?
3. How are creditors' accounts arranged in a subsidiary ledger?
4. How is the equality of general ledger debits and credits maintained when a special journal is used?
5. Why are creditors' accounts arranged alphabetically in a subsidiary ledger rather than numbered?
6. How is the accuracy of the subsidiary ledger proved?
7. What advantage is there in using a three-column ruling in creditors' accounts? A four-column ruling in general ledger accounts?

PROBLEMS

13–1 (1) Record the following purchases of merchandise on account on purchases journa page 5:

February 3, 200— Dye & Akins, invoice No. 1705, $300
            10,   Edward Kalpakian & Sons, invoice No. G-116, $425
            17,   Dye & Akins, invoice No. 1751, $385
            25,   Edward Kalpakian & Sons, invoice No. G-151, $500

   (2) Post to the subsidiary ledger.
   (3) Summarize the purchases journal at the end of the month, and post to the genera ledger.
   (4) Prepare a schedule of accounts payable for the owner, Ruth Ann Davis.

(1)

PURCHASES JOURNAL   Page 2

Dye and Akins

(2)

280- Jan. 15		P1			45000	45000

Edward Kalpakian & Sons

GENERAL JOURNAL

Accounts Payable   No. 21

(3)

			Dr.	Cr.	Balance Dr.	Cr.
200- Jan. 31		P1		45000		45000

Purchases   No. 51

			Dr.	Cr.	Balance Dr.	Cr.

(4)

_____

_____

_____

13–2 (1) Record the following purchases of merchandise on account:

February 1, 200—	Paul Olins, invoice No. 42, $175
5,	Wilson & Shea, invoice No. 513, $200
8,	Island Supply, invoice No. 72A, $265
12,	Wilson & Shea, invoice No. 543, $400
15,	Glen Mfg., Inc., invoice No. 31, $620
19,	Paul Olins, invoice No. 78, $360
22,	Gregory Sims, invoice No. 318, $250
26,	Island Supply, invoice No. 29B, $300

(2) Post to the subsidiary ledger.

(3) Summarize the purchases journal at the end of the month, and post to the general ledger.

(4) Prepare a schedule of accounts payable for the owner, Maria Zagretti.

(1) and (3)   **PURCHASES JOURNAL**   Page 2

ACCOUNTS PAYABLE LEDGER

Glen Mfg., Inc.

(2)

Island Supply

Paul Olins

Gregory Sims

Wilson & Shea

GENERAL LEDGER

Accounts Payable   No. 21

(3)

			Dr.	Cr.	Balance	
					Dr.	Cr.

Purchases   No. 51

			Dr.	Cr.	Balance	
					Dr.	Cr.

(4)

THINK IT OVER

By using a purchases journal, Harold Marino estimates that he saves at least one hour of posting time each week. How is this possible?

CHAPTER **14**

CASH DISBURSEMENTS JOURNAL

A great number of business transactions involve the payment of cash, mostly by check. Such cash disbursements occur when invoices for merchandise purchased on account are paid, as well as payments for equipment, supplies, rent, salaries, and so on.

With each cash disbursement, a credit to cash must be recorded to decrease the Cash account. For each of these transactions, there also is a debit to the other account(s) involved. A typical *general journal* entry for a cash disbursement follows:

200-					
Mar. 2	Accounts Payable / John Reid Co.		54000		
	Cash				54000
	Invoice No. 579, Check No. 318				

Columnar Journal —Special Columns

A general journal entry such as this requires postings to all accounts—Accounts Payable Debit, Cash Credit (in the general ledger), and John Reid Company's account debit (in the subsidiary ledger). It is preferable, therefore, to use a special CASH DISBURSEMENTS JOURNAL, which will require less frequent and fewer postings, and still keep creditors' accounts up to date. The entry shown above has been recorded in Jose Garcia's special journal, along with other typical cash disbursements transactions:

CASH DISBURSEMENTS JOURNAL   Page 1

Date	Account Debited	Ck. No.	PR	General Dr.	Accts. Pay. Dr.	Cash Cr.
200- mar. 2	John Reid Company	318			54000	54000
3	Rent Expense	319		30000		30000
9	Supplies	320		7500		7500
15	Salary Expense	321		15000		15000
16	Union National Bank	322			40000	40000
30	Jose Garcia, Drawing	323		50000		50000
31	Los Angeles Distributing Co.	324			49500	49500

Note that there is a special column for the controlling account—Accounts Payable Dr. While postings are required for each account debited, *special column totals are posted only at the end of the month*. This journal is summarized, and the columns that have *identifiable account title headings* are posted as indicated—Accounts Payable Dr. (21) and Cash Cr. (11). The General Dr. column total is not posted and checked (√) because there is no *single* general ledger account for that total. Furthermore, the individual accounts listed as debited will have been posted.

Summarizing the Journal

Garcia's journal now appears as shown below, summarized and posted:

CASH DISBURSEMENTS JOURNAL   Page 1

Date	Account Debited	Ck. No.	PR	General Dr.	Accts. Pay Dr.	Cash Cr.
200- mar. 2	John Reid Company	318	√		54000	54000
3	Rent Expense	319	54	30000		30000
9	Supplies	320	14	7500		7500
15	Salary Expense	321	55	15000		15000
16	Union National Bank	322	√		40000	40000
30	Jose Garcia, Drawing	323	32	50000		50000
31	Los Angeles Distributing Co.	324	√		49500	49500
31	Totals			103500	143500	246000
				(√)	(21)	(11)

First the columns were pencil footed; debit totals equal credit totals. Then they were written in ink, and the journal was double ruled. The General Dr. column total is always checkmarked, and the special column totals have been posted to the accounts identified in their headings. The postings to creditors' accounts and to the Cash and Accounts Payable accounts follow (General Dr. column account postings are not illustrated here):

GENERAL LEDGER

Cash   No. 11

			Dr.	Cr.	Balance Dr.	Balance Cr.
200–Mar	31	CR	5000 00		5000 00	
	31	CD1		2460 00	2540 00	

Accounts Payable   No. 21

			Dr.	Cr.	Balance Dr.	Balance Cr.
200–Mar	1	Balance ✓				540 00
	31	P1		1995 00		2535 00
	31	CD1	1435 00			1100 00

ACCOUNTS PAYABLE LEDGER

Los Angeles Distributing Company
5001 Santa Monica Boulevard, Los Angeles, CA 90002

			Dr.	Cr.	Balance
200–Mar	4	P1		495 00	495 00
	25	P1		1000 00	1495 00
	31	CD1	495 00		1000 00

John Reid Company
72-05 Canyon Boulevard, Pasadena, CA 91100

			Dr.	Cr.	Balance
200–Mar	1	Balance ✓			540 00
	2	CD1	540 00		—

Union National Bank
452 Ocean Boulevard, San Diego, CA 92101

			Dr.	Cr.	Balance
200–Mar	15	P1		500 00	500 00
	31	CD1	400 00		100 00

Schedule of Accounts Payable

At the end of the month, Jose Garcia's schedule of accounts payable is taken to prove the accuracy of the subsidiary ledger:

Jose Garcia
Schedule of Accounts Payable
March 31, 2700—

Los Angeles Distributing Co.	1 000 00
Union National Bank	100 00
Total Accounts Payable	1 100 00

The balance of the controlling account, Accounts Payable, is also $1,100. The two are equal; the subsidiary ledger proves.

A cash disbursements journal may be expanded to include four or more columns, depending on the needs of the business. For example, if many *cash purchases* of merchandise occur, a special column—*Purchases Dr.*—can be included. Some businesses find it convenient to include a *Salary Expense Dr.* column as well. If these columns are included, it is necessary to checkmark (√) the posting reference column; no posting is needed for each cash purchase entry, inasmuch as *the column total will be posted,* along with all other special column totals, *at the end of the month.*

Examine these entries in a five-column cash disbursements journal:

CASH DISBURSEMENTS JOURNAL   Page 4

Date		Account Debited	Ck. No.	PR	General Dr.	Accts. Pay Dr.	Purchases Dr.	Salary Exp. Dr.	Cash Cr.
2700 Mar.	4	Rent Expense	506		400 00				400 00
	7	Salary Expense	507	√				250 00	250 00
	12	Purchases	508	√			725 00		725 00
	19	Supplies Company	509			75 00			75 00
	26	Purchases	510	√			300 00		300 00
	31	Totals			400 00	75 00	1025 00	250 00	1750 00
					(√)	(√)	(√)	(√)	(√)

At the end of the month, the bookkeeping/accounting clerk can easily see which items need to be posted, and which do not. Those that are already checked *will not be posted*; items appearing in the *General Dr.* and *Accounts Payable Dr.* columns *will be posted* to the accounts identified in the account column. The *special column totals*—Accounts Payable Dr., Purchases Dr., Salary Expense Dr., and Cash Cr.—will be posted.

Source Document for Cash Disbursement

The cash disbursements journal, a multicolumn book of original entry, is used exclusively for entries that result in cash credits, resulting in a decrease in the amount of cash. For each entry, a check stub is identified as the source document in the Check Number (Ck. No.) column.

YOU SHOULD REMEMBER

Creditors' account balances should be kept up to date by frequent postings (daily or weekly).

Special journal column *totals* are *posted* to the accounts identified *in the column heading.*

KNOW YOUR VOCABULARY

Cash disbursements journal   Summary entry

QUESTIONS

1. What advantage is there to using special journals for cash disbursements transactions, compared to using the general journal?
2. How are postings from a cash disbursements journal identified in the general ledger account?
3. What justifies the use of a special column in a cash disbursements journal?
4. How are postings to subsidiary ledger accounts indicated in the cash disbursements journal?
5. When does the check mark ($\checkmark$) indicate not to post?
6. When does the check mark indicate that the item has been posted?
7. How is the accuracy of the subsidiary ledger proved?

PROBLEMS

14-1 Sid Krasnoff uses a four-column cash disbursements journal with a special column for his personal cash withdrawals. Last month, his check stub record indicated the following:

March 1, Paid month's rent, $400; check No. 247

      3, Paid utilities bill, $76.50; check No. 248

      8, Paid Paula Cory on account, $50; check No. 249

     10, Withdrew for personal use, $500; check No. 250

     17, Paid employee's salary, $300; check No. 251

     22, Paid Hilda Piper on account, $90; check No. 252

     24, Withdrew for personal use, $500; check No. 253

     29, Bought new equipment, $1,250; check No. 254

     31, Paid employee's salary, $300; check No. 255

(1) Record each of these transactions, checking any entry that is not to be posted separately.

(2) Summarize the cash disbursements journal, checking any *total that is not to be posted*. Indicate by open parentheses ( ) totals that would be posted.

(1) and (2)   CASH DISBURSEMENTS JOURNAL   Page 3

Date	Account Debited	Ck. No.	PR	General Dr.	Acct. Pay. Dr.	S. Krasnoff Draw. Dr.	Cash Cr.

14–2   Helen Scordas uses a special purchases journal and a three-column cash disbursements journal. Last month, she completed the following transactions:

April 1,   Paid month's rent, $450; check No. 502

4,   Purchased merchandise on account from Abel & Jenks, $600; invoice No. P-311

8,   Withdrew for personal use $400; check No. 503

14,   Paid Abel & Jenks on account $800; check No. 504

15,   Paid employee's salary, $325; check No. 505

20,   Purchased merchandise on account from W. T. Gross, $1,450; invoice No. 5113

22,   Bought supplies, $75; check No. 506

28,   Withdrew for personal use, $500; check No. 507

30,   Paid W. T. Gross part on account, $725; check No. 508

(1)   Record the entries for each transaction.

(2)   Post the entries from the purchases journal.

(3)   Post the entries from the cash disbursements journal.

(4)   Summarize each journal, and post the column totals as indicated in the headings of each special column.

(5)   Prove the accuracy of the subsidiary ledger by preparing a schedule of accounts payable.

(1) and (4)   PURCHASES JOURNAL   Page 2

Date	Account Credited		Inv. No.	PR	Purchases Dr. Acct. Pay. Cr.

(1) and (4)   CASH DISBURSEMENTS JOURNAL   Page 3

Date	Acct. Dr.	Ck. No.	PR	General Dr.	Acct. Pay. Dr.	Cash Cr.

GENERAL LEDGER

Cash   No. 11

Date		PR	Dr.	Cr.	Balance Dr.	Cr.
200- apr. 1	Balance	✓			4500 00	

Supplies   No. 13

Date		PR	Dr.	Cr.	Balance Dr.	Cr.
200- apr. 1	Balance	✓			50 00	

Accounts Payable   No. 21

(2) and (3)

Date		PR	Dr.	Cr.	Balance Dr.	Cr.
200- apr. 1	Balance	✓				800 00

Helen Scordas, Drawing   No. 32

Date		PR	Dr.	Cr.	Balance Dr.	Cr.

Purchases No. 51

Date		PR	Dr.	Cr.	Balance Dr.	Balance Cr.

Rent Expense No. 61

Date		PR	Dr.	Cr.	Balance Dr.	Balance Cr.

Salary Expense No. 62

Date		PR	Dr.	Cr.	Balance Dr.	Balance Cr.

ACCOUNTS PAYABLE LEDGER

(2) and (3)

Abel & Jenks
1200 Mineral Boulevard, Scranton, PA 18501

Date			Dr.	Cr.	Cr. Bal.
200- Apr. 1	Balance	✓			80000

W. J. Gross
805 Keystone Road, Wilkes Barre, PA 18700

Date			Dr.	Cr.	Cr. Bal.

(5)

CHAPTER **15**

SALES OF MERCHANDISE

Sales on Account

For a merchandising business, the sale of merchandise is probably the most frequent of all transactions. In many large businesses, a major part of sales are ON ACCOUNT, that is, credit sales.

A general journal entry to record the sale of merchandise on account follows:

200-					
Apr.	7	Accounts Receivable/Alan Bergstrom	175 00	
		Sales		175 00
		Sales Invoice No. 251		

Sales Journal and Accounts Receivable Ledger

If there were many sales similar to this one during a fiscal period, this entry would be repeated, and each entry would be posted to the Accounts Receivable account as well as to the Sales account. To eliminate the repetitive posting to both Accounts Receivable and Sales, a SALES

137

JOURNAL is used. Customers' accounts are posted for each entry so that up-to-date balances will be available. These accounts are located in another *separate subsidiary ledger*—an ACCOUNTS RECEIVABLE LEDGER—where accounts may be arranged alphabetically or, in some cases, by special account number. Examine the following sales journal entries:

SALES JOURNAL   Page **8**

Date	To Whom Sold – Account Debited	Invoice No.	PR	Accts. Rec.Dr. Sales Cr.
200- apr. 2	Best-West Sewing Machine Company	4834		3096 00
9	Elaine K. Brown	4835		175 00
23	Ralph Mazel & Company	4836		250 00
30	Elaine K. Brown	4837		200 00

Source Documents for Sales Journal Entries

Each of these entries originated with a source document, the invoice or sales slip, completed by the salesperson or the billing department of the seller. This invoice is prepared in TRIP-LICATE copy; one copy is given to the customer, one copy is used by the shipping department, and one copy is sent to the accounting department for a source document to record the transaction. (Refer to the invoice on page 120: Tri-Royal Sales Company is the seller; Best-West Sewing Machine Company is the buyer, or the customer.)

Posting and Summarizing the Sales Journal

The sales journal is posted on a regular basis to customers' accounts in the subsidiary ledger. At the end of the month, this journal, like all special journals, is summarized, and the total is posted to the accounts named in the columns headed "Accounts Receivable Dr." and "Sales Cr." These accounts are in the general ledger, and by posting this total, debits will continue to equal credits.

Review the sales journal below, which has now been posted to both subsidiary and general ledger accounts:

SALES JOURNAL   Page **8**

Date	To Whom Sold – Account Debited	Invoice No.	PR	Accts. Rec.Dr. Sales Cr.
200- apr. 2	Best-West Sewing Machine Company	4834	✓	3096 00
9	Elaine K. Brown	4835	✓	175 00
23	Ralph Mazel & Company	4836	✓	250 00
30	Elaine K. Brown	4837	✓	200 00
30	Total			3721 00
				(13) (41)

ACCOUNTS RECEIVABLE LEDGER

Best-West Sewing Machine Company
296 South Street, Newark, NJ 0A14

Date			PR	Dr.	Cr.	Dr. Bal.
200– apr.	1	Balance	✓			300 00
	2		34	3096 00		3396 00

Elaine K. Brown
11 Harbor Road, Perth Amboy, NJ 08861

Date			PR	Dr.	Cr.	Dr. Bal.
200– apr.	9		S8	175 00		175 00
	30		S8	200 00		375 00

Ralph Mazel & Company
278 Patriots Road, Morristown, NJ 07960

Date			PR	Dr.	Cr.	Dr. Bal.
200– apr.	1	Balance	✓			400 00
	23		S8	250 00		650 00

GENERAL LEDGER

Accounts Receivable   No. 13

				Dr.	Cr.	Balance	
						Dr.	Cr.
200– apr.	1	Balance	✓			70000	
	30		S8	3721 00		4421 00	

Sales   No. 41

				Dr.	Cr.	Balance	
						Dr.	Cr.
200– apr.	30		S8		3721 00		3721 00

The customers' postings are indicated by check marks (√) because these accounts have no numbers—they are arranged alphabetically. The journal total was posted to accounts No. 13 and No. 41 (Accounts Receivable and Sales).

The three-column subsidiary ledger arrangement is used also for customers' accounts. A debit increases the customer's account balance; a credit decreases the customer's account balance.

Schedule of Accounts Receivable

At the end of the month, the accuracy of postings can be proved by preparing a SCHEDULE OF ACCOUNTS RECEIVABLE. This is a listing of customers' accounts and the balance due from each. The total of the schedule should be equal to the balance of the controlling account—Accounts Receivable—which shows in *total* balance the sum of the individual subsidiary account balances.

Tri-Royal Sales Company Schedule of Accounts Receivable April 30, 200—	
Best-West Sewing Machine Company	3396 00
Elaine K. Brown	375 00
Ralph Mazel & Company	650 00
Total Accounts Receivable	4421 00

YOU SHOULD REMEMBER

A sales journal is a book of *original* entry used only to record transactions for the *sale of merchandise on account*.

The sales journal *summary entry* posting is a *debit* to Accounts Receivable and a *credit* to Sales.

The schedule of Accounts Receivable *total* equals the *balance* of the *Accounts Receivable account*.

KNOW YOUR VOCABULARY

Accounts Receivable ledger

On account

Sales journal

Schedule of Accounts Receivable

Triplicate

QUESTIONS

1. What type of transaction is recorded in a sales journal?
2. How are customers' accounts arranged in a subsidiary ledger?
3. How is the equality of general ledger debits and credits maintained when posting a sales journal?

4. How is the accuracy of the subsidiary ledger proved?
5. Why might arranging customers' accounts alphabetically be easier for a small business to manage than numbering them?
6. Why are sales invoice numbers listed in consecutive order in a sales journal?

PROBLEMS

15-1 (1) Record Mear's Department Store's sales of merchandise on account, starting with invoice No. 215:

    March 2, 200— Mrs. Edward Ardyce, $175
        9,   Mr. Herman Gold, $96.50
        16,   Ms. Eliza Fisher, $107.30
        23,   Mrs. Edward Ardyce, $62.45
        30,   Ms. Eliza Fisher, $29.50

(2) Post to the subsidiary ledger.
(3) Summarize the sales journal at the end of the month, and post to the general ledger.
(4) Prepare a schedule of accounts receivable.

(1) and (3) SALES JOURNAL Page 31

Date	To Whom Sold - Account Debited	Invoice No.	PR	Acct. Rec. Dr. Sales Cr.

ACCOUNTS RECEIVABLE LEDGER

(2)

Mrs. Edward Ardyce
305 Riverview Terrace, Cincinnati, OH 45204

Date		PR	Dr.	Cr.	Dr. Bal.

Ms. Eliza Fisher
851 Clarkfield Street, Cincinnati, OH 45201

Date		PR	Dr.	Cr.	Dr. Bal.

Mr. Herman Gold
79 Willowbrook Drive, Cincinnati, OH 45202

Date		PR	Dr.	Cr.	Dr. Bal.
200- Mar. 1	Balance	✓			258 60

GENERAL LEDGER

Accounts Receivable

(3)   No. *13*

Date			PR	Dr.	Cr.	Balance Dr.	Balance Cr.
200- Mar 2	Balance		✓			25860	

Sales

No. *41*

			Dr.	Cr.	Balance Dr.	Balance Cr.

(4)

Mears Department Store
Schedule of Accounts Receivable
March 31, 200-

15–2   (1)   Record the following sales of merchandise on account for Winslow's Emporium, starting with invoice No. 328:

April 2, 200—   Mrs. Fay Wilamowski, $47.50
      6,   Ms. Shirley Callahan, $36.95
      9,   Mr. William Witt, $49.25
      13,   Ms. Shirley Callahan, $107.65
      16,   Mrs. Marjorie Intrator, $76.80
      20,   Mrs. Fay Wilamowski, $52.90
      23,   Mr. William Witt, $59.20
      27,   Mrs. Marjorie Intrator, $67.75
      30,   Ms. Shirley Callahan, $87.00

(2)   Post to the subsidiary ledger.
(3)   Summarize the sales journal at the end of the month, and post to the general ledger.
(4)   Prepare a schedule of accounts receivable.

(1) and (3)   SALES JOURNAL   Page 8

Date	To Whom Sold - Account Debited	Invoice No.	PR	Acct. Rec. Dr. Sales Cr.

ACCOUNTS RECEIVABLE LEDGER

(2)

Ms. Shirley Callahan
186 Mineola Boulevard, Mineola, NY 11501

Date			PR	Dr.	Cr.	Dr. Bal.
200– Apr.	1	Balance	✓			4500

Mrs. Marjorie Intrator
91 Bryn Mawr, New Hyde Park, NY 11501

Mrs. Fay Wilamowski
451 Cornell Drive, Hicksville, NY 11803

200– Apr.	1	Balance	✓			6530

Mr. William Witt
264 Emory Road, Mineola, NY 11501

200– Apr.	1	Balance	✓			9500

GENERAL LEDGER

Accounts Receivable

(3)   No. 13

			Dr.	Cr.	Balance Dr.	Balance Cr.
200- apr. 1	Balance	✓			205 30	

Sales

No. 41

			Dr.	Cr.	Balance Dr.	Balance Cr.

(4)

Winslow's Emporium
Schedule of Accounts Receivable
April 30, 200—

THINK IT OVER

At last count, Lacy's Department Store had approximately 10,000 charge customers. Billing procedures are now fully automated, replacing hand operation. Exactly what has been accomplished (in bookkeeping terms) by the change?

Marshall & Kahn, a neighborhood specialty shop, is considering a change from a one-journal (general journal) bookkeeping/accounting system to using several special journals. What recommendations might be made to help in reaching a decision?

CHAPTER 16

CASH RECEIPTS JOURNAL

Receiving cash from customers is another frequent transaction. Cash is received when a cash sale is made, or when it is received from a customer ON ACCOUNT for an outstanding balance due on a charge sale. Cash is also received when borrowed, whether from a bank or an individual or a cash investment. In each of these transactions, the cash is in the form of either currency or a check.

In each transaction, the result is an increase in the asset cash. Therefore, an entry must be made in which cash is debited. The corresponding credit indicates the source of the cash received. A typical *general journal* entry for a cash receipt follows:

200-						
Apr.	17	Cash			7500	
		Accounts Rec./Alan Bergstrom ✓				7500
		to Apply on Account				

Purpose of Cash Receipts Journal

General journal entries such as these require postings to all accounts—Cash Debit, Accounts Receivable Credit (in the general ledger), and Alan Bergstrom's account credit (in the subsidiary

147

ledger). It is advisable, therefore, to use a special CASH RECEIPTS JOURNAL, which will involve less frequent and fewer postings and still keep customers' accounts up to date.

The same entry as shown above has been recorded in Betty Chan's special cash receipts journal, along with other typical cash receipts transactions:

CASH RECEIPTS JOURNAL   Page 3

Date	Account Credited	PR	General Cr.	Accts. Rec. Cr.	Cash Dr.
200- Apr. 2	Gordon Robbins			5000	5000
7	Betty Chan, Capital		250000		250000
17	Alan Bergstrom			7500	7500
19	Union National Bank		100000		100000
25	Mabel Johnson			10000	10000
30	Equipment		30000		30000

Posting to Accounts

Note that there is a special column for the controlling account—Accounts Receivable Cr. Postings are needed for all accounts credited, and are listed in the General Cr. and Accounts Receivable Cr. columns. Column totals, however, are *posted only at the end of the month*, when the journal is summarized. The columns that have identifiable account title headings are posted as indicated—Accounts Receivable Cr. (13) and Cash Dr. (11). The General Cr. column total is not posted and checked (√) because there is no *single* general ledger account for that total. Furthermore, the individual accounts listed as credited will have been posted.

Summarizing the Cash Receipts Journal

Betty Chan's journal now follows, posted and summarized:

CASH RECEIPTS JOURNAL   Page 3

Date	Account Credited	PR	General Cr.	Accts. Rec. Cr.	Cash Dr.
200- Apr. 2	Gordon Robbins	√		5000	5000
7	Betty Chan, Capital	31	250000		250000
17	Alan Bergstrom	√		7500	7500
19	Union National Bank	22	100000		100000
25	Mabel Johnson	√		10000	10000
30	Equipment	15	30000		30000
30	Totals		380000	22500	402500
			(√)	(13)	(11)

First, the columns were pencil footed; debit totals equal credit totals. Then they were written in ink, and the journal was double ruled. The General Dr. column is always checkmarked, and the special column totals have been posted to the accounts identified in their headings. The postings to customers' accounts and the Cash and Accounts Receivable accounts follow (General Cr. column account postings are not illustrated here):

GENERAL LEDGER

Cash

No. 11

			PR	Dr.	Cr.	Balance Dr.	Balance Cr.
200- apr.	1	Balance	✓			78000	
	30		CR3	402500		480500	
	30		CD4		300000	180500	

Accounts Receivable

No. 13

			PR	Dr.	Cr.	Balance Dr.	Balance Cr.
200- apr.	1	Balance	✓			30000	
	30		S5	120000		150000	
	30		CR3		22500	127500	

ACCOUNTS RECEIVABLE LEDGER

Alan Bergstrom
142 Overlook Drive, Minneapolis, MN 55402

Date			PR	Dr.	Cr.	Dr. Bal.
200- Apr.	7		S5	175 00		175 00
	17		CR3		75 00	100 00
	24		S5	500 00		600 00

Mabel Johnson
7103 River Road, St. Paul, MN 55101

Date			PR	Dr.	Cr.	Dr. Bal.
200- Apr.	1	Balance	✓			100 00
	15		S5	220 00		320 00
	25		CR3		100 00	220 00

Gordon Robbins
3216 Twin Oaks Avenue, Minneapolis, MN 55407

Date			PR	Dr.	Cr.	Dr. Bal.
200- Apr.	1	Balance	✓			200 00
	2		CR3		50 00	150 00
	22		S5	305 00		405 00

Schedule of Accounts Receivable

At the end of the month, Betty Chan's schedule of accounts receivable is taken to prove the accuracy of the subsidiary ledger:

Betty Chan Schedule of Accounts Receivable April 30, 200–		
Alan Bergstrom		600 00
Mabel Johnson		220 00
Gordon Robbins		455 00
Total Accounts Receivable		1275 00

The balance of the controlling account, Accounts Receivable, is also $1,275. Since the balance in the controlling account equals the total of the subsidiary ledger, the accounts receivable ledger has been "proved."

Expanding the Journal

Any cash receipts journal may be expanded to include four or more columns, depending on the needs of the business. For example, if many *cash sales* of merchandise occur, a special column—Sales Cr.—can be included. If this column is used, it is necessary to checkmark (√) the posting reference column; *no posting is needed for each cash sales entry,* inasmuch as the column total will be posted, along with all other *special column totals, at the end of the month.* Examine these entries in a four-column cash receipts journal:

CASH RECEIPTS JOURNAL

Date	Account Debited	PR	General Cr.	Accts. Rec Cr.	Sales Cr.	Cash Cr.
200– May 3	H. L. Wicker			100 00		100 00
7	Sales	√			500 00	500 00
10	Mrs. D. Ginsburg			95 00		95 00
14	Sales	√			625 00	625 00
17	Lawrence Evans, Cap.		4000 00			4000 00
24	Sales	√			595 00	595 00
31	Sales	√			850 00	850 00
31	Totals		4000 00	195 00	2570 00	6765 00
			(√)	( )	( )	( )

The bookkeeping/accounting clerk can easily see which items need to be posted, and which do not. Those that are checked *will not be posted*; items appearing in the *General Cr. and Accounts Receivable Cr. columns will be posted* periodically to the accounts identified in the Account Debited column. The *special column totals*—Accounts Receivable Cr., Sales Cr., and Cash Dr.—*will be posted* at the end of the month.

Source Documents for Cash Receipts

The cash receipts journal is a book of original entry, used exclusively for entries that result in cash debits—to increase the amount of cash. As with all entries, a source document is prepared for each cash receipt transaction; this may be a copy of a hand-prepared cash sales slip or a cash register DETAIL AUDIT TAPE, which accumulates a total of the cash register activity for each salesperson.

YOU SHOULD REMEMBER

Customers' account balances should be kept up to date by frequent (daily, weekly or monthly) posting.

Source documents are *business forms* that serve as *evidence of every transaction*, such as invoices (one copy is evidence of a sale on account, a duplicate copy is evidence of a purchase on account) and detail audit tapes.

KNOW YOUR VOCABULARY

Cash receipts journal   On account

Detail audit tape

QUESTIONS

1. What type of transaction is exclusively entered in a cash receipts journal?
2. What justifies the use of a special column in a cash receipts journal?
3. How are postings to subsidiary ledger accounts from the cash receipts journal indicated?
4. When does a check mark indicate a posting reference?
5. When does a check mark indicate that an item is not to be posted?
6. How is the accuracy of the accounts receivable ledger proved?

PROBLEMS

16–1   Raul Garcia, owner of the Rose of Texas Specialty Gift Shop, uses a four-column cash receipts journal. Subtotals are indicated in pencil for the first 3 weeks' entries.

    (1) Continue by recording the following entries for the cash receipts transactions for the remainder of the month:

        April 23,   Garcia invested an additional $2,000 cash in his business
              24,   Borrowed $2,500 from Lone Star Bank; received a check for that amount
              25,   Received $85 from J. R. Dallas on account
              26,   Received $60 from Margo Chase on account
              27,   Sold old office typewriter (equipment) for $95 cash
              28,   Received $75 from Frances Lima on account
              29,   Cash sales for the week amounted to $1,765

(2) Summarize the journal at the end of the month. Checkmark all items *not to be posted* separately.

(3) Post the summary entry only.

(1) and (2)

CASH RECEIPTS JOURNAL   Page 6

Date	Accts. Cr.	PR	General Cr.	Accts. Rec. Cr.	Sales Cr.	Cash Dr.
200- Apr. 23			750 00	1435 00	5976 00	8161 00

GENERAL LEDGER

Cash   No. 11

Date		PR	Dr.	Cr.	Balance Dr.	Balance Cr.
200- Apr. 1	Balance	✓			1935 00	

Accounts Receivable   No. 13

Date		PR	Dr.	Cr.	Balance Dr.	Balance Cr.
200- Apr. 1	Balance	✓			1729 50	

Sales   No. 41

Date		PR	Dr.	Cr.	Balance Dr.	Balance Cr.
200- Mar. 31		S4		3500 00		3500 00
31		CR5		6250 00		9750 00
31		J3	9750 00		—	—

16-2 Pat Norrell is a wholesaler who sells beauty shop supplies to barber shops and beauty salons. She uses a sales journal to record all sales of merchandise *on account*. She uses a four-column cash receipts journal with a sales credit column for sales made to customers to whom she sells merchandise for cash.

(1) Enter the following sales and cash receipts transactions for the month, starting with invoice No. 7156:

May 1, Sold merchandise on account:
Willow's Beauty Shoppe, $465
Lee's Unisex, $395
7, Cash sales for week, $252.50
10, Received $200 from Goddess of Love
12, Sold merchandise on account:
Goddess of Love, $268.50
Jayne's Curls & Waves, $175
14, Cash sales for week, $307.25
15, Invested an additional $3,000 cash
17, Sold merchandise on account:
Willow's Beauty Shoppe, $192
19, Received $395 from Lee's Unisex
21, Cash sales for week, $296.80
25, Received $265 from Willow's Beauty Shoppe on account
28, Cash sales for week, $319.90
29, Sold merchandise on account:
Jayne's Curls & Waves, $225
Lee's Unisex, $315.20
31, Cash sales for 3 days, $191.40

(2) Post current entries on a *weekly basis*, posting first the sales journal, then the cash receipts journal.
(3) Summarize the journals; post totals from the sales journal first, then the cash receipts journal.
(4) Prepare a schedule of accounts receivable.

(1) SALES JOURNAL Page 9

Date	To Whom Sold – Account Debited	Invoice No.	PR	Acct. Rec. Dr. Sales Cr.

CASH RECEIPTS JOURNAL   Page 6

Date	Account Credited	PR	General Cr.	Accts. Rec. Cr.	Sales Cr.	Cash Dr.

ACCOUNTS RECEIVABLE LEDGER

(2) and (3)

Goddess of Love
110 Chemung Avenue, Binghamton, NY 13901

Date		PR	Dr.	Cr.	Dr. Bal.
200- May 1	Balance	✓			200 00

Jayne's Curls & Waves
39 Tompkins Avenue, Cortland, NY 13045

Lee's Unisex
451 College Heights Road, Ithaca, NY 14850

Willow's Beauty Shoppe
58 Twain Boulevard, Elmira, NY 14901

GENERAL LEDGER

Cash

(3)   Page *11*

Date		PR	Dr.	Cr.	Balance Dr.	Balance Cr.
200- may 1	Balance	✓			1078 50	

Accounts Receivable

No. *13*

Date		PR	Dr.	Cr.	Balance Dr.	Balance Cr.
200- may 1	Balance	✓			200 00	

Pat Norrell, Capital

No. *31*

Date		PR	Dr.	Cr.	Balance Dr.	Balance Cr.
200- may 1	Balance	✓				25000 00

Sales

No. *41*

Date		PR	Dr.	Cr.	Balance Dr.	Balance Cr.

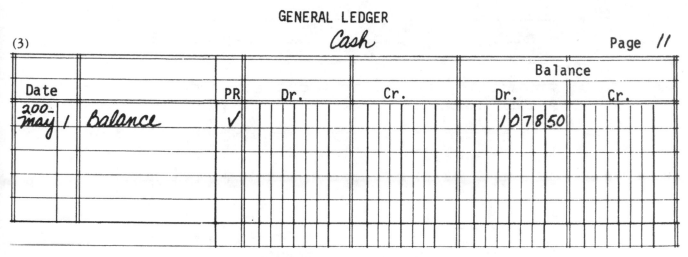

(4)

CHAPTER 17

GENERAL JOURNAL, FOUR-COLUMN FORMAT

There are several reasons why customers may return merchandise that was sold to them. It may be damaged, the wrong size, the wrong color, or otherwise unsatisfactory. In other cases, customers may retain possession of the merchandise but receive a reduction in the selling price.

Sales Returns and Allowances, and Purchases Returns and Allowances

In either case, a new account is involved in each of these transactions—either SALES RETURNS AND ALLOWANCES or PURCHASES RETURNS AND ALLOWANCES. A *general journal* entry illustrating the first of these follows:

200-					
May 23	Sales Returns and Allowances	44		25 75	
	Accts. Receivable / J. Falkin	✓			25 75
	Credit Memo No. 135				

Posting references are given to show how this is handled. Because Sales Returns and Allowances represent decreases in Sales, the special numbering sequence for such VALUATION ACCOUNTS is indicated by the use of a decimal figure, as account No. 41.1. (Purchases Returns and Allowances would be account No. 51.1, which indicates decreases in Purchases.) Accounts Receivable was posted to account No. 13, and Judith Falkin was posted (√) to a subsidiary ledger account.

Source Documents

The source document for such an entry is a CREDIT MEMORANDUM, a form that is similar in appearance to the original invoice but has the words "Credit Memorandum" printed at the top and is often printed on pink paper. A copy is given to the customer (the buyer) who returns merchandise and/or is being given an allowance (by the seller).

Note the use of the diagonal line in the Posting Reference column for the credit part of this entry. Both accounts are posted—one to a general ledger account, and one to a subsidiary ledger account.

Examine carefully how the same entry is recorded in a *four-column general journal*, using columns for controlling accounts: Accts. Pay. Dr. and Accts. Rec. Cr.

GENERAL JOURNAL   P4

Date			PR	General Dr.	General Cr.	Accts. Pay. Dr.	Accts. Rec. Cr.
200- May 23	*Sales Returns and Allowances*		41.1	25 75			
	Judith Falkin		√				25 75
	Credit Memo No. 135						

Only two postings are needed for this entry—Sales Returns and Allowances and Judith Falkin. At the end of the month, the journal is summarized. The totals for the General Dr. and General Cr. columns are checkmarked, and the special columns are posted to the accounts indicated in their headings. Compare this to the entry on page 159.

A four-column general journal with typical entries follows. Explanations are given below the journal.

GENERAL JOURNAL
P4

Date			PR	General Dr.	General Cr.	Accts. Pay. Dr.	Accts. Rec. Cr.
200– May	2	Priscilla Deutsch	✓	50 00			
		Priscilla Deutsch	✓		50 00		
		Correct Posting Error 4/10					
	9	Martin Hande, Drawing	32	26 00			
		Purchases	51		26 00		
		Merchandise for Personal Use					
	23	Sales Returns and Allowances	41.1	25 75			
		Judith Falkin					25 75
		Credit Memo No. 135					
	25	Kevin Sullivan & Company	✓			15 00	
		Purchases Returns and	51.1		15 00		
		Allowances					
		Debit Memo No. 52					
	29	Equipment	15	275 00			
		Martin Hande, Capital	31		275 00		
		Transferred Typewriter to					
		Business					
	31	Totals		610 75 610 75	660 00 660 00	15 00 15 00	25 75 25 75
				(✓)	(✓)	( )	( )

Correcting Errors in Ledger Postings

On May 2, a CORRECTING ENTRY was made. Because of similarity in names, a posting error was made last month. A charge to Priscilla Deutsch for merchandise sold on account was posted to Priscilla Deitch. It appears as a debit in the wrong account. It should be in the Deutsch account. This entry corrects the error and can be entered in the General Dr. and General Cr. columns, inasmuch as it *does not affect* the Accounts Receivable account balance.

On May 9, the owner, Martin Hande, withdrew *merchandise* for personal use. Merchandise *purchased* for resale to customers is, therefore, reduced by the cost price of whatever was withdrawn. Since purchases are debits, *withdrawals of merchandise are credits to the Purchases account.*

On May 23, a charge customer, Judith Falkin, returned damaged merchandise for credit. Credit memorandum No. 135 was completed, and a copy (source document) used for this entry, which *decreases the customer's account balance.* Since this amount is entered in the controlling account column, it will also decrease that account balance when the column total is posted at the end of the month.

On May 25, the owner returned merchandise purchased on account to a creditor, Kevin Sullivan & Company. This is a DEBIT MEMORANDUM, a copy of the original memorandum completed by the seller. This entry *decreases the balance owed to the creditor*, as well as the controlling account when the column total is posted at the end of the month.

On May 29, the owner transferred to his business a typewriter formerly used at home. This increases his owner's equity, as any investment would.

At the end of the month, the general journal summary entry shows that the General Dr. and General Cr. column totals are checkmarked. They are not to be posted. The individual items in these two columns will be posted daily (or as soon as possible) during the month. The special account column totals will be posted to accounts identified in their headings. In this way, the controlling accounts—Accounts Receivable and Accounts Payable—will continue to show in totals what individual customers' and creditors' accounts show in their respective subsidiary ledgers.

Statement of Account

Periodically—at the end of each month, or at set dates during the month—the seller of merchandise sends each charge customer a STATEMENT OF ACCOUNT. This "bill" may be in the form of a detailed list of all transactions. Illustrated below is a statement sent by a seller to one of its charge customers:

BOSTON WHOLESALE SUPPLY COMPANY
1219 Beacon Street
Boston, MA 02105

May 31   200—

Mr. James Wolff
351 Tremont Street
Brighton, MA   02135

		CHARGES			
May 4	200—	Sales Slip No. 408	25 00		
22	200—	Sales Slip No. 573	40 00	65 00
		PAYMENTS/RETURNS			
May 28	200—	Check No. 79	25 00		
28	200—	Credit Memo No. 91	15 00	40 00
		Balance Due			25 00

The charges are debit postings to this customer's account. The payment/returns are credit postings. The balance due is the same as the last balance in the customer's account. Occasionally a *customer may overpay* an account (the balance due). Should this happen, there would be a *credit balance* in the customer's account, an account that normally has a debit balance. (If a creditor's account is overpaid, there would be a *debit balance* in an account that normally has a credit balance.)

A *cash refund or allowance* may be given to a *customer*. This is a cash disbursements journal entry in which Sales Returns and Allowances is debited and Cash is credited. If the *buyer* is given the cash refund or allowance, a cash receipts journal entry will be made in which Purchases Returns and Allowances is credited and Cash is debited.

YOU SHOULD REMEMBER

A four-column general journal includes special columns for any *debits* to *Accounts Payable* and any *credits* to *Accounts Receivable*.

General debit and credit *column totals* are *checkmarked* to indicate that those *totals are not to be posted.*

Valuation accounts (returns and allowance accounts) *reduce* the balance of the account to which they are "related."

KNOW YOUR VOCABULARY

Correcting entry

Credit memorandum

Debit memorandum

Purchases returns and allowances

Sales returns and allowances

Statement of account

Valuation account

QUESTIONS

1. What are the column headings of a four-column general journal?
2. What is the posting procedure from a four-column general journal?
3. What kinds of entries are recorded in a general journal?
4. Henry Jones sold merchandise to Claire Smith on account. Part of it is returned for credit. What entry is made in Jones's records? What entry is made in Smith's records?
5. What is the source document for Jones's entry? What is the source document for Smith's entry?
6. What information is reported in a customer's statement of account?

PROBLEMS

17–1   (1)   Record the following entries on journal page 7 for Philip Scheiber, the owner of Scheiber's Music Emporium:

May 2,   Allowed Jane McDonald $35 credit for damaged merchandise; credit memo No. 18

5,   Correct $65 posting error for sale on account to Hedy Nachtigal, posted incorrectly to Netty Nachtigal

9,   Received $100 allowance on merchandise purchased from Baldwin Piano Company; debit memo No. 53

15,   Took a $95 guitar as a gift for nephew

22,   Allowed Molly Shapiro $80 credit for return of damaged merchandise; credit memo No. 19

29,   Transferred a $185 desk from home to the business office

GENERAL JOURNAL

Date		PR	General Dr.	General Cr.	Accts. Pay. Dr.	Accts. Rec. Cr.

17–2 (1) Record the following entries on journal page 5 for Carol Dambroff, owner of Carol's Quality Draperies:

> May 3, Returned to Home Decorator's Corp. $160 worth of poor quality merchandise purchased on account last month; debit memo No. AR-51
>
> 10, Paid $38 cash refund to customer who returned merchandise; check No. 326
>
> 17, Granted a $77 credit to Robin Moore for merchandise returned; credit memo No. 39
>
> 24, Received a $50 cash refund for wrong-size merchandise paid for last month
>
> 28, Correct $140 posting error for purchase on account from C. Wilton Fabric Company, credited incorrectly to Carl Walton Furniture Company's account

(2) Summarize the general ledger and indicate by a check mark any column total *not to be posted.*

(1) and (2)   GENERAL JOURNAL   Page __5__

Date			PR	General Dr.	General Cr.	Accts. Pay. Dr.	Accts. Rec. Cr.

CASH RECEIPTS JOURNAL   Page *12*

Date	Acct. Cr.	PR	Gen. Cr.	Acct. Rec. Cr.	Sales Cr.	Cash Dr.

CASH DISBURSEMENTS JOURNAL   Page *11*

Date	Acct. Dr.	Ck. No.	PR	Gen. Dr.	Acct. Pay. Dr.	Purch. Dr.	Cash Cr.

17–3　Below is the ledger account for a customer, Pearl Nathanson, of Hudson's Department Store. Prepare a statement of account, dated May 20.

Ms. Pearl Nathanson
972 Riverside Dr.
St. Louis, MO 63104

200- May						
May	1		S3	6000		6000
	5		S4	7500		13500
	12		J2		3500	10000
	15		CR5		2000	7500
	18		S5	4500		12000

STATEMENT OF ACCOUNT

Hudson's Department Store
100 Gateway Plaza
St. Louis, MO 63101

SOLD TO

_____　　_____ 20 ____

_____

_____

		CHARGES		
		PAYMENTS/CREDITS		

17–4 Comprehensive Five-Journal Problem.

Daniel Shaw owns and operates a retail jewelry business. He uses special journals for

(1) sales of merchandise on account,
(2) purchases of merchandise on account,
(3) cash disbursements,
(4) cash receipts, and
(5) all other transactions are recorded in a general journal.

(1) Record the following transactions in the appropriate journals:

May 1, 20--	Paid Winslow Jewelers $465; check No. 392
	Paid rent for month $450; check No. 393
3,	Received cash on account from:
	Marc Green, $150
	Gian Polidoro, $95
4,	Sold merchandise on account to:
	Antonio Lorenzo, $300; invoice No. B192
	Edward Grabczak, $250; invoice No. B193
8,	Correct $35 posting error for supplies incorrectly posted to Equipment
11,	Sold merchandise on account to Marc Green, $275; invoice No. B194
13,	Withdrew $500 *cash* for personal use; check No. 394
14,	Paid clerks' salaries, $300; check No. 395
17,	Purchased merchandise on account:
	Schmidt & Brendle, $375
	Winston Jewelers, $1,200
22,	Received cash on account from:
	Antonio Lorenzo, $50
	Edward Grabczak, $125
24,	Allowed $75 credit to Marc Green for damaged merchandise; credit memo No. 35
28,	Paid Schmidt & Brendle $375; check No. 396
29,	Paid $40 refund to customer for returned merchandise; check No. 397
31,	Cash sales to date, $2,740
31,	Took a $200 ring home as gift for wife

(2) Summarize all journals. Checkmark any items, current entries and totals, that are not to be posted.

PURCHASES JOURNAL   Page *10*

Date	Account Credited		Inv. No.	PR	Purchases Dr. Acct. Pay. Cr.

SALES JOURNAL

Date	Account Debited		PR	Acct. Rec. Dr Sales Cr.

CASH RECEIPTS JOURNAL

Date		PR	Gen. Cr.	Acct. Rec. Cr	Sales Cr.	Cash Dr.
19— May 1	Balance on hand $1,500	✓				

CASH DISBURSEMENTS JOURNAL

Date		Ck. No.	PR	Gen. Dr.	Acct. Pay. Dr.	Purch. Dr.	Cash Cr.

GENERAL JOURNAL

Date		PR	General Dr.	General Cr.	Accts. Pay. Dr.	Accts. Rec. Cr.

CHAPTER

EIGHT-COLUMN WORK SHEET

Up to this point in a merchandising business, the bookkeeping/accounting cycle has followed these steps:

(1)   A business transaction occurs, resulting in a source document — an invoice (sales and purchases), a check, a debit or credit memorandum, and so on.
(2)   The transaction is journalized.
(3)   The journal entry is posted to ledger accounts; summary entries are posted.

Trial Balance

To complete all the work required in the cycle, a trial balance is prepared. This may be a separate, formal statement, or it may be completed as the first two columns of an EIGHT-COLUMN WORK SHEET. This trial balance is a listing of *all general ledger accounts*, including those that do not have balances—Revenue and Expense Summary, and certain expenses as well.

Adjusting Entries

An eight-column work sheet provides columnar space to adjust the accounts that have not been kept up to date. Some changes in account balances were not recorded in the journals, and therefore not posted to accounts. It is now necessary to bring them up to date. This is accomplished by entering ADJUSTMENTS in the special work sheet columns.

MERCHANDISE INVENTORY

In a merchandising business, one of the major assets is the MERCHANDISE INVENTORY. As merchandise is purchased and sold, however, no entries are made to the Merchandise Inventory account. All purchases are debits to the Purchases account; all sales are credits to the Sales account. However, the cost value (or possibly some other basis for evaluating merchandise) is an asset value. At the end of each fiscal period, the new, closing, or ending inventory is taken. The beginning, or opening, inventory (last fiscal period's ending inventory) has undoubtedly been sold, and is, therefore, part of the revenue and expense for the fiscal period.

To record this change in inventory values, adjusting entries are made on the work sheet. See adjusting entry (A) in the sample work sheet on page 173, which *debits Revenue and Expense Summary* and *credits Merchandise Inventory*, using the amount of the *old, beginning inventory.* This actually "zeroes out" the Merchandise account balance. To record the new, ending inventory, adjusting entry (B) *debits Merchandise Inventory* and *credits Revenue and Expense Summary,* using the amount of the inventory at the *end of the fiscal period.*

SUPPLIES

The trial balance lists the SUPPLIES account at its beginning balance, plus any supplies acquired during the fiscal period. The fact that some of these supplies may have been used during the fiscal period has not been recorded. Therefore a supplies inventory is taken to determine the value on hand at the end of the fiscal period. To find the *amount used* during that time, the ending inventory is subtracted from the account balance. The *difference is the expense* for supplies. See adjusting entry (C), which *debits Supplies Expense* and *credits Supplies* for that *difference.*

OTHER PREPAID EXPENSES

Other PREPAID EXPENSES—assets such as prepaid insurance, which become expenses by being used up in a relatively short period—are adjusted in the same way. Their respective expense accounts are debited, and the prepaid assets are credited for *the amount used* during the fiscal period.

Extending Updated Balances

Each of the amounts is extended to one of the remaining columns to complete the work sheet. Examine each account, its debits and/or credits, in the first four columns, in order to determine the updated balance or amount to be extended to one of the remaining four columns in either the Income Statement or the Balance Sheet column. Revenue and Expense Summary adjustment figures are carried to *both* Income Statement columns; each of the other account balances is extended to only one column.

Determining Net Income or Net Loss

When the extensions are completed properly, the *differences between the total debits and credits in the Income Statement columns and the total debits and credits in the Balance Sheet columns should be equal.* The amount is either a net income or a net loss for the fiscal period — *net income* if the Income Statement credit column total is greater than the debit column; *net loss* if the reverse is true.

The amount of net income is entered in each pair of columns, to be added to the smaller column total, thus giving two equal totals for each pair of columns. In the Income Statement columns, the total is entered in the debit column; in the Balance Sheet columns, it is entered in the credit column. The final equal totals are then double ruled, and the words "Net Income" are written on the proper line in the Account Title column.

Shields and Ross
Work Sheet
For Year Ended December 31, 200-

Account Title	A.N.	Trial Balance Debit	Trial Balance Credit	Adjustments Debit	Adjustments Credit	Income Statement Debit	Income Statement Credit	Balance Sheet Debit	Balance Sheet Credit
Cash	111	235000						235000	
Petty Cash	112	5000						5000	
Accounts Receivable	113	317500						317500	
Merchandise Inventory	114	1550000		(a) 1360000	(A) 1550000			1360000	
Equipment	115	1500000						1500000	
Supplies	116	229000			(c) 95000			134000	
Accounts Payable	211		205000						205000
O.L. Fields, Capital	311		1159500						1159500
O.L. Fields, Drawing	311.1	1200000						1200000	
B.W. Ross, Capital	312		1361000						1361000
B.W. Ross, Drawing	312.1	1200000						1200000	
Income and Expense Summary	313			(A) 1550000	(b) 1360000	1550000	1360000		
Sales	411		7600000				7600000		
Sales Returns & Allow.	411.1	175000				175000			
Purchases	511	3000000				3000000			
Purchases Returns & Allow.	511.1		58000				58000		
Advertising Expense	611	120000				120000			
Miscellaneous Expense	612	12000				12000			
Rent Expense	613	240000				240000			
Salary Expense	614	600000				600000			
Supplies Expense	615			(c) 95000		95000			
		10383500	10383500	3005000	3005000	5792000	9018000	5951500	2725500
Net Income						3226000			3226000
						9018000	9018000	5951500	5951500

Notice that the completed work sheet on page 173 is for a PARTNERSHIP, Fields and Ross. In a partnership, two or more individuals combine their investments and operate a business according to an agreement. The amounts invested, the responsibilities of the partners, and the method for sharing net income or net losses should be spelled out in detail. In that way future disagreements may be avoided.

YOU SHOULD REMEMBER

The Revenue and Expense Summary account is used to *make certain adjusting entries* (for merchandise inventory) at the end of a fiscal period.

Prepaid expenses *are assets when first acquired*, but become expenses as they are used, thus requiring an adjustment to record this change.

KNOW YOUR VOCABULARY

Adjustments (adjusting entries)   Partnership

Eight-column work sheet   Prepaid assets

Merchandise inventory

QUESTIONS

1. What are the four headings for the four pairs of columns in an eight-column work sheet?
2. How is the end-of-fiscal-period merchandise inventory determined?
3. What does the first merchandise adjusting entry (A) accomplish?
4. What does the second merchandise adjusting entry (B) accomplish?
5. How are the Balance Sheet column extended amounts determined for
   a) merchandise inventory, and
   b) prepaid expenses?
6. Why do prepaid expenses have to be adjusted at the end of a fiscal period?
7. How is a net income for the fiscal period determined?
8. How is a net loss for the fiscal period determined?

PROBLEMS

(Save your work for use in Chapters 19 and 20.)

18-1 Daniel Green's general ledger account balances are given below:

Cash	$ 1,200
Accounts Receivable	2,500
Merchandise Inventory	5,000
Equipment	6,000
Supplies	400
Accounts Payable	1,800
Daniel Green, Capital	14,200 ($12,200 plus additional $2,000 investment)
Daniel Green, Drawing	1,500
Revenue and Expense Summary	---
Sales	6,500
Sales Returns and Allowances	250
Purchases	3,000
Purchase Returns and Allowances	150
Miscellaneous Expense	100
Rent Expense	1,200
Salary Expense	1,500
Supplies Expense	---

Complete the work sheet on page 176 for the quarter ended June 30, using the following information for adjustments:

Merchandise inventory, June 30	$5,175
Supplies on hand	$ 300

18-2 Timothy Sullivan's general ledger is given on pages 177–180. Complete the eight-column work sheet on page 181, using the following additional information:

Merchandise Inventory, Jan. 31	$3,950
Supplies on hand	$ 205
Prepaid insurance	$ 250

Account Title	A. N.	Trial Balance		Adjustments		Income Statement		Balance Sheet	
		Debit	Credit	Debit	Credit	Debit	Credit	Debit	Credit

Cash   No. 11

Date		PR	Dr.	Cr.	Balance Dr.	Balance Cr.
200- Jan. 1	Balance	✓			1500 00	
31		CR2	3650 00		5150 00	
31		CP3		1790 00	3360 00	

Accounts Receivable   No. 12

Date		PR	Dr.	Cr.	Balance Dr.	Balance Cr.
200- Jan. 1	Balance	✓			500 00	
31		S2	3200 00		3700 00	
31		CR2		150 00	3550 00	
31		J1		35 00	3515 00	

Merchandise Inventory   No. 13

Date		PR	Dr.	Cr.	Balance Dr.	Balance Cr.
200- Jan. 1	Balance	✓			3800 00	

Supplies   No. 14

Date		PR	Dr.	Cr.	Balance Dr.	Balance Cr.
200- Jan. 1	Balance	✓			275 00	
3		CP2	50 00		325 00	

Prepaid Insurance   No. 15

Date		PR	Dr.	Cr.	Balance Dr.	Balance Cr.
200- Jan. 1	Balance	✓			300 00	

Accounts Payable   No. 21

Date		PR	Dr.	Cr.	Balance Dr.	Balance Cr.
200- Jan. 1	Balance	✓				1000 00
31		P2		1200 00		2200 00
31		CP3	400 00			1800 00

Timothy Sullivan, Capital   No. 31

Date		PR	Dr.	Cr.	Balance Dr.	Balance Cr.
200- Jan. 1	Balance	✓				5375 00
10		CR3		2500 00		7875 00

Timothy Sullivan, Drawing   No. 32

Date		PR	Dr.	Cr.	Balance Dr.	Balance Cr.
200- Jan. 15		CP2	150 00		150 00	
30		CP2	150 00		300 00	

Revenue and Expense Summary — No. 33

Date		PR	Dr.	Cr.	Balance Dr.	Balance Cr.

Sales — No. 41

Date		PR	Dr.	Cr.	Balance Dr.	Balance Cr.
200- Jan 31		S2		3200 00		3200 00
31		C.R1		1000 00		4200 00

Sales Returns and Allowances — No. 411

Date		PR	Dr.	Cr.	Balance Dr.	Balance Cr.
200- Jan 20		J2	35 00		35 00	

Purchases — No. 51

Date		PR	Dr.	Cr.	Balance Dr.	Balance Cr.
200- Jan 31		P2	1200 00		1200 00	
31		C.P3	500 00		1700 00	

Advertising Expense   No. 61

Date		PR	Dr.	Cr.	Balance Dr.	Cr.
200- Jan 3		CP2	100 00		100 00	

Insurance Expense   No. 62

Date		PR	Dr.	Cr.	Balance Dr.	Cr.

Miscellaneous Expense   No. 63

Date		PR	Dr.	Cr.	Balance Dr.	Cr.
200- Jan 12		CP2	25 00		25 00	
27		CP2	15 00		40 00	

Rent Expense   No. 64

Date		PR	Dr.	Cr.	Balance Dr.	Cr.
200- Jan 2		CP2	400 00		400 00	

Supplies Expense   No. 65

Date		PR	Dr.	Cr.	Balance Dr.	Cr.

Account Title	A.N.	Trial Balance		Adjustments		Income Statement		Balance Sheet	
		Debit	Credit	Debit	Credit	Debit	Credit	Debit	Credit

THINK IT OVER

A delivery truck that cost $12,500 three years ago has been used by a business. It is now worth $6,500, either on a trade-in deal for a new truck, or by selling it privately. What has happened during the three years of use? Has the owner of the truck considered all possible expenses in operating his business? What has been omitted? How does this change the net income or net loss for each of the three years the truck has been used? How would you recommend handling this situation in the future?

CHAPTER

FINANCIAL STATEMENTS

At the end of each fiscal period, financial statements are prepared to summarize the operations of a business. This information allows the owner(s) to see how profitable (or unprofitable) the business has been, to compare one fiscal period with prior periods, and to determine future courses of action. In addition, this information may be requested by banks, and by the Internal Revenue Service if tax returns are examined.

Income Statement

An INCOME STATEMENT describes the way in which a business has operated during a fiscal period. It is prepared from information on the work sheet in the special Income Statement columns. The income statement for Fields and Ross (see work sheet, page 173) follows:

Fields and Ross
Income Statement
For Year Ended December 31, 200-

Income:			
Sales		7600000	
Less Sales Returns and Allowances		175000	
Net Sales			7425000
Cost of Goods Sold:			
Merchandise Inv., Jan 1		1550000	
Purchases	30,000		
Less Purchases Returns and Allowances	580		
Net Purchases		2942000	
Merchandise Available for Sale		4492000	
Less Merchandise Inv., Dec. 31		1360000	
Cost of Goods Sold			3132000
Gross Profit on Sales			4293000
Expenses:			
Advertising Expense		120000	
Miscellaneous Expense		12000	
Rent Expense		240000	
Salary Expense		600000	
Supplies Expense		95000	
Total Expenses			1067000
Net Income			3226000

The customary three-line heading indicates the answers to WHO, WHAT, and WHEN. The statement is divided into five parts:

(1) An *income* section, listing all operating income earned during the fiscal period—sales, less sales returns and allowances.

> Sales − Sales Returns and Allowances = Net Sales

(2) A *cost of goods sold* section, which includes the following: beginning inventory, plus net purchases (purchases, less purchases returns and allowances), less ending inventory.

Beginning Inventory + Net Purchases − Ending Inventory = Cost of Goods Sold

(3) The *gross profit*, which is the difference between net sales and cost of goods sold.

Net Sales − Cost of Goods Sold = Gross Profit

(4) The *expenses* section, listing all operating expenses for the fiscal period (overhead).

(5) The *net income*, which is the difference between gross profit on sales and total expenses.

Gross Profit − Total Expenses = Net Income (or Net Loss)

In the event that total expenses exceed gross profit on sales, the result is a net loss for the fiscal period.

Briefly stated, an income statement shows

Net Sales

− Cost of Goods Sold

= Gross Profit on Sales

− Total Expenses

= Net Income (or Net Loss)

An income statement for a business owned by a single owner does not differ from one for a business owned by two or more people (a partnership).

Capital Statement

This information is included in the CAPITAL STATEMENT, which shows how each partner's owner's equity changed during the fiscal period.

There must be an agreement as to how partners are to share any net income or net loss. If Fields and Ross in our example share equally, each partner would receive $16,130 (one half of $32,260). If partners share in any other way, this must be clearly stated in the ARTICLES OF PARTNERSHIP, the written agreement establishing the business. Assume in the case of Fields and Ross that the agreement provides for the partners to share income and losses *in the ratio* of 3 to 2 (3:2). This means that Fields would receive three fifths ($\frac{3}{5}$) or 60%, and Ross two fifths ($\frac{2}{5}$) or 40%, of any net income or any net loss.

Fields's share of the net income is, therefore, $19,356 ($\frac{3}{5}$ or 60% of $32,260), and Ross's share is $12,904 ($\frac{2}{5}$ or 40% of $32,260).

Fields and Ross
Capital Statement
For Year Ended December 31, 200—

A. G. Fields:			
Beginning Balance, Jan. 1		1159500	
Plus 3/5 of Net Income	19,356		
Less Withdrawals	12,000		
Net Increase in Capital		735600	
Ending Balance, Dec. 31			1895100
B. W. Ross:			
Beginning Balance, Jan. 1		1061000	
Plus: Additional Investment	2,000		
2/5 of Net Income	12,904		
	14,904		
Less Withdrawals	12,000		
Net Increase in Capital		290400	
Ending Balance, Dec. 31			1351400
Total Owner's Equity, Dec. 31			3246500

Examine the following capital statement for Lois Berlowitz, who had a loss for the fiscal period:

Lois Berlowitz
Capital Statement
For Six Months Ended June 30, 200—

Beginning Balance, Jan. 1			2876500
Additional Investment			250000
			3126500
Less: Net Loss		520000	
Withdrawals		600000	
Total Decrease in Capital			1120000
Ending Balance, June 30			2006500

Balance Sheet

The next financial statement to be prepared is a BALANCE SHEET. This shows the financial condition of a business at the end of the fiscal period. The form presented below is the REPORT FORM balance sheet, listing items (assets, liabilities, and owners' equity) vertically, one under the other. Notice, however, that the fundamental bookkeeping/accounting equation is maintained and is emphasized by double-ruling *total assets* and *total liabilities plus owners' equity*.

Fields and Ross
Balance Sheet
December 31, 200–

Assets		
Cash	225000	
Petty Cash	5000	
Accounts Receivable	317500	
Merchandise Inventory	1360000	
Equipment	1500000	
Supplies	44000	
Total Assets		3451500
Liabilities		
Accounts Payable		205000
Owners' Equity		
A. G. Fields, Capital	1895100	
B. W. Ross, Capital	1351400	
Total Owners' Equity		3246500
Total Liabilities and Owners' Equity		3451500

YOU SHOULD REMEMBER

The income statement shows:
  Net Sales
  less Cost of Goods Sold
  equals Gross Profit (or Loss)
  less Total Expenses
  equals Net Income (or Loss).
Increases in *owner's equity* are caused by investments and net income.
Decreases in *owner's equity* are caused by withdrawals and net loss.

KNOW YOUR VOCABULARY

Articles of partnership   Gross profit
Balance Sheet   Income statement
Capital statement   Partnership
Cost of goods sold   Report form balance sheet

QUESTIONS

1. What information is shown on each of the following?
    a) An income statement.
    b) A capital statement.
    c) A balance sheet.
2. How is the cost of goods sold calculated?
3. What determines whether there is a net income or a net loss for a fiscal period?
4. How does a report form balance sheet differ from an account form balance sheet?

PROBLEMS

19-1   Using the completed work sheet for Daniel Green (Problem 18-1), complete:
    1) An income statement.
    2) A capital statement (assume that Green's $14,200 capital includes a $2,000 additional investment).
    3) A balance sheet.

1) _____

_____

_____

2)

3)

19–2 Using the completed work sheet for Timothy Sullivan (Problem 18–2), complete:
   1) An income statement.
   2) A capital statement (examine Sullivan's capital account for any additional investment; see pp. 178–181).
   3) A balance sheet.

1) _____
   _____
   _____

2)

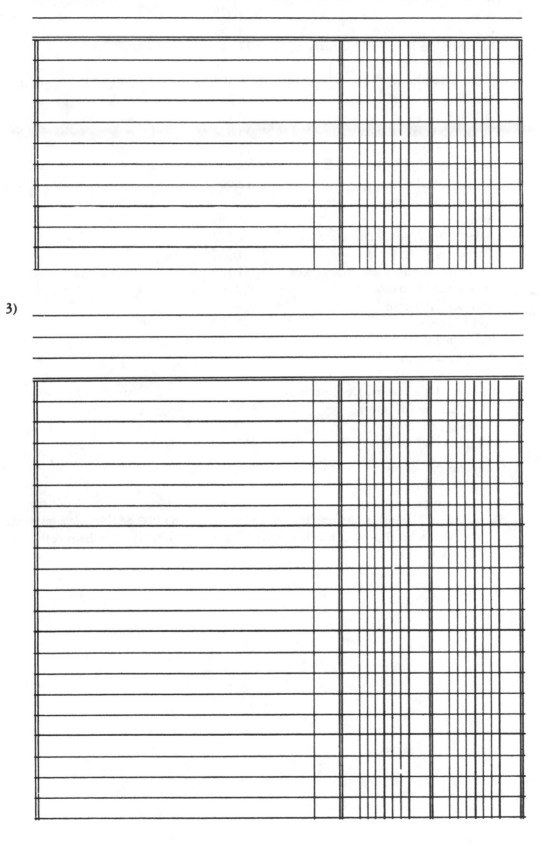

3)

19–3   Abdullah and Pahlevi are partners who share profits and losses in the ratio of 4:3. Their general ledger account balances at the end of the year are as follows:

Cash	$ 3,625
Accounts Receivable	18,260
Merchandise Inventory, January 1	22,320
Equipment	7,500
Prepaid Insurance	500
Supplies	275
Accounts Payable	3,105
T. G. Abdullah, Capital	33,802
T. G. Abdullah, Drawing	10,000
S. H. Pahlevi, Capital	28,404
S. H. Pahlevi, Drawing	12,000
Revenue and Expense Summary	– –
Sales	51,790
Sales Returns and Allowances	2,570
Purchases	31,380
Purchases Returns and Allowances	1,529
Advertising Expense	600
Insurance Expense	– –
Rent Expense	3,600
Salary Expense	6,000
Supplies Expense	– –

Additional Information, December 31:

Merchandise Inventory	$23,195
Prepaid Insurance	$400
Supplies on Hand	$178.50

Complete the following:
1)   A work sheet.
2)   An income statement.
3)   A capital statement (assume that Abdullah made a $5,000 additional investment during the fiscal period, which was included in his capital account balance).
4)   A balance sheet.

Account Title	A. N.	Trial Balance		Adjustments		Income Statement		Balance Sheet	
		Debit	Credit	Debit	Credit	Debit	Credit	Debit	Credit

(2)

(3)

4) _____

_____

_____

_____

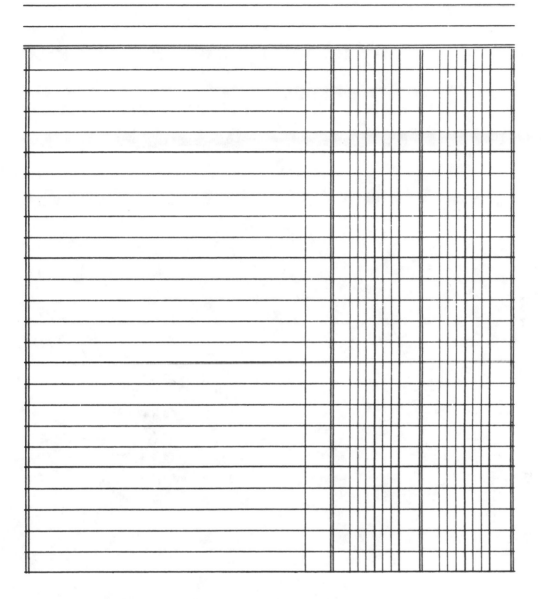

THINK IT OVER

Paul Garrison believes his balance sheet does not reflect a correct end-of-fiscal-period financial condition. He is concerned because several of his charge customers (accounts receivable) have been unable to pay him amounts that are due. In past years, he has seen a similar situation: there are always some uncollectible accounts.

Does this situation affect the value of Garrison's assets? What adjustment might be made to account for an estimated loss on "bad debts" at the end of each fiscal period?

How would this adjustment affect Garrison's operating expenses if he estimates that approximately $500 may be uncollectible accounts receivable and, therefore, another operating expense? How would this affect Garrison's net income or net loss for the fiscal period?

CHAPTER **20**

ADJUSTING AND CLOSING THE GENERAL LEDGER

In Chapters 18 and 19, work sheets with adjustments were completed, and certain accounts were brought up to date. These ADJUSTING ENTRIES reflected the changes that had taken place but had not been recorded in the actual accounts. *General ledger accounts* must now be brought up to date at the end of the fiscal period so that these changes become part of the permanent bookkeeping/accounting records.

Adjusting Accounts

Examine the Adjustments columns of the work sheet for Fields and Ross, page 173. Entries, with debits and credits identified by letters A, B, and C, pair off each adjustment. These are recorded in a general journal (using the General Dr. and General Cr. columns of a four-column general journal). The illustration below shows these adjusting entries *posted* to general ledger accounts.

GENERAL JOURNAL

Date			PR	General Dr.	General Cr.	Accts. Pay. Dr.	Accts. Rec. Cr.
200–		*Adjusting Entries*					
Dec	31	Revenue and Expense Summary	313	1550000			
		Merchandise Inventory	114		1550000		
	31	Merchandise Inventory	114	1360000			
		Revenue and Expense Summary	313		1360000		
	31	Supplies Expense	615	95000			
		Supplies	116		95000		

GENERAL LEDGER

Merchandise Inventory   No. 114

Date			PR	Dr.	Cr.	Balance Dr.	Balance Cr.
200–Jan	1	Balance	✓			1550000	
Dec.	31		J4		1550000		
	31		J4	1360000		1360000	

Supplies   No. 116

Date			PR	Dr.	Cr.	Balance Dr.	Balance Cr.
200–Jan	1	Balance	✓			50000	
May	15		CP3	60000		110000	
Nov.	3		CP8	29000		139000	
Dec.	31		J4		95000	44000	

Revenue and Expense Summary   No. 313

Date		PR	Dr.	Cr.	Balance Dr.	Balance Cr.
200- Dec. 31		J4	1550000		1550000	
31		J4		1360000	190000	

Supplies Expense   No. 615

Date		PR	Dr.	Cr.	Balance Dr.	Balance Cr.
200- Dec. 31		J4	95000		95000	

The ledger Posting Reference column indicates postings from general journal page 4 (J4). These accounts—Merchandise Inventory, Supplies, and Supplies Expense—are now up to date.

Closing Accounts

The next step at the end of the fiscal period is the closing procedure. Examine once again the Fields and Ross work sheet, page 173. The accounts listed in the Income Statement columns—all *revenue, cost, and expense accounts,* and the *Revenue and Expense Summary account*—and, in the Balance Sheet debit column, the *drawing accounts* are temporary accounts that are to be closed or "zeroed out." They show information for one fiscal period only and do not carry over to succeeding periods. CLOSING ENTRIES will close these temporary accounts.

First, close the accounts listed in the Income Statement credit column, starting with the Sales Account. They are *debited* to "zero out," and their total is *credited* to Revenue and Expense Summary.

Second, close the accounts listed in the Income Statement debit column, starting with the Sales Returns and Allowance account. They are *credited* to "zero out," and their total is *debited* to Revenue and Expense Summary.

Third, close the Revenue and Expense Summary account. The amount of the *net income* is *debited* to Revenue and Expense Summary to "zero out" and is *credited* to owners' *capital accounts* in the ratio for sharing profits and losses. (If there was a *net loss,* the debits and credits would be reversed.)

Fourth, close the drawing accounts. Owners' capital accounts are *debited*, and their drawing accounts are *credited* to "zero out."

Closing entries continue in the general journal, immediately following the adjusting entries:

		Closing Entries				
	31	Sales	411	76000 00		
		Purchases Returns and Allow.	511.1	580 00		
		Revenue and Expense Summary	313			76580 00
	31	Revenue and Expense Summary	313	42420 00		
		Sales Returns and Allowances	411.1			1750 00
		Purchases	511			30000 00
		Advertising Expense	611			1200 00
		Miscellaneous Expense	612			120 00
		Rent Expense	613			2400 00
		Salary Expense	614			6000 00
		Supplies Expense	615			950 00
	31	Revenue and Expense Summary	313	32260 00		
		Q. H. Fields, Capital	311			19356 00
		B. W. Ross, Capital	312			12904 00
	31	Q. H. Fields, Capital	311	12000 00		
		B. W. Ross, Capital	312	12000 00		
		Q. H. Fields, Drawing	311.1			12000 00
		B. W. Ross, Drawing	312.1			12000 00

The illustration below shows the closing entries for the Revenue and Expense Summary Account, posted and closed.

Revenue and Expense Summary. No. 313

Date		PR	Dr.	Cr.	Dr.	Cr.
200-Dec	31	J4	15500 00		15500 00	
	31	J4		13600 00	1900 00	
	31	J4		76580 00		74680 00
	31	J4	42420 00			32260 00
	31	J4	32260 00		—	

(Other temporary accounts—not illustrated—will be closed as well.)

Post-Closing Trial Balance

To prove that the adjusting and closing work has been completed correctly, a last POST-CLOSING TRIAL BALANCE is taken. The accounts that are open at this point will have balances that carry over to succeeding fiscal periods. These are balance sheet accounts—*assets, liabilities,* and *capital.* Below is the post-closing trial balance for Fields and Ross. (If a complete general ledger had been illustrated here, all of these account balances would now be shown, and they would be the source of the information listed.)

Fields and Ross
Post-closing Trial Balance
December 31, 200-

Cash	225000	
Petty Cash	5000	
Accounts Receivable	317500	
Merchandise Inventory	1360000	
Equipment	1500000	
Supplies	44000	
Accounts Payable		205000
A. G. Fields, Capital		1895100
B. W. Ross, Capital		1351400
	3451500	3451500

YOU SHOULD REMEMBER

Adjusting and closing entries are not transactions; they are the bookkeeper's way of first *bringing accounts up to date, and then zeroing out income, cost, expense and drawing account balances* at the end of each fiscal period.

A post-closing trial balance lists only accounts which have *balances that carry over to the succeeding fiscal period.*

KNOW YOUR VOCABULARY

Adjusting entry   Post-closing trial balance
Closing Entry

QUESTIONS

1. How are debits and credits for each adjustment shown on the work sheet?
2. Why is it necessary to journalize and post adjusting entries, inasmuch as they are included on the work sheet?
3. Which columns of the work sheet contain information needed for journalizing closing entries?
4. What does the first closing entry accomplish?

5. What does the second closing entry accomplish?
6. What is the third closing entry when there has been a net income for the fiscal period? A net loss for the fiscal period?
7. What does the fourth closing entry accomplish?
8. How does the posting of the third closing entry affect the owner's equity?
9. How does the posting of the fourth closing entry affect the owner's equity?
10. Why are balance sheet accounts the only accounts listed on a post-closing trial balance?
11. What does the post-closing trial balance prove?

PROBLEMS

20–1 Refer to Problem 18–1. Using a four-column general journal, page 7, complete the following:
   1) The adjusting entries.
   2) The closing entries.

(1) and (2)   GENERAL JOURNAL   Page _____

Date			PR	General Dr.	General Cr.	Accts. Pay. Dr.	Accts. Rec. Cr.

20-2 Refer to Problem 18-2. Using a two-column general journal, page 6, complete the following:

1) Record the adjusting entries and post.
2) Record the closing entries and post.
3) Take a post-closing trial balance.

(1) and (2)   **GENERAL JOURNAL**   **Page**

Date	Account Title	PR	Debit	Credit

(3) _____
_____
_____

20–3 Refer to Problem 19–3. Using a four-column general journal, page 9, do the following:
1) Record the adjusting entries.
2) Record the closing entries.

(1) and (2) GENERAL JOURNAL Page _____

Date		PR	General Dr.	General Cr.	Accts. Pay. Dr.	Accts. Rec. Cr.

3) Can you prepare a post-closing trial balance from the information in this problem, even though you have no ledger? If so, how? See solution and explain how each account balance was found.

CHAPTER 21

USING A COMBINATION JOURNAL

In chapters 1–20, basic bookkeeping and accounting principles were developed. These may be applied to personal as well as business use. Some individuals and many small businesses prefer to use the simplest forms possible. This can be accomplished using a COMBINATION JOURNAL, a columnar book which combines a general journal with whatever special journals — cash receipts, cash disbursements, sales, and purchases — may be needed.

Combination Journal For Personal Use

The arrangement of columns will differ from one individual to another. Most, however, will have special columns for cash receipts (Cash Dr.) and cash disbursements (Cash Cr.) as well as two general columns (General Dr. and General Cr.)

Examine carefully the combination journal below for Alan Daniels:

COMBINATION JOURNAL

Date	Explanation / Account	PR	General Dr.	General Cr.	Cash Dr.	Cash Cr.
200- May 1	Balance on hand 675	✓				
5	Salary Income			600 00	600 00	
8	Stern's (charge acct.)		76 90			76 90
10	Auto Expense (gas)		12 50			12 50
31	Insurance Expense		275 00			275 00
31	Totals		2175 40 2175 40	2400 00 2400 00	2400 00 2400 00	2175 40 2175 40
			(✓)	(✓)	( )	( )

At the end of the month, Daniels can verify the cash balance by adding the beginning balance and the cash debit total, less the cash credit total:

$$\begin{array}{r} 675.00 \\ \underline{2400.00} \\ 3075.00 \\ \underline{2175.40} \\ 899.60 \end{array}$$ — **This amount should equal the balance** of cash on hand and/or in the bank.

Note that pencil footings are used to prove the debit column totals equal the credit column totals, *before* those amounts are written in ink. If Daniels posts to ledger accounts, the cash *totals* are posted as the column headings indicate (Dr. and Cr.) and *each item* in the general debit and credit columns is posted to the account identified in the explanation column. The general column totals *are not* posted.

Combination Journal For Business Use

Depending upon their need, the arrangement of columns will differ from one business to another. Most combination journals will include special columns for cash receipts (Cash Dr.) and cash disbursements (Cash Cr.) as well as two general columns (General Dr. and General Cr.). In addition, there may be special columns for customers' accounts (Accounts Receivable Dr. and Cr.), sales of merchandise (Sales Cr.), creditors' accounts (Accounts Payable Dr. and Cr.), and purchases of merchandise (Purchases Dr.).

If similar transactions occur frequently in a relatively short time, a special column may be used for that account. An example of this might be for the purchase of supplies used in a business (Supplies Dr. or Supplies Expense Dr.)

Examine carefully the combination journal opposite for Karen and Kenneth's Promotional's business:

p. 5

COMBINATION JOURNAL

Date	Explanation	PR	General Dr.	General Cr.	Accounts Receivable Dr.	Accounts Receivable Cr.	Sales Credit	Accounts Payable Dr.	Accounts Payable Cr.	Purchases Dr.	Supplies Dr.	Dr.	Cr.
200- May 1	Balance 1500.00	✓											
3	Thomas Co.					500 00						500 00	
6	Wiley Inc.	✓			750 00		750 00						
8	Supplies										40 00		40 00
10	Equipment		250 00										250 00
15	H.L. Mfg. Co.	✓							350 00	350 00			
20	Sales						1500 00					1500 00	
31	Rent Expense		600 00										600 00
31	Totals		1750 00	50 00	2100 00	2980 00	3750 00	800 00	850 00	850 00	340 00	4750 00	2900 00

Note that footings are used to prove the equality of debits and credits:

Debits —

General	1,790.00
Cash	4,750.00
Accts. Rec.	2,100.00
Accts. Pay.	800.00
Purchases	950.00
Supplies	340.00
	10,730.00

Credits —

General	50.00
Cash	2,900.00
Accts. Rec.	2,980.00
Sales	3,950.00
Accts. Pay.	850.00
	10,730.00

Totals are then written in ink and double-lined. All special column totals are to be posted, indicated by open parentheses, to the accounts indicated in the column headings. Items that are check-marked are not to be posted—the general debit and credit column totals and any accounts in the explanation column *for which there are special columns.*

It is assumed there are subsidiary ledgers for customers' and creditors' accounts. Since these accounts are arranged alphabetically, a check mark instead of an account number will be entered in the posting reference column as each one is posted.

Computer Spreadsheets

A combination journal can be adapted to a computer spreadsheet. A program could be utilized so that entries are extended automatically to designated columns, with cumulative totals for instant information. Such a spreadsheet could be used for a travel agency.

Assume Aliza Jordan, a college student, is a part-time agent for Global Travel, Inc. She earns half of the commissions paid for tour packages (12%), hotels (10%), car rentals (10%), air (8%), and cruises (12%), each of which is coded A, B, C, D, or E. As clients pay their travel arrangements, the total commissionable amount is entered by code and automatically extended to the appropriate column. At any time, Jordan could find her commission in each category of travel, as well as her total commissionable sales.

A similar computer program could be used for the Global Travel agency with similar extensions. This would indicate the total of all business travel transactions for each of the categories indicated above. As can be seen, a program is the key to how a computer spreadsheet is used, not only for single-entry records, but double-entry bookkeeping records, too.

YOU SHOULD REMEMBER

A combination journal replaces special journals to simplify bookkeeping procedures. All transactions are entered in one journal.

Columnar headings and arrangement will vary from one individual and/or business to another.

For every entry, bookkeeping/accounting double-entry theory applies. The amount(s) debited equal the amount(s) credited. In that way, if the journal is properly proved and posted, a trial balance should be in balance.

KNOW YOUR VOCABULARY

Combination Journal   Verify Cash Balance

QUESTIONS

1. What determines which accounts will be used as special columns?
2. Which transactions will be check-marked as they are entered in a combination journal?
3. How is a combination journal proved?
4. Which column totals are posted?
5. Which column totals are not to be posted?

PROBLEMS

21-1   Dana and David use a combination journal for their family records. They have decided to use special columns—one for all household operating expenses, and another for all automobile expenses. On May 1st, their balance of cash on hand and in the bank was $1,675.00.

   (1)   Record the following transactions:

     May   1, 200— Paid the rent, $695.00
        3,   Paid for personal expenses, $37.95
        5,   Gas for their car, $14.60
        8,   Electricity bill, $79.50
      10,   Food shopping, $63.45
      12,   Quarterly premium on household insurance, $108.75
      15,   Two weeks' salary, cash received, $1,048.30
      21,   Automobile insurance for year, $355.20
      24,   Food shopping, $59.25
      25,   Personal expenses, $48.95
      26,   Automobile tune-up, $66.50
      28,   Medical bill, $80.00
      29,   Two weeks' salary, cash received, $1,048.30
      30,   Paid charge accounts, $91.85
      31,   Telephone bill, $54.30

   (2)   Summarize the journal and prove the equality of debits and credits.
   (3)   Rule the combination journal. Checkmark any column totals that should not be posted.
   (4)   Verify the cash balance on May 31.

21–1   COMBINATION JOURNAL   *p.5*

Date	Explanation	PR	General		House	Auto	Cash	
			Dr.	Cr.	Exp. Dr.	Exp. Dr.	Dr.	Cr.

21–2   Antonina and Salvatore Moffo use a combination journal for their personal household records. Because Mrs. Moffo is a diabetic and under a doctor's care, they use a special column for medical expenses, as well as one for their home and food expenses.

(1) Record their transactions for the month:

June 1, Cash balance on hand and in the bank, $1,162.00

     1, Paid month's rent, $900

     2, Food shopping, $68.75

     4, Movies and refreshments, $16.50

     5, Gas and electric bill, $96.25

     8, Doctor's visit, $45 and medication, $22.50

    12, Food shopping, $72.50

    15, Visited local museum, $6.00 and went to dinner, $32.45

    19, Doctor's visit, $45 and lab fees, $30

    22, Telephone bill, $42.92

    25, Food shopping, $61.47

    27, Paid charge account, Stern Bros., $52.50

    29, Donation to the Diabetes Foundation, $25.00

    30, Monthly pay check, $2,400.00

    30, Movies and refreshments, $15.00

(2) Summarize the journal and prove the equality of debits and credits.

(3) Rule the combination journal. Checkmark any column totals that should not be posted.

(4) Verify the cash balance on June 30.

21–2 COMBINATION JOURNAL *p. 12*

Date	Explanation	PR	General Dr.	General Cr.	House Exp. Dr.	Medical Exp. Dr.	Cash Dr.	Cash Cr.

21–3 Paula Dambroff is an attorney who uses a combination journal for her law practice's bookkeeping records. She uses special columns for cash (Cash Dr. and Cash Cr.), her clients (Accounts Receivable Dr. and Accounts Receivable Cr.), her income from legal fees (Fees Income Cr.), and the major categories of expenditures (Office Expenses Dr. and Travel and Auto Expenses Dr.).

(1) Record the following transactions:

June 1, Cash balance on hand and in bank, $1,042.35

  1, Paid office rent, $650.00

  3, Paid for stationery and cards, $32.90

  5, Settled H. L. Thompson case. Client awarded $12,000 in damages. Davis will receive 33⅓% plus reimbursed expenses, $362.40 (Debit Accounts Receivable and credit Fees Income.)

  8, Purchased from Apex Furniture Company a desk and two chairs, $2,250; cash deposit $750, balance on account

  11, Paid telephone bill, $67.88

  15, Paid for legal forms, $28.25

  20, Tolls and mileage to visit a client, $16.50

  22, Received cash for settlement in Thompson case

  24, Purchased new file cabinet for cash, $350.00

  27, Paid for postage, $10.00

  29, Paid for gasoline, $14.00

  30, Davis withdrew for personal use, $1,200.00

  30, Returned defective file cabinet; received full refund

(2) Summarize the journal and prove the equality of debits and credits.

(3) Rule the combination journal. Checkmark any column totals that should not be posted.

(4) Verify the cash balance on June 30.

21-3 (1) and (2)

p. 2

COMBINATION JOURNAL

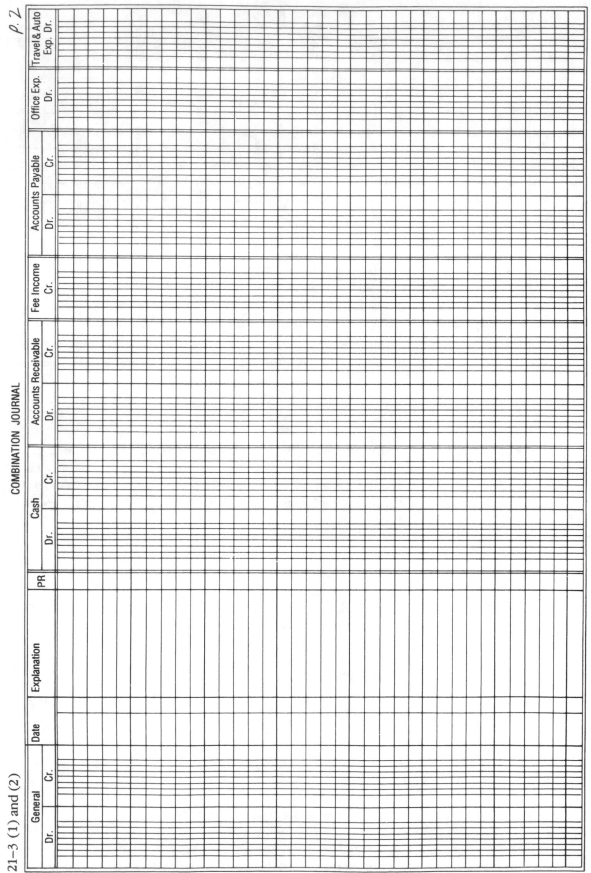

Date	Explanation	PR	Cash Dr.	Cash Cr.	Accounts Receivable Dr.	Accounts Receivable Cr.	Fee Income Cr.	Accounts Payable Dr.	Accounts Payable Cr.	Office Exp. Dr.	Travel & Auto Exp. Dr.	General Dr.	General Cr.

21–4 Chris Bayer and Lee Falk are partners who use a combination journal for their whole-sale business.

(1) Record the following transactions for the month of June:

June 1, Cash balance on hand and in the bank, $5,162.00

1, Paid rent for the month, $1,200.00

3, Sales on account to Smythe Co., $1,950.00

5, Paid on account Maxwell Inc., $1,600.00

8, Received cash on account from PVP & Co., $995.00

12, Purchased merchandise on account from Khan & Farah, $3,000.00

13, Bought office supplies, $62.50

15, Paid salaries, $2,000.00

19, Received cash on account from Bill Bros., $1,535.50

21, Paid for advertising in trade journal, $125.00

24, Each partner withdrew cash for personal use, $350.00

27, Purchased merchandise from Peck & Persky Inc., $1,500.00

29, Paid on account Khan & Farah, $1,000.00

30, Paid telephone bill, $182.75

30, Received on account from Smythe Co., $1,950.00

30, Sold an office desk and chair; received $250.00

(2) Summarize the journal, and prove the equality of debits and credits.

(3) **Rule the combination journal. Checkmark any column totals that should not be posted.**

(4) **Verify the cash balance on June 30.**

COMBINATION JOURNAL

21-4

Cash		Date 20__	General		Accounts Receivable		Sales	Accounts Payable		Purchases
Dr.	Cr.		Dr.	Cr.	Dr.	Cr.	Cr.	Dr.	Cr.	Dr.
		June								

CYCLE TWO
EXAMINATION

Part I   Indicate by a check (√) in the column at the right whether each statement is TRUE or FALSE.

	T	F
Example: Debts owed to creditors are accounts payable.	√	
1. A purchases journal is used for recording the purchase of all merchandise on account.		
2. Cost accounts increase by debits.		
3. A major advantage of special journals is the elimination of repetitive posting.		
4. A source document for each transaction is identified in the ledger account.		
5. A controlling account is found in each subsidiary ledger.		
6. A summary entry proves that debits equal credits in each journal.		
7. A check mark posting reference to a customer's account indicates that the item has been posted.		
8. General Debit and General Credit column totals are posted to general ledger accounts.		
9. A subsidiary ledger's accuracy is proved by taking a trial balance.		
10. Invoices usually are prepared in multiple copies.		
11. The use of special journals eliminates the need for controlling accounts.		
12. A correcting entry usually is recorded in the general journal.		
13. A charge to the wrong customer's account is corrected by debiting that account and crediting the correct one.		
14. A withdrawal of merchandise by the owner is debited to the Sales account.		
15. A statement of account is sent to each charge customer to indicate the balance due.		
16. An eight-column work sheet includes special columns for closing entries.		
17. Prepaid expenses are adjusted at the end of each fiscal period by the amounts of their ending inventory values.		
18. Partners automatically share net income equally unless a written agreement specifies otherwise.		
19. Gross profit on sales is found by subtracting cost of goods sold from net sales.		
20. A post-closing trial balance includes general ledger accounts with adjusted balances.		

Part II Match the definition with the term by writing the appropriate *letter* in the column at the right. (A term is used once only.)

Terms	Definitions	Letter
	Example: A charge purchase of merchandise, rather than a purchase for cash	K
A. Adjusting entries	1. A special grouping of similar accounts	1.
B. Capital statement	2. A source document that describes a sale of merchandise	2.
C. Cash payments journal	3. The totaling of all special journals to prove that debits equal credits	3.
D. Cash receipts journal	4. A special journal for all cash disbursements	4.
E. Closing entries	5. The journal in which a withdrawal of merchandise by the owner is recorded.	5.
F. Debit	6. The normal balance of a customer's account	6.
G. Credit		
H. General journal	7. A valuation account	7.
	8. Entries made at the end of the fiscal period to bring certain accounts up to date	8.
I. Income statement		
J. Invoice	9. The financial statement that shows changes in owner's equity	9.
K. On account		
L. Purchases returns and allowances	10. Proving that general ledger debits and credits are equal	10.
M. Subsidiary ledger		
N. Summary entry		
O. Trial balance		

Part III (1) Record each of the following transactions for Rex Drug Company in the journals provided:

June 1, Paid month's rent, $375; check No. 147

3, Purchased $500 worth of merchandise on account from J. L. Rossini Company

5, Sold merchandise on account to Dr. George Tyler, $165

8, The owner, Jordan Glaser, withdrew $50 worth of merchandise for personal use

10, Paid J. L. Rossini Company $500 on account; check No. 148

12, Issued credit memo No. 7 for $15 to Dr. George Tyler for merchandise returned

15, Cash sales to date were $2,950

19, Paid telephone bill, $46; check No. 149

22, Received $150 from Dr. George Tyler for balance due on account

26, Sold $125 worth of merchandise to Sona Parisian on account

29, Purchased $300 worth of merchandise from Fred Pulaski Wholesalers, Inc., on account

30, Cash sales to date were $3,750

(2) Summarize each journal, and checkmark any totals not to be posted.

(1) and (2) GENERAL JOURNAL Page _3_

Date			PR	General Dr.	General Cr.	Accts. Pay. Dr.	Accts. Rec. Cr.

1) and 2)   PURCHASES JOURNAL   Page 2

Date	Account Credited			PR	Purchases Dr. Accts. Pay. Cr.

1) and 2)   SALES JOURNAL   Page 4

Date	Account Debited		PR	Acct. Rec. Dr. Sales Cr.

1) and 2)

CASH RECEIPTS JOURNAL

Date		PR	General Cr.	Accts. Rec. Cr.	Sales Cr.	Cash Dr.
200- June 1	Balance on hand $2,500	✓				
200- June 1	Balance on hand $2,500	✓				

(1) and (2)

Page 3

CASH DISBURSEMENTS JOURNAL

Date	Account Debited	Ck. No.	PR	General Dr.	Accts. Pay. Dr.	Purchases Dr.	Salary Exp. Dr.	Cash Cr.

Part IV From the completed work sheet below do the following:
- (1) Prepare an income statement.
- (2) Complete a capital statement, assuming that Fowler made a $1,000 investment during the fiscal period.
- (3) Prepare a balance sheet.
- (4) Journalize the adjusting and closing entries.

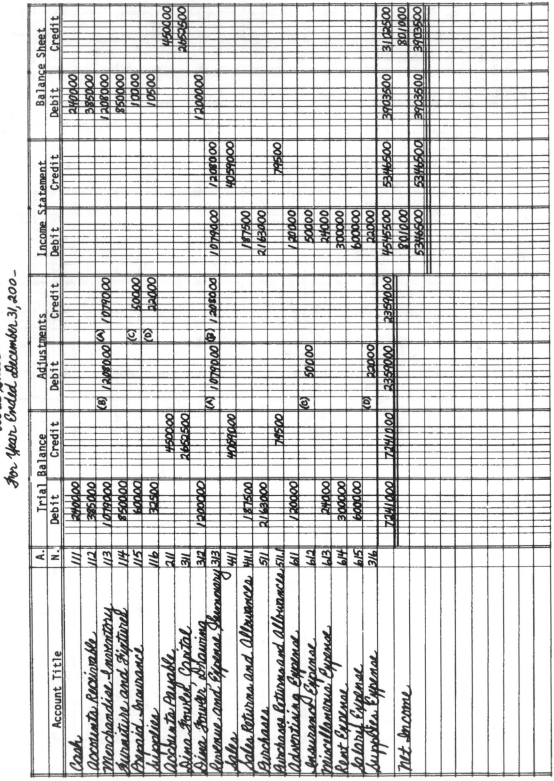

Fowler's Crystal Palace
Work Sheet
For Year Ended December 31, 200–

A.N.	Account Title	Trial Balance Debit	Trial Balance Credit	Adjustments Debit	Adjustments Credit	Income Statement Debit	Income Statement Credit	Balance Sheet Debit	Balance Sheet Credit
111	Cash	240000						240000	
112	Accounts Receivable	385000						385000	
113	Merchandise Inventory	1079000		(B) 1208000	(A) 1079000			1208000	
114	Furniture and Fixtures	850000						850000	
115	Prepaid Insurance	60000			(C) 50000			10000	
116	Supplies	32500			(D) 22000			10500	
211	Accounts Payable		450000						450000
311	Dina Fowler, Capital		2652500						2652500
312	Dina Fowler, Drawing	1200000						1200000	
313	Revenue and Expense Summary			(A) 1079000	(B) 1208000	1079000	1208000		
411	Sales		4059000				4059000		
411.1	Sales Returns and Allowances	187500				187500			
511	Purchases	2163000				2163000			
511.1	Purchases Returns and Allowances		74500				74500		
611	Advertising Expense	120000				120000			
612	Insurance Expense			(C) 50000		50000			
613	Miscellaneous Expense	24000				24000			
614	Rent Expense	300000				300000			
615	Salary Expense	600000				600000			
316	Supplies Expense			(D) 22000		22000			
		7236000	7236000	2359000	2359000	4545500	5346500	3903500	3102500
	Net Income					801000			801000
						5346500	5346500	3903500	3903500

(1) _____
_____
_____

(2) _____
_____
_____

(3) _____

_____

_____

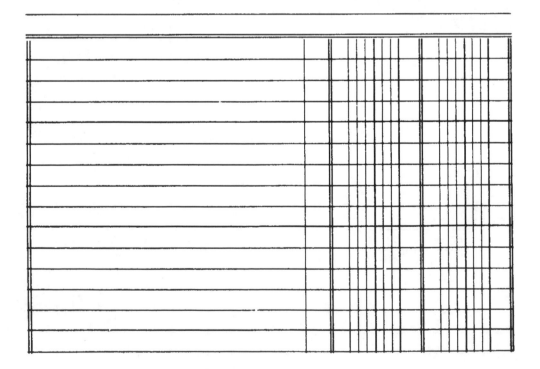

(EXTRA FORM)

_____

_____

_____

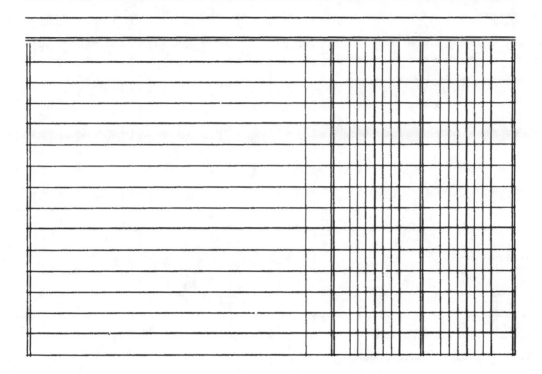

(4)   GENERAL JOURNAL   Page _____

Date			PR	General Dr.	General Cr.	Accts. Pay. Dr.	Accts. Rec. Cr.

GENERAL JOURNAL   Page _____

Date			PR	General Dr.	General Cr.	Accts. Pay. Dr.	Accts. Rec. Cr.

ANSWERS

Chapter 1

QUESTIONS

Item	Classification
Example: Cash on hand	Asset
1. Automobile	1. Asset
2. Balance owed on loan	2. Liability
3. Gerald Smith's capital	3. Owner's Equity
4. Supplies on hand	4. Asset
5. Personal clothes	5. Asset
6. Charge account balances	6. Liability
7. One's net worth	7. Owner's Equity
8. Bank loan	8. Liability
9. Allison Paris, account receivable	9. Asset
10. Panos & George, account payable	10. Liability

PROBLEMS

1–1

1.	$ 11,500.00
2.	3,700.00
3.	17,500.00
4.	16,087.10
5.	8,569.07
6.	106,930.96
7.	210,818.34
8.	40,314.48
9.	571,657.75
10.	1,116,743.28

THINK IT OVER

Winslow's liabilities total $5,000. She is in a stronger financial situation.

Chapter 2

QUESTIONS

	Classification	Side
1.	Asset	Left
2.	Liability	Right
3.	Owner's equity	Right
4.	Asset	Left
5.	Liability	Right
6.	Asset	Left
7.	Asset	Left
8.	Liability	Right
9.	Asset	Left
10.	Owner's equity	Right

PROBLEMS

2-1	A	=	L	+	OE
1. Decrease	Decrease				
2. None					
3. Increase	Increase				
4. None					
5. None					
6. Increase					Increase
7. None					
8. Decrease					Decrease

2-2		A	=	L	+	OE
	1.	-$ 2,000				
		+ 2,000				
		$29,250		$ 4,250		$25,000
	2.	+ 7,500		+ 7,500		
		$36,750		$11,750		$25,000
	3.	-$ 450				
		+ 450				
		$36,750		$11,750		$25,000
	4.	-$12,000				
		+ 12,000				
		$36,750		$11,750		$25,000
	5.	- 1,500		- 1,500		
		$35,250		$10,250		$25,000

THINK IT OVER

Loan for $14,000 ($20,000 – $6,000)

Fundamental equation:

   Assets increase $14,000   Liabilities increase $14,000

       Owner's Equity, no change

Chapter 3

QUESTIONS

1. Who? What? When?
2. 30 days—April, June, September, November
   31 days—January, March, May, July, August, October, December
   28 or 29 Days—February
3. July 1—September 30
   January 1—March 31
   October 1—December 31
4. Assets = Liabilities + Owner's Equity
5. Assets – Liabilities = Owner's Equity
6. Total—$30,977

PROBLEMS

3-1	Classification
1.	Asset
2.	Liability
3.	Asset
4.	Owner's equity
5.	Asset
6.	Asset
7.	Liability
8.	Liability
9.	Owner's equity
10.	Liability

3-2	Left Side	Right Side
1.	Asset	
2.		Liability
3.	Asset	
4.		Liability
5.	Asset	
6.	Asset	
7.	Asset	
8.		Owner's equity
9.	Asset	
10.		Owner's equity

3-3

Maria's Beauty Salon

Balance Sheet

August 31, 200-

Assets		Liabilities	
Cash	1750 00	Regal Laundry	275 00
Furn. & Fixtures	8900 00	Marvelle Corp.	2500 00
Beauty Supplies	600 00	Total Liab.	2775 00
		Owner's Equity	
		Maria Lopez, Cap.	8475 00
Total Assets	11250 00	Total Liab. & OE	11250 00

3-4   Total Assets, $7,685

Total Liabilities,	$ 825
Capital	6,860
Total Liab. + OE	$7,685

3-6   Total Assets, $104,050

Total Liabilities,	$ 28,925.00
Capital	75,125.00
Total Liab. + OE	$104,050.00

3-5   Total Assets, $1,389.50

Total Liabilities,	$ 197.75
Capital	1,191.75
Total Liab. + OE	$1,389.50

THINK IT OVER

Answers will vary for each person.

Chapter 4

QUESTIONS

1. (a) true
   (b) false
2. A transaction may result in two increases (example: buying supplies on credit) or two decreases (example: paying cash for a liability).
3. Assets have debit balances.
4. Assets decrease by credits; liabilities and owner's equity decrease by debits.

PROBLEMS

4-1 (1)

Cash		Equipment		Supplies	
1,245		3,670		430	

L.D. Brown		J.C. Tucker		Emilee Suzanne, Cap.	
	400		175		4,770

4-1 (2)   Total Assets, $5,345

Total Liabilities,	$ 575
Capital	<u>4,770</u>
Total Liab. + OE	$5,345

Therefore: <u>Emilee Suzanne, Capital</u>

              | 4,770

4-2 (1)

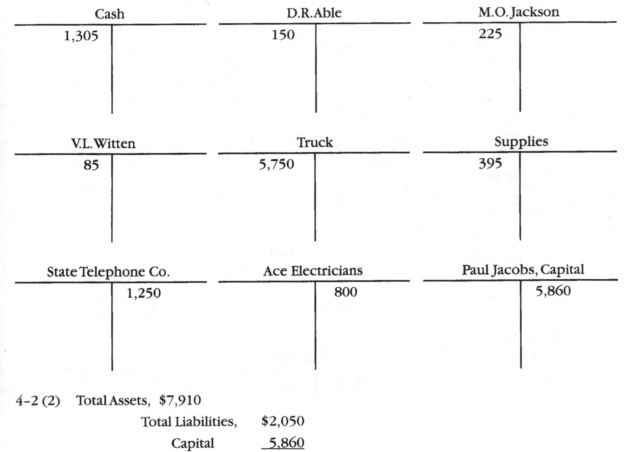

Cash		D.R. Able		M.O. Jackson	
1,305		150		225	

V.L. Witten		Truck		Supplies	
85		5,750		395	

State Telephone Co.		Ace Electricians		Paul Jacobs, Capital	
	1,250		800		5,860

4-2 (2)   Total Assets, $7,910

Total Liabilities,	$2,050
Capital	<u>5,860</u>
Total Liab. + OE	$7,910

4-3

Cash			Equipment	
4,075	*Ex.* 150		12,500	
(2) 1,000	(1) 75		(4) 500	
(3) 2,500				

Supplies			Regal Bank Company	
200			*Ex.* 150	2,000
(1) 75				(2) 1,000

Bixby Company			Kimberley Travis, Capital	
	(4) 500			14,775
				(3) 2,500

4-4

Trans. No.	Assets	Liabilities	Owner's Equity
Example	Decrease	Decrease	
(1)	No change		
(2)	Increase	Increase	
(3)	Increase		Increase
(4)	Increase	Increase	

4-5 (1) and (2)

Cash			H.L. Rhodes MD			Mary Turner MD	
437.50	(b) 65.00		50.00	(a) 50.00		50.00	(e) 25.00
(a) 50.00	(c) 75.00						
(d) 500.00							
(e) 25.00							

T.W. Vine DDS			Equipment			Supplies	
35.00			2,650.00			25.00	
						(c) 75.00	

State Telephone Co.			Ace Electricians			Lori Luing, Capital	
	215.00		(b) 65.00	65.00			2,967.50
							(d) 500.00

4-5 (3) Total Assets $3,247.50

Total Liabilities, $ 280.00

Capital <u>2,967.50</u>

Total Liab. + OE $3,247.50

THINK IT OVER

Reasons for being in business:

1) to be successful

2) to make a profit

3) to serve a useful purpose

The profit motive combines 1) and 2) above.

Chapter 5

QUESTIONS

1. (a) shorten trousers, waist adjustments

(b) hair setting, manicure

(c) plans for new or rebuilding homes

(d) drawing up legal documents, defending a client

(e) tooth extraction, cleaning teeth

(f) preparing financial statements, tax returns

2. (a) heat, light, supplies

(b) equipment, salaries

(c) architect's tables and tools

(d) salaries, legal forms

(e) salaries, supplies

(f) supplies, auto expense

PROBLEMS

5-1 (1) and (2)

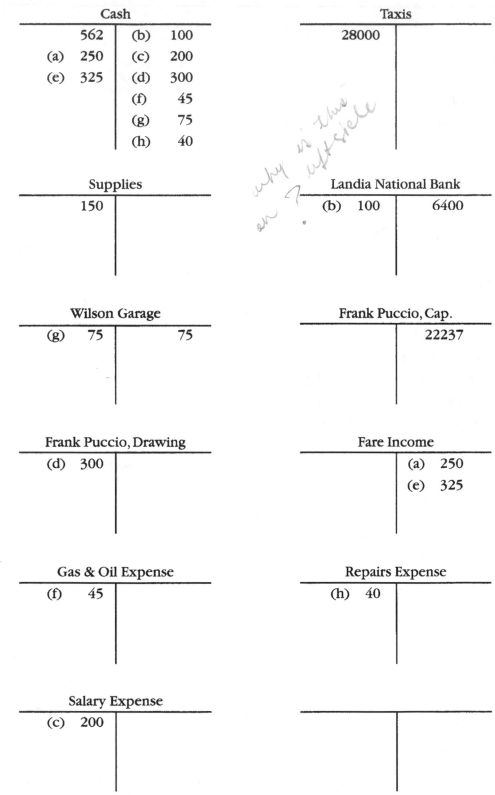

Cash			
	562	(b)	100
(a)	250	(c)	200
(e)	325	(d)	300
		(f)	45
		(g)	75
		(h)	40

Taxis	
28000	

Supplies	
150	

Landia National Bank	
(b) 100	6400

Wilson Garage	
(g) 75	75

Frank Puccio, Cap.	
	22237

Frank Puccio, Drawing	
(d) 300	

Fare Income	
	(a) 250
	(e) 325

Gas & Oil Expense	
(f) 45	

Repairs Expense	
(h) 40	

Salary Expense	
(c) 200	

5-1 (3)	Cash	377.00		5-2 (1)	Cash	902.00
	Taxis	28,000.00			Accounts Receivable	425.00
	Supplies	150.00			Delivery Equipment	12,000.00
	Salary Expense	200.00			Supplies	160.00
	Gas and Oil Expense	45.00			Tucker, Drawing	600.00
	Puccio, Drawing	300.00			Advertising Expense	95.00
	Repair Expense	40.00			Telephone Expense	140.00
	Total Debits	29,112.00			Trucking Expense	150.00
	Landia	6,300.00			Total	14,472.00
	Puccio, Capital	22,237.00			Accounts Payable	1075.00
	Fare Income	575.00			Tucker, Capital	12,297.00
	Total Credits	29,112.00			Delivery Income	1,100.00
					Total	14,472.00

5-2 (2)	Total Assets,	$13,487
	Total Liabilities,	$ 1,075
	Capital	12,412
	Total Liab. + OE	$13,487

THINK IT OVER

Separate each store's bookkeeping records to determine how profitable each one is.

Chapter 6

QUESTIONS

1. at least 250 postings to ledger accounts
2. Dates of entries are needed, for each transaction to follow logically.
3. day-by-day entries to record transactions
4. debits entered first, next to date column
   credits entered on next line, indented

PROBLEMS

6-1

Date		Account Title	PR	Debit	Credit
200-Oct	2	Salary Expense		175 00	
		Cash			175 00
		Employee's Salary			
	7	Cash		600 00	
		Design Income			600 00
		Received for a design			
	14	Supplies		200 00	
		Cash			200 00
		Supplies and Material			
	16	Cash		1000 00	
		Vernon Trust Co.			1000 00
		Borrowed from bank			
	21	Cash		500 00	
		Design Income			500 00
		Received for a design			
	23	Equipment		360 00	
		Cash			160 00
		Textile Equipment Co.			200 00
		new drawing table			
	30	Rose Klein, Drawing		400 00	
		Cash			400 00
		Withdrawal			
	31	Cash		100 00	
		Mary Wu			100 00
		Received on account			

JOURNAL   Page

6-2   Oct. 2—Check stub

               7—check received

          14—check stub and/or seller's receipt

          16—bank loan form

          21—check received

          23—statement from Textile Equipment Co. and check stub

          30—check stub

          31—check received

THINK IT OVER

Bredhoff should change to a system using the journal approach.

Cosmos should journalize first to logically follow the flow of her business activity.

Chapter 7

QUESTIONS

1. Steps in posting journal entries:

    (1) For the account debited, enter the amount on the debit side of the account.

    (2) Enter the year, month, and day in the date column (do not repeat the year or month).

    (3) Enter the journal page number in the posting reference column of the account.

    (4) Enter the account number in the posting reference column of the journal.

2. Account balances are normally found on the side the account increases.

3. (a) Journal posting refers to the account.

    (b) Account posting refers to the journal page.

4. A clerk resumes posting work after the last account posting indicated in the journal.

5. A trial balance "in balance" proves that debit and credit column totals are correct.

PROBLEMS

7-1 (ledger postings only)

Cash   No. 11

200-Oct.	1	Balance	√	1 7 5 0 00	200-Oct.	18		6	5 0 0 00
	10		6	2 5 0 0 00		25		6	2 5 0 00

Equipment   No. 12

200-Oct.	1	Balance	√	3 0 0 0 00					
	1		6	1 0 0 0 00					

Lamders Mfg. Company   No. 21

200-Oct.	25		6	2 5 0 00	200-Oct.	1		6	1 0 0 0 00

L.D. Berger Drawing   No. 32

200-Oct.	18		6	5 0 0 00					

Service Income   No. 32

					200-Oct.	10			2 5 0 0 00

7-2 (1) and (2)

Cash	2,020.00
Equipment	3,965.00
Supplies	60.00
Korn, Drawing	500.00
Advertising Expense	100.00
Utilities Expense	50.00
Total	6,695.00
Hi-Tech	1,925.00
Comp-Software	465.00
Korn, Capital	3,060.00
Services Income	1,245.00
Total	6,695.00

7-3 (1) and (2)

GENERAL JOURNAL   Page

Date		Account Title	PR	Debit	Credit
200-Oct.	2	Supplies	13	125 00	
		Cash	11		125 00
	7	Cash	11	200 00	
		Fee Income	41		200 00
	11	Jessup Bank	21	50 00	
		Cash	11		50 00
	21	Cash	11	240 00	
		Fee Income	41		240 00
	27	Miscellaneous Expense	51	65 00	
		Cash	11		65 00
	31	Anita Schaffer, Drawing	32	300 00	
		Cash	11		300 00

7-3 (2) and (3)

Cash | No. 11

200-Oct.	1	Balance	√	1375 00	200-Oct.	2		3	125 00
	7		3	200 00		11		3	50 00
	21		3	240 00		27		3	65 00
						31			300 00

1275.00   1815.00   540.00

Equipment | No. 12

200-Oct.	1	Balance	√	1642 50					

Supplies | No. 13

200-Oct.	1	Balance	√	230 00					
	2		3	125 00					

355.00

Jessup Bank | No. 21

200-Oct.	11		3	50 00	200-Oct.	1	Balance	√	875 00

Anita Schaffer, Capital | No. 31

					200-Oct.	10	Balance	√	2372 50

Anita Schaffer, Drawing | No. 32

200-Oct.	11		3	300 00					

Fee Income | No. 41

					200-Oct.	7		3	200 00
						21			240 00

440.00

Miscellaneous Expense | No. 51

200-Oct.	27		3	65 00					

7-3 (3)	Cash	1,275.00
	Equipment	1,642.50
	Supplies	355.00
	Schaffer, Drawing	300.00
	Miscellaneous Expense	65.00
	Total	3,637.50
	Jessup Bank	825.00
	Schaffer, Capital	2,372.50
	Fee Income	440.00
	Total	3,637.50

7-3 (4)

Anita Schaffer
Trial Balance
October 31, 200-

	Debit	Credit
Cash	127500	
Equipment	164250	
Supplies	35500	
Anita Schaffer, Drawing	30000	
Miscellaneous Expense	6500	
Jessup Bank		82500
Anita Schaffer, Capital		237250
Fee Income		44000
	363750	363750

THINK IT OVER

Fowler should retrace the steps in the procedure:

1) check trial balance column totals
2) verify that accounts are entered in proper debit or credit column
3) verify correct account balances
4) check posting procedure for each entry
5) verify proper journal entry

Jacobs neglected to journalize and post an entry for the same amount—$50—thus not affecting the equality of debits and credits in the trial balance.

Another error might be posting a debit or credit to an incorrect account—a debit to Supplies, for example, instead of to equipment.

Chapter 8

QUESTIONS

1. To locate an error in the trial balance:
    (a) Total columns, re-add.
    (b) Verify that each account is properly listed as a debit or a credit.
    (c) Verify correct postings from journal to accounts.
    (d) Verify correct account balances.
2. Any of the above done incorrectly will cause a trial balance to be "out of balance."
3. Errors that will not cause a trial balance to be out of balance include
    (a) omitting an entire entry.
    (b) posting to an incorrect account—a debit to a debit, or a credit to a credit.
    (c) posting an incorrect amount to both a debit and a credit.
    (d) posting a transaction journalized twice.
4. The net income or net loss is determined in the work sheet by subtracting one column total from the other in the Income Statement columns. The same result is found in the Balance Sheet column totals.

PROBLEMS

8-1

J. R. Price

Work Sheet

For Month Ended November 30, 200-

Account Title	A.N.	Trial Balance Dr.	Trial Balance Cr.	Income Statement Dr.	Income Statement Cr.	Balance Sheet Dr.	Balance Sheet Cr.
Cash	11	264500				264500	
Equipment	12	150000				150000	
Truck	13	750000				750000	
County Mfg. Co.	21		55000				55000
J. R. Price, Capital	31		1057000				1057000
J. R. Price, Drawing	32	50000				50000	
Commissions Income	41		165000		165000		
Advertising Expense	51	10000		10000			
Miscellaneous Expense	52	5000		5000			
Rent Expense	53	17500		17500			
Salary Expense	54	30000		30000			
		1277000	1277000	62500	165000	1214500	1112000
Net Income				102500			102500
				165000	165000	1214500	1214500

8-2 (1)

Accounts Payable ($600.00) should go in the Credit column.

8-2 (2)

Trial Balance totals, $7,251.40

8-2 (3)

Net Income, $1,450

Danziger Designs

Work Sheet

For the Quarter Ending Sept. 30, 200-

Account Title	A. N.	Trial Balance Dr.	Trial Balance Cr.	Income Statement Dr.	Income Statement Cr.	Balance Sheet Dr.	Balance Sheet Cr.
Cash		176250				176250	
Accts. Receivable		73890				73890	
Equipment		260500				260500	
Supplies		39500				39500	
Accts. Payable			60000				60000
Ann Danziger, Capital			425140				425140
Ann Danziger, Drawing		80000				80000	
Fee Income			240000		240000		
Advertising Expense		16000		16000			
Insurance Expense		4000		4000			
Materials Expense		10000		10000			
Rent Expense		25000		25000			
Salary Expense		40000		40000			
		725140	725140	95000	240000	650140	485140
Net Income				145000			145000
				240000	240000	650140	650140

8-3 (1) Service Income ($1,875.50) should go in the Credit column.

8–3 (2)

Gayle's Reliable Service

Trial Balance

October 31, 200-

Account Title	A.N.	Trial Balance Dr.	Trial Balance Cr.	Income Statement Dr.	Income Statement Cr.	Balance Sheet Dr.	Balance Sheet Cr.
Cash		760 00				760 00	
Accts. Receivable		142 50				142 50	
Automobile		9200 00				9200 00	
Supplies		350 00				350 00	
County Bank & Trust Co.			3600 00				3600 00
Rebecca Gayle, Capital			6302 00				6302 00
Rebecca Gayle, Drawing		600 00				600 00	
Service Income			1875 50		1875 50		
Advertising Expense		200 00		200 00			
Auto Expense		400 00		400 00			
Miscellaneous Expense		50 00		50 00			
Telephone Expense		75 00		75 00			
		11777 50	11777 50	725 00	1875 50	11052 50	9902 00
Net Income				1150 50			1150 50
				1875 50	1875 50	11052 50	11052 50

THINK IT OVER

See Think It Over for Chapter 7, p.54, for reasons trial balance is not in balance.

The $100 error overstates the credit total by $100 and understates the debit total by $100. The transposed error understates the debit total by $9. The difference is $209 ($200 + $9).

Chapter 9

QUESTIONS

1. Financial statements are prepared from a work sheet.
2. Income statements are prepared first, followed by capital statements and a balance sheet.
3. Owner's equity will increase by additional investments and a net income.
4. Owner's equity will decrease by a withdrawal and a net loss.
5. The work sheet capital balance is not up-to-date—it is a carryover from the end of the previous fiscal period.
6. The dating on an income statement indicates the length of the fiscal period. The dating on a balance sheet indicates the last day of the fiscal period.

PROBLEMS

9-1 (1)

J. R. Price
Income Statement
For Month Ended November 30, 200-

Revenue:			
Commissions Income			1650 00
Expenses:			
Advertising Expense		100 00	
Miscellaneous Expense		50 00	
Rent Expense		175 00	
Salary Expense		300 00	
Total Expenses			625 00
Net Income			1025 00

9-1 (2)

J. R. Price
Capital Statement
For Month Ended November 30, 200-

Beginning Balance, Nov. 1, 200-			10570 00
Plus: Net Income		1025 00	
Less: Withdrawals		500 00	
Net Increase in Capital			525 00
Ending Balance, Nov. 30, 200-			11095 00

9-1 (3)

J. R. Price
Balance Sheet
November 30, 200-

Assets		Liabilities	
Cash	2645 00	County Mfg. Company	550 00
Equipment	1500 00	Owner's Equity	
Truck	7500 00	J. R. Price, Capital, Nov. 30	11095 00
Total Assets	11645 00	Total Liab. & OE	11645 00

9–2 (1)

Damziger Designs

Income Statement

For the Quarter Ending Sept. 30, 200-

Revenue:				
Fee Income				2400 00
Expenses:				
Advertising Expense		160 00		
Insurance Expense		40 00		
Materials Expense		100 00		
Rent Expense		250 00		
Salary Expense		400 00		
Total Expenses				950 00
Net Income				1450 00

9–2 (2)

Damziger Designs

Capital Statement

For the Quarter Ending Sept. 30, 200-

Beginning Balance, July 1, 200-			4251 40
Net Income		1450 00	
Less Withdrawal		800 00	
Net Increase in Capital			650 00
Ending Balance, Sept. 30, 200-			4901 40

9–2 (3)

Danziger Designs

Balance Sheet

September 30, 200-

Assets		Liabilities	
Cash	1762 50	Accts. Payable	600 00
Accts. Reveivable	738 90	Owner's Equity	
Equipment	2605 00	Ann Danziger, Capital	
Supplies	395 00	Sept. 30	4901 40
Total Assets	5501 40	Total Liab. & OE	5501 40

9-3 (1)

Gayle's Reliable Service
Income Statement
For Month Ended October 31, 200-

Revenue:			
Service Income			1875 50
Expenses:			
Advertising Expense		200 00	
Auto Expense		400 00	
Miscellaneous Expense		50 00	
Telephone Expense		75 00	
Total Expenses			725 00
Net Income			1150 50

9-3 (2)

Gayle's Reliable Service
Capital Statement
For Month Ended October 31, 200-

Beginning Balance, Oct. 1, 200-			6302 00
Plus Net Income		1150 50	
Less Withdrawals		600 00	
Net Increase in Capital			550 50
Ending Balance, Oct. 31, 200-			6852 50

9-3 (3)

Gayle's Reliable Service
Balance Sheet
October 31, 200-

Assets		Liabilities	
Cash	760 00	County Bank & Trust Co.	3600 00
Accts. Reveivable	142 50	Owner's Equity	
Automobile	9200 00	Rebecca Gayle, Capital	6852 50
Supplies	350 00		
Total Assets	10452 50	Total Liab. & OE	10452 50

9-4 (1)

Walter Finnegan Associates

Work Sheet

For Month Ending Nov. 30, 200-

Account Title	A.N.	Trial Balance Dr.	Trial Balance Cr.	Income Statement Dr.	Income Statement Cr.	Balance Sheet Dr.	Balance Sheet Cr.
Cash		5648 00				5648 00	
Equipment		10400 00				10400 00	
Supplies		420 00				420 00	
Accounts Receivable		2655 00				2655 00	
Truck		15000 00				15000 00	
Accounts Payable			8600 00				8600 00
Walter Finnegan, Capital			28243 00				28243 00
Walter Finnegan, Drawing		2500 00				2500 00	
Fees Income			3680 00		3680 00		
Advertising Expense		800 00		800 00			
Miscellaneous Expense		400 00		400 00			
Rent Expense		1200 00		1200 00			
Salary Expense		1500 00		1500 00			
		40523 00	40523 00	3900 00	3680 00	36623 00	36843 00
Net Loss					220 00	220 00	
				3900 00	3900 00	36843 00	36843 00

9-4 (2a)

Walter Finnegan Associates

Income Statement

For Month Ending Nov. 30, 200-

Revenue:			
Fees Income			3680 00
Expenses:			
Advertising Expense		800 00	
Miscellaneous Expense		400 00	
Rent Expense		1200 00	
Salary Expense		1500 00	
Total Expenses			3900 00
Net Loss			220 00

9–4 (2b)

Walter Finnegan Associates

Capital Statement

For Month Ended November 30, 200-

Beginning Balance, Nov. 1, 200-			25243 00
Plus Additional Investment			3000 00
			28243 00
Less Withdrawal		2500 00	
Net Loss		220 00	
			2720 00
Walter Finnegan Cap. Nov. 30, 200-			25523 00

Form may vary—Ending Capital remains the same, $25,523.00

9–4 (2c)

Walter Finnegan Associates

Balance Sheet

November 30, 200-

Assets		Liabilities	
Cash	5648 00	Accts. Payable	8600 00
Equipment	10400 00	Owner's Equity	
Supplies	420 00	Walter Finnegan, Capital, Nov. 30	25523 00
Accts. Receivable	8655 00		
Truck	15000 00		
Total Assets	34123 00	Total Liab. & OE	34123 00

THINK IT OVER

A Balance Sheet is a "picture" at a given moment, a specific date—June 30 or December 31. An Income Statement shows activity over a period of time, for the period ending December 31.

Chapter 10

QUESTIONS

1. Net increases and/or decreases are transferred to the capital account by recording and posting closing entries.
2. Closing entries in correct order:
   (a) income accounts and credits in the income statement columns
   (b) expense accounts and debits in the income statement columns
   (c) the net income or net loss indicated on the work sheet
   (d) the drawing account balance in the balance sheet debit column
3. A credit balance in the Revenue and Expense Summary account indicates a net income.
4. Debit the owner's capital account, credit Revenue and Expense Summary.
5. Revenue and Expense Summary is closed by a debit, crediting Capital for a net income, or a debit to Capital and credit to Revenue and Expense Summary for a net loss. (Revenue accounts are closed by a debit, crediting the Revenue and Expense Summary account.)
6. Expense accounts are closed by a debit, crediting the Revenue and Expense Summary account.
7. Accounts with balances that remain open at the end of a fiscal period are assets, liabilities, and capital.

PROBLEMS

10-1 Net Income, $3,350 from completed Income Statement columns on work sheet

		Closing Entries				
200- Dec.	31	Consulting Fees Income		3 7 5 0 00		
		Royalty Income		5 0 0 00		
		Revenue and Expense Summary			4 2 5 0 00	
	31	Revenue and Expense Summary		9 0 0 00		
		Advertising Expense			1 0 0 00	
		Miscellaneous Expense			6 00	
		Rent Expense			2 5 0 00	
		Salary Expense			4 0 0 00	
		Telephone Expense			9 00	
	31	Revenue and Expense Summary		3 3 5 0 00		
		Gwen Vreeland, Capital			3 3 5 0 00	
	31	Gwen Vreeland, Capital		1 8 0 0 00		
		Gwen Vreeland, Drawing			1 8 0 0 00	

10–2 Trial Balance amounts:

2,800.00	6,000.00
3,895.00	12,920.00
4,000.00	8,500.00
12,500.00	
750.00	
1,500.00	
600.00	
175.00	
300.00	
900.00	
Total 27,420.00	Total 27,420.00

Net Income $6,525.00

10–2 (1)

Allen Insurance Agency

Work Sheet

For Month Ended Nov. 30, 200–

Account Title	A.N.	Trial Balance Dr.	Trial Balance Cr.	Income Statement Dr.	Income Statement Cr.	Balance Sheet Dr.	Balance Sheet Cr.
Cash		280000				280000	
Accts. Receivable		389500				389500	
Equipment		400000				400000	
Automobile		1250000				1250000	
Supplies		75000				75000	
Accts. Payable			600000				600000
Elliot Allen, Capital			1292000				1292000
Elliot Allen, Drawing		150000				150000	
Commissions Income			850000		850000		
Auto Expense		60000		60000			
Office Expense		17500		17500			
Rent Expense		30000		30000			
Salary Expense		90000		90000			
		2542000	2542000	197500	850000	2544500	1892000
Net Income				652500			652500
				850000	850000	2544500	2544500

10-2 (2)

			Closing Entries					
200-Nov.	30		Commissions Income		850000			
			Revenue & Expense Summary				850000	
	30		Revenue & Expense Summary		197500			
			Auto Expense				60000	
			Office Expense				17500	
			Rent Expense				30000	
			Salary Expense				90000	
	30		Revenue & Expense Summary		652500			
			Elliot Allen, Capital				652500	
	30		Elliot Allen, Capital		150000			
			Elliot Allen, Drawing				150000	

10-3 (1) Trial Balance totals, $35,675.75

Net Income, $4,850.00 (on completed work sheet)

10-3 (2a)

Earl Alpert, Esquire
Income Statement
For 3 Months Ended June 30, 200-

Revenue				
Legal Fees Income				950000
Expenses:				
Miscellaneous Expense		15000		
Office Expense		22500		
Rent Expense		120000		
Salary Expense		300000		
Travel Expense		7500		
Total Expenses				465000
Net Income				485000

10-3 (2b)

Earl Alpert, Esquire
Capital Statement
June 30, 200-

Beginning Balance, April 1		23300 75
Plus: Additional Investment	100000	
Net Income	485000	
	585000	
Less: Withdrawals	480000	
Net Increase in Capital		105000
Ending Balance, June 30, 200-		24350 75

10-3 (2c)

Earl Alpert, Esquire
Balance Sheet
June 30, 200-

Assets		Liabilities	
Cash	160500	Accts. Payable	187500
Accts. Receivable	1458000	Owner's Equity	
Office Equipment	396000	Earl Alpert, Capital	2435075
Furniture	525000		
Supplies	83075		
Total Assets	2622575	Total Liability & OE	2622575

10-3 (3)

			Closing Entries				
200- June	30		Revenue and Expense Summary		9 5 0 0 00		
			Legal Fees Income				9 5 0 0 00
	20		Miscellaneous Expense		1 5 0 00		
			Office Expense		2 2 5 00		
			Rent Expense		1 2 0 0 00		
			Salary Expense		3 0 0 0 00		
			Telephone Expense		7 5 00		
			Revenue and Expense Summary				4 6 5 0 00
	20		Revenue and Expense Summary		4 8 5 0 00		
			Earl Alpert, Capital				4 8 5 0 00
	20		Earl Alpert, Capital		4 8 0 0 00		
			Earl Alpert, Drawing				4 8 0 0 00

10-4 (1) Net income $1,485.00

10-4 (1), (3), and (4)

Cash No. *11*

200- Dec.	1	Balance	√	1 0 0 0 00	200- Dec.	20		5	2 5 0 00
	10		4	5 0 0 00		30		5	1 7 5 00
	22		5	7 5 0 00		31		6	1 0 0 00
			6	1 3 5 0 00		31		6	9 0 00
		2185.00		3 6 0 0 00		31		6	8 0 0 00
						31	Balance	√	1 4 1 5 00 2 1 8 5 00
				3 6 0 0 00					3 6 0 0 00
200- Jan.	1	Balance	√	2 1 8 5 00					

Accounts Receivable No. *12*

200- Dec.	1	Balance	√	2 0 0 0 00	200- Dec.	22		5	7 5 0 00
		1250.00				31	Balance	√	1 2 5 0 00
				2 0 0 0 00					2 0 0 0 00
200- Jan.	1	Balance	√	1 2 5 0 00					

Equipment No. 13

200- Dec.	1	Balance	√		350000	200- Dec.	31	Balance	√		500000
	15		4		150000						
					500000						
					500000						500000
200- Jan.	1	Balance	√		500000						

Supplies No. 14

200- Dec.	1	Balance	√		58000						

Accounts Payable No. 21

200- Dec.	20		5		25000	200- Dec.	1	Balance	√		45000
	31	Balance	√		170000		15		4		150000
					195000			1700.00			195000
											195000
						200- Jan.	1	Balance	√		170000

Pamela Washington, Capital No. 31

200- Dec.	31		7		80000	200- Dec.	1	Balance	√		663000
	31	Balance	√		731500		31		7		148500
					811500						811500
						200- Jan.	1	Balance	√		731500

Pamela Washington, Drawing No. 32

200- Dec.	31		6		80000	200- Dec.	31		7		80000

Revenue and Expense Summary No. 33

200- Dec.	31		7		36500	200- Dec.	31		7		185000
	31		7		148500						
					185000						185000

Fees Income No. *41*

200- Dec.	31		7	1 8 5 00	200- Dec.	10		4	5 0 00
						31		6	1 3 5 00
									1 8 5 00
				1 8 5 00					1 8 5 00

Automobile Expense No. *51*

200- Dec.	31		6	9 0 00	200- Dec.	31		7	9 0 00

Office Expense No. *52*

200- Dec.	31		6	1 0 0 00	200- Dec.	31		7	1 0 0 00

Rent Expense No. *53*

200- Dec.	30		5	1 7 5 00	200- Dec.	31		7	1 7 5 00

10-4 (2)

Pamela Washington

Work Sheet

For Month Ended Dec. 31, 200-

Account Title	A. N.	Trial Balance		Income Statement		Balance Sheet	
		Dr.	Cr.	Dr.	Cr.	Dr.	Cr.
Cash		2 1 8 5 00				2 1 8 5 00	
Accounts Receivable		1 2 5 0 00				1 2 5 0 00	
Equipment		5 0 0 0 00				5 0 0 0 00	
Supplies		5 8 0 00				5 8 0 00	
Accounts Payable			1 7 0 0 00				1 7 0 0 00
P. Washington, Capital			6 6 3 0 00				6 6 3 0 00
P. Washington, Drawing		8 0 0 00				8 0 0 00	
Revenue & Exp. Summary							
Fees Income			1 8 5 0 00		1 8 5 0 00		
Automobile Expense		9 0 00		9 0 00			
Office Expense		1 0 0 00		1 0 0 00			
Rent Expense		1 7 5 00		1 7 5 00			
		1 0 1 8 0 00	1 0 1 8 0 00	3 6 5 00	1 8 5 0 00	9 8 1 5 00	8 3 3 0 00
Net Income				1 4 8 5 00			1 4 8 5 00
				1 8 5 0 00	1 8 5 0 00	9 8 1 5 00	9 8 1 5 00

10-4 (2a)

Pamela Washington

Income Statement

For the Month Ended December 31, 200-

Revenue:			
Fees Income			1850 00
Expenses:			
Auto Expenses	90 00		
Office Expenses	100 00		
Rent Expenses	175 00		
Total Expenses			365 00
Net Income			1485 00

10-4 (2b)

Pamela Washington

Capital Statement

For the Month Ended December 31, 200-

Beginning Balance, Dec. 1		6630 00
Plus: Net Income	1485 00	
Less: Withdrawal	800 00	
Net Increase in Capital		685 00
Ending Balance, Dec. 31		7315 00

10-4 (2c)

Pamela Washington

Balance Sheet

December 31, 200-

Assets		Liabilities	
Cash	2185 00	Accts. Payable	1700 00
Accts. Receivable	1250 00	Owner's Equity	
Equipment	5000 00	Pamela Washington,	
Supplies	580 00	Capital, Dec. 31	7315 00
Total Assets	9015 00	Total Liability & OE	9015 00

10-4 (3)

GENERAL JOURNAL

Page 7

Date		Account Title	PR	Debit	Credit
200- Dec.	31	*Closing Entries*			
		Fees Income	41	1 8 5 0 00	
		Revenue & Expense Summary	33		1 8 5 0 00
	31	*Revenue & Expense Summary*	33	3 6 5 00	
		Auto Expense	51		9 0 00
		Office Expense	52		1 0 0 00
		Rent Expense	53		1 7 5 00
	31	*Revenue & Expense Summary*	33	1 4 8 5 00	
		Pam Washington, Capital	31		1 4 8 5 00
	31	*Pam Washington, Capital*	31	8 0 0 00	
		Pam Washington, Drawing	32		8 0 0 00

10-4 (5)

Pamela Washington

Post-Closing Trial Balance

December 31, 200-

	Debit	Credit
Cash	2 1 8 5 00	
Accounts Receivable	1 2 5 0 00	
Equipment	5 0 0 0 00	
Supplies	5 8 0 00	
Accounts Payable		1 7 0 0 00
Pamela Washington, Capital		7 3 1 5 00
	9 0 1 5 00	9 0 1 5 00

THINK IT OVER

Green will mix financial records and not be able to determine his profit or loss for a given fiscal period. IRS will not accept these mixed records. He will have to reexamine his work to separate one period from the next in order to prepare acceptable tax returns.

Chapter 11

QUESTIONS

1. Three parties to a check are the drawer, drawee, and payee.
2. A signature card is used by the drawer's bank (the drawee) to verify the drawer's handwritten name and signature.
3. The service charge entry should debit Miscellaneous Expense and credit Cash.
4. A reconciliation statement is prepared to bring together the checkbook balance and the bank statement balance because
   (a) omitted deposits (a deposit in transit) are not included on the bank statement.
   (b) outstanding checks are not on the bank statement.
   (c) bank service charges are not deducted in the checkbook until the bank statement is received.

PROBLEMS

11-1

	DOLLARS	CENTS
CASH	1049	00
COINS	8	72
CHECKS	148	65
	79	15
TOTAL ITEMS TOTAL	1285	52

11-2 (1)

NO. _118_	$ _40.00_	
DATE _Jan 15_	20 - -	
TO _K-Mart_		
FOR _Cleaning supplies_		

	DOLLARS	CENTS
BAL BRO'T FOR'D	136	50
AMT. DEPOSITED		
TOTAL		
AMT. THIS CHECK	40	00
BAL. CAR'D FOR'D	96	50

No. _118_

1-830 / 860

January 15 20 - -

Pay to the order of _K-Mart_ $ _40.00_

Forty and —————————————— 00/100 Dollars

BOLTON NATIONAL BANK
of New York, NY

Louann Pringle

⑆0860⑈0830⑆1848⑈6 7 1⑆

NO. _119_	$ _15.00_	
DATE _Jan 19_	20 - -	
TO _Brown's Cab_		
FOR _Taxi service_		

	DOLLARS	CENTS
BAL BRO'T FOR'D	96	50
AMT. DEPOSITED		
TOTAL		
AMT. THIS CHECK	15	00
BAL. CAR'D FOR'D	81	50

No. _119_

1-830 / 860

January 19 20 - -

Pay to the order of _Brown's Cab_ $ _15.00_

Fifteen and —————————————— 00/100 Dollars

BOLTON NATIONAL BANK
of New York, NY

Louann Pringle

⑆0860⑈0830⑆1848⑈6 7 1⑆

NO. _120_	$ _50.00_	
DATE _Jan 22_	20 - -	
TO _Cash_		
FOR _Personal_		

	DOLLARS	CENTS
BAL BRO'T FOR'D	81	50
AMT. DEPOSITED	75	00
TOTAL	156	50
AMT. THIS CHECK	50	00
BAL. CAR'D FOR'D	106	50

No. _120_

1-830 / 860

January 22 20 - -

Pay to the order of _Cash_ $ _50.00_

Fifty and —————————————— 00/100 Dollars

BOLTON NATIONAL BANK
of New York, NY

Louann Pringle

⑆0860⑈0830⑆1848⑈6 7 1⑆

11-2 (2)

FOR DEPOSIT TO THE ACCOUNT OF

NAME   _Louann Pringle_

ADDRESS   _Bolton_

DATE   _Jan 23_   20 - -

BOLTON NATIONAL BANK
New York, NY

CHECKS AND OTHER ITEMS ARE RECEIVED FOR FOR DEPOSIT SUBJECT TO THE TERMS AND CONDITIONS OF THE BANK'S COLLECTION AGREEMENT

	DOLLARS	CENTS
BILLS	75	00
COINS		
CHECKS AS FOLLOWS. PROPERLY ENDORSED		
TOTAL DEPOSIT	75	00

⑆0860⑈0830⑆1848⑈6 7 1⑆

11-3

Checkbook Balance	420.90	Bank Balance	397.40
Deduct: Service Charge	4.00	Add: Omitted deposit	250.00
Correct checkbook bal.	416.90		647.40
		Deduct: Outstanding checks	
		#217— 75.00	
		219—105.50	
		220— 50.00	
			230.50
		Correct Bank Balance	416.90

11-4 (1)

Bank Reconciliation Statement

Checkbook Balance	708.92	Bank Balance	626.66
Deduct: Service Charge	3.60	Add: Omitted deposit	375.00
Correct checkbook bal.	705.32		1,001.66
		Deduct: Outstanding checks	
		#641— 92.50	
		644—107.25	
		646— 37.80	
		647— 58.79	
			296.34
		Correct Available Balance	705.32

11-4 (2)

Jan.	31	Miscellaneous Expense			3 40	
		Cash				3 40
		Bank Service Charge. Jan.				

THINK IT OVER

Hankins assumes no legal responsibility by his qualified endorsement. The bank may attempt to recover from the drawer of the check who had insufficient funds in his/her checking account.

Chapter 12

QUESTIONS

1. One person handling the petty cash fund limits responsibility to just one person.
2. To establish the petty cash fund, draw a check payable to Petty Cash. To replenish the fund, draw a check payable to Petty Cash. List on the checkstub the amount spent on each expense with the replenishing check for the total spent.
3. The entry to establish petty cash should debit Petty Cash and credit Cash.
4. The entry to replenish the fund should debit each account for which petty cash was spent and credit the cash account.
5. Petty cash is proved by subtracting the sum of all petty cash vouchers from the original amount in the petty cash fund. The difference should equal the amount of cash remaining in the fund.

PROBLEMS

12-1 (1)

NO. 138	$ 35.00				No. 138
DATE April 1 20 - -					1-830
TO Petty Cash				April 1 20 - -	860
FOR To establish a Petty					
Cash fund		Pay to the order of Petty cash			$ 35.00
	DOLLARS / CENTS				
BAL BRO'T FOR'D	1406 / 92	Thirty-five and			00 / 100 Dollars
AMT. DEPOSITED					
TOTAL	1406 / 92	BOLTON NATIONAL BANK			
AMT. THIS CHECK	35 / 00	of New York, NY		Hilda Marcello	
BAL. CAR'D FOR'D	1371 / 92	⑆0860⑈0830⑆1843⑈671⑈		(or student's name)	

12-1 (2)

No. 1	SPACE TRAVEL SERVICES
	Petty Cash Voucher

		Date April 2 20 - -
Pay to Messenger		
For Delivery package		Amount $ 2.75
Delivery Expense		
XYZ		Student's Name
Payment Received		Authorized

No. _2_

SPACE TRAVEL SERVICES
Petty Cash Voucher

Date _April 9_ 20_- -_

Pay to _Post Office_

For _Postage_

Office Expense

Amount
$ 8.00

ABC

Student's Name

Payment Received

Authorized

No. _3_

SPACE TRAVEL SERVICES
Petty Cash Voucher

Date _April 16_ 20_- -_

Pay to _Mobil_

For _Gasoline_

Auto Expense

Amount
$ 10.00

JKL

Student's Name

Payment Received

Authorized

No. _4_

SPACE TRAVEL SERVICES
Petty Cash Voucher

Date _April 23_ 20_- -_

Pay to _Stationery Store_

For _Business cards_

Misc. Expense

Amount
$ 7.50

LMN

Student's Name

Payment Received

Authorized

No. _5_

SPACE TRAVEL SERVICES
Petty Cash Voucher

Date _April 30_ 20_--_

Pay to _Post Office_

For _Postage_

Office Expense

Amount
$ *4.00*

_____ _ABC_   _____ *Student's Name*

Payment Received   Authorized

12-1 (3) sort:

Delivery Exp	Auto Exp	Office Exp	Misc Exp
$ 2.75	$10.00	$ 8.00	$7.50
		4.00	
		12.00	

$ 2.75
+10.00
+12.00
+ 7.50
$32.25   amount of replenishing check

12-1 (3)

NO.	156	$	32.25
DATE	April 30	20 --	
TO	Petty Cash		
FOR	Auto Exp. 10.00—Del.		
	Exp. 2.75—Office Exp.		
	12.00—Misc. Exp. 7.50		

	DOLLARS	CENTS
BAL. BRO'T FOR'D	1091	37
AMT. DEPOSITED	500	00
TOTAL	1591	37
AMT. THIS CHECK	32	25
BAL. CAR'D FOR'D	1559	12

SPACE TRAVEL SERVICES

No. _156_

1-830
860

April 30 20 _--_

Pay to the order of _Petty cash_ $ _32.25_

Thirty-two and —————————————— 25/100 **Dollars**

BOLTON NATIONAL BANK
of New York, NY

⑈0860⑈0830⑈1243⑈671⑈

Hilda Marcello
(or student's name)

12-2

200-Apr.	1	Petty cash			3 5 00	
		Cash				3 5 00
		To establish fund				
	30	Auto Expense			1 0 00	
		Delivery Expense			2 75	
		Miscellaneous Expense			7 50	
		Office Expense			1 2 00	
		Cash				3 2 25
		To replenish fund				

THINK IT OVER

Responsibility should be separated between the drawer of checks from the regular checking account and the person in charge of the petty cash fund. If the fund requires frequent replenishment, it should be increased to a larger amount.

Cycle One Examination

Part I

1. T	11. T
2. F	12. T
3. T	13. F
4. T	14. T
5. F	15. F
6. T	16. T
7. T	17. T
8. F	18. F
9. F	19. F
10. F	20. T

Part II

1. I	9. W
2. L	10. E
3. Q	11. B
4. V	12. N
5. F	13. A
6. G	14. K
7. R	15. H
8. T	16. U

Part III

	Account Dr.	Account Cr.
1.	J	A
2.	B	A
3.	A	D
4.	G	F
5.	B	A, C
6.	E	A
7.	F	H, I, J
8.	F	D
9.	D	F
10.	D	E

Part IV (1) Complete Chet Gorski's work sheet.

County-Wide Plumbing

Work Sheet

For the Year Ended December 31, 200-

Account Title	A.N.	Trial Balance Dr.	Trial Balance Cr.	Income Statement Dr.	Income Statement Cr.	Balance Sheet Dr.	Balance Sheet Cr.
Cash		1 4 7 2 50				1 4 7 2 50	
Petty Cash		2 5 00				2 5 00	
Accounts Receivable		3 8 5 00				3 8 5 00	
Supplies		2 4 2 50				2 4 2 50	
Truck		1 4 8 5 0 00				1 4 8 5 0 00	
Accounts Payable			9 7 0 00				9 7 0 00
Chet Gorski, Capital			1 4 6 8 5 00				1 4 6 8 5 00
Chet Gorski, Drawing		9 5 0 0 00				9 5 0 0 00	
Fees Income			1 8 6 2 0 00		1 8 6 2 0 00		
Advertising Expense		4 8 0 00		4 8 0 00			
Automobile Expense		2 4 0 0 00		2 4 0 0 00			
Miscellaneous Expense		1 2 0 00		1 2 0 00			
Rent Expense		3 6 0 0 00		3 6 0 0 00			
Telephone Expense		1 2 0 0 00		1 2 0 0 00			
		5 4 2 7 5 00	5 4 2 7 5 00	7 8 0 0 00	1 8 6 2 0 00	2 6 4 7 5 00	1 5 6 5 5 00
Net Income				1 0 8 2 0 00			1 0 8 2 0 00
				1 8 6 2 0 00	1 8 6 2 0 00	2 6 4 7 5 00	2 6 4 7 5 00

Part IV (2)

<u>County-Wide Plumbing</u>

<u>Capital Statement</u>

<u>December 31, 200-</u>

Beginning Capital, Jan. 1, 200-		9685 00
Plus: Additional Investment	5000 00	
Net Income	10820 00	
	15820 00	
Less: Withdrawals	9500 00	
Net Increase in Capital		6320 00
Ending Capital, Dec. 31, 200-		16005 00

Part IV (3)

<u>County-Wide Plumbing</u>

<u>Balance Sheet</u>

<u>December 31, 200-</u>

Assets		Liabilities	
Cash	14725 0	Accounts Payable	970 00
Petty Cash	25 00	Owner's Equity	
Accounts Receivable	385 00	Chet Gorski, Capital	16005 00
Supplies	242 50		
Truck	14850 00		
Total Assets	16975 00	Total Liabilities & OE	16975 00

Part IV (4)

GENERAL JOURNAL

		Closing Entries			
200- Dec.	31	*Fees Income*	1862000		
		Revenue and Expense Summary		1862000	
	31	*Revenue and Expense Summary*	780000		
		Advertising Expense		48000	
		Automobile Expense		240000	
		Miscellaneous Expense		12000	
		Rent Expense		360000	
		Telephone Expense		120000	
	31	*Revenue and Expense Summary*	1082000		
		Chet Gorski, Capital		1082000	
	31	*Chet Gorski, Capital*	950000		
		Chet Gorski, Drawing		950000	

Part V (1)

NO. 207	$ 35.50
DATE *January 7* 20 --	
TO *Wilson Supply Co.*	
FOR *Smoke Alarm*	
(Equipment)	

	DOLLARS	CENTS
BAL BRO'T FOR'D	382	47
AMT. DEPOSITED	225	00
TOTAL	607	47
AMT. THIS CHECK	35	50
BAL. CAR'D FOR'D	571	97

No. 207

1-830 / 860

January 7 20 --

Pay to the order of *Wilson Supply Company* $ *35.50*

Thirty-five and 50/100 **Dollars**

BOLTON NATIONAL BANK
of New York, NY

Student's Name

⑈086〇⑈0830⑈ 1248 ⑈ 671⑈

Part V (2)

JOURNAL

200- Jan.	31	*Equipment*	3550	
		Cash		3550
		Bought smoke alarm		

Chapter 13

QUESTIONS

1. A service type of business sells the services to be performed—plumbing, electrical, TV repair, and the like. A merchandising business sells goods—clothing, appliances, furniture and such.
2. A purchases journal is used to record the purchase of merchandise on account.
3. Creditors' accounts may be arranged either alphabetically or numerically in a subsidiary ledger.
4. Instead of listing each creditor's account in the general ledger, a controlling account—Accounts Payable—with a credit balance will maintain the equality of debits and credits.
5. This would be true if there are a limited number of creditors' accounts.
6. The sum of all creditors' account balances should equal the balance of the controlling account—Accounts Payable—in the general ledger.
7. A three-column ruling in creditors' accounts and a four-column ruling in the general ledger accounts indicate the balance of each account with a minimum of adding and subtracting, and eliminates the balancing-and-ruling procedure at the end of a fiscal period.

PROBLEMS

13-1 (1) and (3)

PURCHASES JOURNAL   PAGE *5*

Date		From Whom Purchased Account Credited		Invoice No.	PR	Purchases Dr. Acct. Pay. Cr.
200- Feb.	3	Dye & Akins		1705	✓	300 00
	10	Edward Kalpakian & Sons		G-116	✓	425 00
	17	Dye & Akins		1751	✓	385 00
	25	Edward Kalpakian & Sons		G-151	✓	500 00
	28	Total				1610 00
						(51) (21)

13-1 (2)

ACCOUNTS PAYABLE LEDGER

Dye & Akins
1011 Mountain Avenue, Denver, CO 80201

Date			PR	Dr.	Cr.	Cr. Bal.
200- Jan	15		P1		450 00	450 00
Feb	3		P5		300 00	750 00
	17		P5		385 00	1135 00

Edward Kalpakian & Sons
379 Valley View Drive, Denver, CO 80204

Date			PR	Dr.	Cr.	Cr. Bal.
200- Feb	10		P5		425 00	425 00
	25		P5		500 00	925 00

13-1 (3)

GENERAL LEDGER
Accounts Payable No. 2

Date			PR	Dr.	Cr.	Balance Dr.	Balance Cr.
200- Jan.	31		P1		450 00		450 00
Feb.	28		P5		1610 00		2010 00

Purchases No. 5

Date			PR	Dr.	Cr.	Dr.	Cr.
200- Feb.	28		P5	1610 00		1610 00	

13-1 (4)

Ruth Ann Davis

Schedule of Accounts Payable

February 28, 200-

Dye & Atkins	1135 00
Edward Kalpakian & Sons	925 00
Total Accounts Payable	2060 00

13-2 (1) and (3)

PURCHASES JOURNAL   PAGE 2

Date		From Whom Purchased Account Credited		Invoice No.	PR	Purchases Dr. Acct. Pay. Cr.
200- Feb.	1	Paul Olins		#42	✓	175 00
	5	Wilson & Shea		513	✓	200 00
	8	Island Supply		72A	✓	265 00
	12	Wilson & Shea		543	✓	400 00
	15	Glen Mfg. Inc.		31	✓	620 00
	19	Paul Olins		78	✓	360 00
	22	Gregory Sims		318	✓	250 00
	26	Island Supply		29B	✓	300 00
	30	Total				2570 00
						(51) (21)

13–2 (2)

ACCOUNTS PAYABLE LEDGER

Glen Mfg., Inc.

200– Feb.	15		P2		6 2 0 00		6 2 0 00

Island Supply

200– Feb.	8		P2		2 6 5 00		2 6 5 00
	26		P2		3 0 0 00		5 6 5 00

Paul Olins

200– Feb.	1		P2		1 7 5 00		1 7 5 00
	19		P2		3 6 0 00		5 3 5 00

Gregory Sims

200– Feb.	22		P2		2 5 0 00		2 5 0 00

Wilson & Shea

200– Feb.	5		P2		2 0 0 00		2 0 0 00
	12		P2		4 0 0 00		6 0 0 00

13-2 (3)

GENERAL LEDGER

Accounts Payable No. *21*

			PR	Dr.	Cr.	Balance Dr.	Cr.
200- Feb.	28		P2		2 5 7 0 00		2 5 7 0 00

Purchases No. *51*

			PR	Dr.	Cr.	Balance Dr.	Cr.
200- Feb.	28		P2	2 5 7 0 00		2 5 7 0 00	

13-2 (4)

Maria Zagretti

Schedule of Accounts Payable

February 28, 200-

Glen Mfg., Inc.		6 8 0 00
Island Supply		5 6 5 00
Paul Olins		5 3 5 00
Gregory Sims		2 5 0 00
Wilson & Shea		6 0 0 00
Total Accounts Payable		2 5 7 0 00

THINK IT OVER

Marino does not have to post to the purchases account for each purchase. Instead, he posts once from the total of the purchases journal.

Chapter 14

QUESTIONS

1. A special journal for cash disbursements reduces the amount of time and expense in posting credits to the cash account. Only one posting is made at the end of the fiscal period for a credit to Cash.
2. Postings from the cash disbursements journal are identified by the letters *CD* and page number.
3. How often an account title is used determines the use of a special column.
4. Special column totals will have account numbers as posting references to general ledger accounts; other account postings will be indicated by an account number or a check mark.
5. A check mark indicates "do not post" for a general Dr. column total.
6. A check mark for a subsidiary account indicates that the item has been posted.
7. The sum of all subsidiary accounts at the end of a fiscal period should equal the balance of the controlling account in the general ledger.

PROBLEMS

14-1 (1) and (2)

CASH DISBURSEMENTS JOURNAL   Page 3

Date	Account Debited	Ck. No.	PR	General Dr.	Acct. Pay. Dr.	S. Krasnoff Draw. Dr.	Cash Cr.
200- Mar 1	Rent Expense	247		400 00			400 00
3	Utilities Expense	248		76 50			76 50
8	Paula Cory	249			50 00		50 00
10	Sid Krasnoff, Drawing	250	✓			500 00	500 00
17	Salary Expense	251		300 00			300 00
22	Hilda Piper	252			90 00		90 00
24	Sid Krasnoff, Drawing	253	✓			500 00	500 00
29	Equipment	254		1250 00			1250 00
31	Salary Expense	255		300 00			300 00
31	Totals			2326 50 2326 50	140 00 140 00	1000 00 1000 00	3466 50 3466 50
				(✓)	( )	( )	( )

14-2 (1), (2), and (4)

PURCHASES JOURNAL

PAGE **2**

Date		From Whom Purchased Account Credited		Invoice No.	PR	Purchases Dr. Acct. Pay. Cr.
200-Apr.	4	Abel Jenks		P-311	✓	600 00
	20	W. T. Gross		S-113	✓	1450 00
	30	Total				2050 00
						2050 00
						(51) (21)

14-2 (1), (3), and (4)

CASH DISBURSEMENTS JOURNAL

Page **3**

Date		Acct. Dr.	Ck. No.	PR	General Dr.	Acct. Pay. Dr.	Cash Cr.
200-Apr.	1	Rent Expense	502	65	450 00		450 00
	8	Helen Scordas, Drawing	503	32	400 00		400 00
	14	Abel & Jenks	504	✓		800 00	800 00
	15	Salary Expense	505	67	325 00		325 00
	22	Supplies	506	15	75 00		75 00
	28	Helen Scordas, Drawing	507	32	500 00		500 00
	30	W.T. Gross	508	✓		725 00	725 00
	30	Totals			1750 00	1525 00	3275 00
					1750 00	1525 00	3275 00
					(✓)	(21)	( )

14-2 (2) and (3)

ACCOUNTS PAYABLE LEDGER

Abel & Jenks

140 Rocky Mountain Street, Boise, ID 83701

Date			PR	Dr.	Cr.	Cr. Bal.
200-Apr	1	Balance	✓			800 00
	4		P2		600 00	1400 00
	14		CD3	800 00		600 00

W.T. Gross

205 Columbia Avenue, Boise, ID 83702

Date			PR	Dr.	Cr.	Cr. Bal.
200- Apr	20		P2		1 450 00	1 450 00
	30		CD3	725 00		725 00

GENERAL LEDGER

Cash No. **11**

Date			PR	Dr.	Cr.	Balance Dr.	Balance Cr.
200- Apr	1	Balance	✓			4500 00	
	30		CD3		3275 00	1225 00	

14–2 (2) and (3)

Supplies No. **15**

Date			PR	Dr.	Cr.	Balance Dr.	Balance Cr.
200- Apr	1	Balance	✓			50 00	
	22		CD3	75 00		125 00	

Accounts Payable No. **21**

Date				Dr.	Cr.	Balance Dr.	Balance Cr.
200- Apr	1	Balance	✓				800 00
	30		P2		2050 00		2850 00
	30		CD3	1525 00			1325 00

Helen Scordas, Drawing No. **32**

Date				Dr.	Cr.	Balance Dr.	Balance Cr.
200- Apr	8		CD3	400 00		400 00	
	28		CD3	500 00		900 00	

Purchases   No. *51*

200-				Dr.		Cr.		Balance Dr.		Cr.	
Apr	30		P2	2 0 5 0 00				2 0 5 0 00			

Rent Expense   No. *65*

200-				Dr.		Cr.		Balance Dr.		Cr.	
Apr	1		CD3	4 5 0 00				4 5 0 00			

Salary Expense   No. *67*

200-				Dr.		Cr.		Balance Dr.		Cr.	
Apr	15		CD3	3 2 5 00				3 2 5 00			

14-2 (5)

Helen Scordas

Schedule of Accounts Payable

April 30, 200-

Abel & Jenks	6 0 0 00
W. T. Gross	7 2 5 00
Total Accounts Payable	1 3 2 5 00

Chapter 15

QUESTIONS

1. Sales of merchandise on account are recorded in a sales journal.
2. Customers' accounts may be arranged alphabetically or numerically in a subsidiary ledger.
3. Instead of listing each customer's account in the general ledger, a controlling account—Accounts Receivable—with a debit balance will maintain the equality of debits and credits.
4. The total of all customers' accounts in the subsidiary ledger should equal the balance of the controlling account in the general ledger.
5. A small business might have fewer customers to whom merchandise is sold on account.
6. Sales invoice numbers are in consecutive order in the sales journal because they are numbered that way in the sales book or on the form used for such sales.

PROBLEMS

15-1 (1), (2), and (3)

SALES JOURNAL   Page *31*

Date		To Whom Sold – Account Debited	Invoice No.	PR	Acct. Rec. Dr. Sales Cr.
200- *Mar*	2	*Mrs. Edward Ardyce*	215	✓	175 00
	9	*Mr. Herman Gold*	216	✓	96 50
	16	*Ms. Eliza Fisher*	217	✓	107 30
	23	*Mrs. Edward Ardyce*	218	✓	62 45
	30	*Ms. Eliza Fisher*	219	✓	29 50
	31	*Total*			470 75
					(13) (41)

15-1 (2)

ACCOUNTS RECEIVABLE LEDGER

Mrs. Edward Ardyce

305 Riverview Terrace, Cincinnati, OH 45204

				Dr.	Cr.	Dr. Bal.
200- *Mar*	2		S31	175 00		175 00
	23		S31	62 45		237 45

Ms. Eliza Fisher
851 Clarkfield Street, Cincinnati, OH 45201

				Dr.	Cr.	Dr. Bal.
200- Mar	16		S31	107 30		107 30
	30		S31	29 50		136 80

Mr. Herman Gold
79 Willowbrook Drive, Cincinnati, OH 45202

				Dr.	Cr.	Dr. Bal.
200- Mar	1	Balance	✓			258 60
	9		S31	96 50		355 10

15-1 (3)

GENERAL LEDGER

Accounts Receivable   No. 13

				Dr.	Cr.	Balance Dr.	Balance Cr.
200- Mar	1	Balance	✓			258 60	
	9		S31	470 75		729 35	

Sales   No. 41

				Dr.	Cr.	Balance Dr.	Balance Cr.
200- Mar	31		S31		470 75		470 75

15-1 (4)

Mears Department Store

Schedule of Accounts Receivable

March 31, 200-

Mrs. Edward Ardyce			2 3 7 45
Ms. Eliza Fisher			1 3 6 80
Mr. Herman Gold			3 5 5 10
Total Accounts Receivable			7 2 9 35
			7 2 9 35

15-2 (1) and (3)

SALES JOURNAL   Page *8*

Date		To Whom Sold – Account Debited	Invoice No.	PR	Accts. Rec. Dr. Sales Cr.
200- Mar	2	Mrs. Fay Wilamowski	328	✓	4 7 50
	6	Ms. Shirley Callahan	329	✓	3 6 95
	9	Mr. William Witt	330	✓	4 9 25
	13	Shirley Callahan	331	✓	1 0 7 65
	16	Mrs. Marjorie Intrator	332	✓	7 6 80
	20	Fay Wilamowski	333	✓	5 2 90
	23	William Witt	334	✓	5 9 20
	27	Marjorie Intrator	335	✓	6 7 75
	30	Shirley Callahan	336	✓	8 7 00
	30	Total			5 8 5 00
					(13) (41)

15-2 (2)

ACCOUNTS RECEIVABLE LEDGER

Ms. Shirley Callahan

186 Mineola Boulevard, Mineola, NY 11501

Date			PR	Dr.	Cr.	Dr. Bal.
200- Apr	1	Balance	✓			45 00
	6		S8	36 95		81 95
	13		S8	107 65		189 60
	30		S8	87 00		276 60

Mrs. Marjorie Intrator

91 Bryn Mawr, New Hyde Park, NY 11040

Date			PR	Dr.	Cr.	Dr. Bal.
200- Apr	16		S8	76 80		76 80
	27		S8	67 75		144 55

Mrs. Fay Wilamowski

451 Cornell Drive, Hicksville, NY 11803

Date			PR	Dr.	Cr.	Dr. Bal.
200- Apr	1	Balance	✓			65 30
	2		S8	47 50		112 80
	20		S8	52 90		165 70

Mr. William Witt

451 Emory Road, Mineola, NY 11501

Date			PR	Dr.	Cr.	Dr. Bal.
200- Apr	1	Balance	✓			95 00
	9		S8	49 25		144 25
	23		S8	59 20		203 45

15-2 (3)

GENERAL LEDGER

Accounts Receivable   No. *13*

200-				Dr.	Cr.	Balance Dr.	Balance Cr.
Apr	1	Balance	✓			2 0 5 30	
	30		S8	5 8 5 00		7 9 0 30	

Sales   No. *13*

200-			Dr.	Cr.	Balance Dr.	Balance Cr.
Apr	30	S8		5 8 5 00		5 8 5 00

15-2 (4)

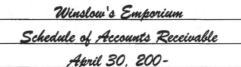

Winslow's Emporium

Schedule of Accounts Receivable

April 30, 200-

Ms. Shirley Callahan		2 7 6 60
Mrs. Marjorie Intrator		1 4 4 55
Mrs. Fay Wilamowski		1 6 5 70
Mr. William Witt		2 0 3 45
Total Accounts Receivable		7 9 0 30

THINK IT OVER

Automated billing procedures eliminate hand procedures for posting to customers' accounts, thus saving time and expense. Marshall & Kahn will have better control of their records by using a special journal, thus saving time and expense even with a hand procedure.

Chapter 16

QUESTIONS

1. All transactions that would result in debits to cash are entered in the cash receipts journal.
2. A special column would be used if the account for which cash is received is used frequently.
3. Special column total postings are indicated by general ledger account numbers; other account postings are indicated by check marks for subsidiary ledger accounts or numbers for general ledger accounts.
4. Check marks for subsidiary ledger accounts indicate that they have been posted.
5. Check marks for general ledger accounts indicate that they have not been posted.
6. The sum of all customers' account balances in the subsidiary ledger should equal the balance of the controlling account—Accounts Receivable—in the general ledger.

PROBLEMS

16-1 (1), (2), and (3)

CASH RECEIPTS JOURNAL   Page 6

Date	Account Credited	PR	General Cr.	Accts. Rec. Cr.	Sales Cr.	Cash Dr.
200- Apr 23		✓	750 00	1435 00	5976 00	8161 00
23	Raul Garcia, Capital		2000 00			2000 00
24	Lone Star Bank		2500 00			2500 00
25	J.R. Dallas			85 00		85 00
26	Margo Chase			60 00		60 00
27	Equipment		95 00			95 00
28	Frances Lima			75 00		75 00
29	Sales	✓			1765 00	1765 00
30	Totals		5345 00	1655 00	7741 00	14741 00
			(✓)	(13)	(41)	(11)

(Note: In a complete problem, items listed in the
General Cr. and Accts. Rec. Cr. columns
would be posted. Post references
would appear, therefore, in the PR column.)

16–1 (3)

GENERAL LEDGER

Cash   No. *11*

Date			PR	Dr.	Cr.	Balance Dr.	Balance Cr.
200- Apr	1	Balance	✓			1 9 3 5 00	
	30		CR6	1 4 7 4 1 00		1 6 6 7 6 00	

Accounts Receivable   No. *13*

Date				Dr.	Cr.	Balance Dr.	Balance Cr.
200- Apr	1	Balance	✓			1 7 2 9 50	
	30		CR6		1 6 5 5 00	7 4 50	

Sales   No. *41*

Date				Dr.	Cr.	Balance Dr.	Balance Cr.
200- Mar	31		S4		3 5 0 0 00		3 5 0 0 00
	31		CR5		6 2 5 0 00		9 7 5 0 00
	31		J3	9 7 5 0 00			—
Apr	30		CR6		7 7 4 1 00		7 7 4 1 00

16–2 (1) and (2)

Date		To Whom Sold – Account Debited	Invoice No.	PR	Accts. Rec. Dr. Sales Cr.
200- May	1	Willow's Beauty Shoppe	7156	✓	4 6 5 00
	1	Lee's Unisex	7157	✓	3 9 5 00
	12	Goddess of Love	7158	✓	2 6 8 00
	12	Jayne's Curls & Waves	7159	✓	1 7 5 00
	17	Willow's Beauty Shoppe	7160	✓	1 9 2 00
	29	Jayne's Curls & Waves	7161	✓	2 2 5 00
	29	Lee's Unisex	7162	✓	3 1 5 20
	31	Total			2 0 3 5 70 2 0 3 5 70
					(13) (41)

16-2 (1), (2), and (3)

CASH RECEIPTS JOURNAL   Page 6

Date	Account Credited	PR	General Cr.	Accts. Rec. Cr.	Sales Cr.	Cash Dr.
200- May 7	Sales	✓			25250	25250
10	Goddess of Love	✓		20000		20000
14	Sales	✓			30725	30725
15	Pat Norrell	31	300000			300000
19	Lee's Unisex	✓		39500		39500
21	Sales	✓			29680	29680
25	Willow's Beauty Shoppe	✓		26500		26500
28	Sales	✓			31990	31990
31	Sales	✓			19140	19140
31	Totals		300000	86000	136785	522785
			(✓)	(13)	(41)	(11)

GENERAL LEDGER

Cash   No. 11

Date		PR	Dr.	Cr.	Balance Dr.	Balance Cr.
200- May 1	Balance	✓			107850	
31		CR6	522785		630635	

Accounts Receivable   No. 13

Date			Dr.	Cr.	Balance Dr.	Balance Cr.
200- May 1	Balance	✓			20000	
31		S9	203570		223570	
31		CR6		86000	137570	

Pat Norrell, Capital   No. 31

Date			Dr.	Cr.	Balance Dr.	Balance Cr.
200- May 1	Balance	✓				2500000
15		CR6		300000		2800000

Sales   No. 41

Date			Dr.	Cr.	Balance Dr.	Balance Cr.
200- May 31		S9		203570		203570
31		CR6		136785		340355

16-2 (2) and (3)

ACCOUNTS RECEIVABLE LEDGER

Goddess of Love

110 Chemung Avenue, Binghamton, NY 13901

Date			PR	Dr.	Cr.	Dr. Bal.
200- May	1	Balance	✓			200 00
	10		CR6		200 00	—
	12		S9	268 50		268 50

Jayne's Curls & Waves

39 Tompkins Avenue, Cortland, NY 13045

Date			PR	Dr.	Cr.	Dr. Bal.
200- May	12		S9	175 00		175 00
	29		S9	225 00		400 00

Lee's Unisex

451 College Heights Road, Ithaca, NY 14850

Date			PR	Dr.	Cr.	Dr. Bal.
200- May	1		S9	395 00		395 00
	19		CR6		395 00	—
	29		S9	315 20		315 20

Willow's Beauty Shoppe

58 Twain Boulevard, Elmira, NY 14901

Date			PR	Dr.	Cr.	Dr. Bal.
200- May	1		S9	465 00		465 00
	17		S9	192 00		657 00
	25		CR6		265 00	392 00

16-2 (4)

Pat Norrell			
Schedule of Accounts Receivable			
May 31, 200-			
Goddess of Love			2 6 8 50
Jayne's Curls & Waves			4 0 0 00
Lee's Unisex			3 1 5 20
Willow's Beauty Shoppe			3 9 2 00
Total Accounts Receivable			1 3 7 5 70

Chapter 17

QUESTIONS

1. (We have changed this to show the new formats for a 4-column journal)
2. Posting procedure: Each account is posted to either a general ledger account or a subsidiary ledger account; column totals are posted to Accounts Payable and Accounts Receivable; General Dr. and General Cr. column totals are checked (not posted).
3. All entries not entered in special journals are recorded in a general journal.
4. Jones' record: Dr.   Sales Returns & Allowances
                          Cr. Claire Smith (Acct. Rec. Cr.)
   Smith's record: Dr.   Henry Jones (Accts. Pay. Dr.)
                          Cr. Purchases Returns & Allowances
5. A credit memorandum is the source document for each of these entries: a credit memo and copy for Jones' entry and a debit memo for Smith's entry.
6. A statement of account lists a customer's charges and payments and returns, with a balance due.

PROBLEMS

17-1 (1) and (2)

GENERAL JOURNAL   Page 7

Date		PR	General Dr.	General Cr.	Accts. Pay. Dr.	Accts. Rec. Cr.
200- May 2	Sales Returns & Allowances		35 00			
	Jane Mc Donald					35 00
	Credit Memo No. 18					
5	Hedy Nachtigal		65 00			
	Netty Nachtigal			65 00		
	Correct posting error					
9	Baldwin Piano Company				100 00	
	Purchases Returns & Allowances			100 00		
	Debit Memo No. 53					
15	Philip Scheiber, Drawing		95 00			
	Purchases			95 00		
	Withdrew guitar for nephew					
22	Sales Returns & Allowances		80 00			
	Molly Shapiro					80 00
	Credit Memo No. 19		185 00			
29	Equipment			185 00		
	Philip Screiber, Capital					
	Invested desk		460 00	445 00	100 00	115 00
			460 00	445 00	100 00	115 00
31	Totals		(✓)	(✓)		

17–2

GENERAL JOURNAL

Date			PR	General Dr.	General Cr.	Accts. Pay. Dr.	Accts. Rec. Cr.
200- May	3	Home Decor. Corp.				160 00	
		Purch. Ret. & Allow.			160 00		
		Memo AR -1					
	17	Sales Ret. & Allow.		77 00			
		Mrs. R. Muir					77 00
		Memo 39					
	28	Carl Walton Furn. Co.		140 00			
		C. Wilton Fabric Co.			140 00		
		Posting error					

17-2

CASH RECEIPTS JOURNAL

Page *12*

Date	Acct. Cr.	PR	General Cr.	Accts. Rec. Cr.	Sales Cr.	Cash Dr.
200- May 24	Purchases Ret. & Allow.		50 00			50 00

CASH DISBURSEMENTS JOURNAL

Page *11*

Date	Acct. Dr.	Ck. No.	PR	General Dr.	Accts. Pay. Dr.	Purch. Dr.	Cash Cr.
200- May 10	Sales Ret. & Allow.	326		38 00			38 00

17-3

STATEMENT OF ACCOUNT

Hudson's Department Store
100 Gateway Plaza
St. Louis, MO 63101

SOLD TO

Ms. Pearl Nathanson
972 Riverside Dr.
St. Louis, MO 63104

May 20, 200-

		CHARGES			
May	1		60 00		
	5		75 00		
	18		45 00		
				180 00	
		PAYMENTS/CREDITS			
	12		35 00		
	15		20 00		
				55 00	
	18	Balance Due		125 00	

17-4 (1) and (2)

PURCHASES JOURNAL   Page *10*

Date		Account Credited			PR	Purchases Dr. Acct. Pay. Cr.
200- May	17	Schmidt & Brendle				375 00
	17	Winston Jewelers				1200 00
	31	Totals				1575 00
						( ) ( )

17–4 (1) and (2)

		SALES JOURNAL			Page *14*

<table>
<tr><td colspan="2">Date</td><td>Account Debited</td><td>Invoice No.</td><td>PR</td><td>Accts. Rec. Dr.
Sales Cr.</td></tr>
<tr><td>200-
May</td><td>4</td><td>Antonio Lorenzo</td><td>B192</td><td></td><td>3 0 0 00</td></tr>
<tr><td></td><td>4</td><td>Edward Grabezak</td><td>B193</td><td></td><td>2 5 0 00</td></tr>
<tr><td></td><td>11</td><td>Marc Green</td><td>B194</td><td></td><td>2 7 5 00</td></tr>
<tr><td></td><td>31</td><td>Totals</td><td></td><td></td><td>8 2 5 00</td></tr>
<tr><td></td><td></td><td></td><td></td><td></td><td>( )   ( )</td></tr>
</table>

17–4 (1) and (2)

		CASH RECEIPTS JOURNAL					Page *19*

<table>
<tr><td colspan="2">Date</td><td></td><td>PR</td><td>General
Cr.</td><td>Accts. Rec.
Cr.</td><td>Sales
Cr.</td><td>Cash
Dr.</td></tr>
<tr><td>200-
May</td><td>1</td><td>Balance on hand $1,500</td><td>✓</td><td></td><td></td><td></td><td></td></tr>
<tr><td></td><td>3</td><td>Marc Green</td><td></td><td></td><td>1 5 0 00</td><td></td><td>1 5 0 00</td></tr>
<tr><td></td><td>3</td><td>Gian Polidoro</td><td></td><td></td><td>9 5 00</td><td></td><td>9 5 00</td></tr>
<tr><td></td><td>22</td><td>Antonio Lorenzo</td><td></td><td></td><td>5 0 00</td><td></td><td>5 0 00</td></tr>
<tr><td></td><td>23</td><td>Edward Grabezak</td><td></td><td></td><td>1 2 5 00</td><td></td><td>1 2 5 00</td></tr>
<tr><td></td><td>31</td><td>Sales</td><td>✓</td><td></td><td></td><td>2 7 4 0 00</td><td>2 7 4 0 00</td></tr>
<tr><td></td><td>31</td><td>Totals</td><td></td><td>—</td><td>4 2 0 00</td><td>2 7 4 0 00</td><td>3 1 6 0 00</td></tr>
<tr><td></td><td></td><td></td><td></td><td>(✓)</td><td>( )</td><td>( )</td><td>( )</td></tr>
</table>

17–4 (1)

		CASH DISBURSEMENTS JOURNAL					

<table>
<tr><td colspan="2">Date</td><td></td><td>Ck.
No.</td><td>PR</td><td>General
Dr.</td><td>Accts. Pay.
Dr.</td><td>Purch.
Dr.</td><td>Cash
Cr.</td></tr>
<tr><td>200-
May</td><td>1</td><td>Winslow Jewelers</td><td>392</td><td></td><td></td><td>4 6 5 00</td><td></td><td>4 6 5 00</td></tr>
<tr><td></td><td>1</td><td>Rent Expense</td><td>393</td><td></td><td>4 5 0 00</td><td></td><td></td><td>4 5 0 00</td></tr>
<tr><td></td><td>13</td><td>Daniel Shaw, Drawing</td><td>394</td><td></td><td>5 0 0 00</td><td></td><td></td><td>5 0 0 00</td></tr>
<tr><td></td><td>14</td><td>Salary Expense</td><td>395</td><td></td><td>3 0 0 00</td><td></td><td></td><td>3 0 0 00</td></tr>
<tr><td></td><td>28</td><td>Schmidt & Brendle</td><td>396</td><td></td><td></td><td>3 7 5 00</td><td></td><td>3 7 5 00</td></tr>
<tr><td></td><td>29</td><td>Sales Returns & Allowances</td><td>397</td><td></td><td>4 0 00</td><td></td><td></td><td>4 0 00</td></tr>
<tr><td></td><td>31</td><td>Totals</td><td></td><td></td><td>1 2 9 0 00</td><td>8 4 0 00</td><td>—</td><td>2 1 3 0 00</td></tr>
<tr><td></td><td></td><td></td><td></td><td></td><td>(✓)</td><td>( )</td><td>—</td><td>( )</td></tr>
</table>

17-4 (1) and (2)

GENERAL JOURNAL

Page 5

Date			PR	General Dr.	General Cr.	Accts. Pay. Dr.	Accts. Rec. Cr.
200-May	8	Supplies		35 00			
		Equipment			35 00		
		Posting Error					
	24	Sales Ret. & Allow.		75 00			
		Marc Green					75 00
		Credit Memo 35					
	31	Daniel Shaw, Draw		200 00			
		Purchases			200 00		
		Ring for wife					
	31	Totals		310 00	235 00	—	75 00
				(✓)	(✓)	(—)	( )

Chapter 18

QUESTIONS

1. An 8-column work sheet has a pair of columns for a trial balance, adjustments, income statement, and balance sheet.

2. End-of-period merchandise inventory may be estimated or taken by a physical count or by records for purchases and sales.

3. The first merchandise adjustment transfers the old or beginning inventory to Revenue and Expense Summary.

4. The second merchandise adjustment transfers the new or ending inventory to Revenue and Expense Summary.

5. Balance sheet amount for merchandise is the new inventory—the old inventory is zero, the result of a Dr. in the trial balance column and a Cr. in the adjustments column.

6. Prepaid accounts such as supplies are used and therefore are expenses that are recorded by an adjustment at the end of each fiscal period.

7. The net income is determined on the work sheet by subtracting the Income Statement debit column total from the credit column total; the same difference will result by subtracting one total from the other in the Balance Sheet columns.

8. The net loss is determined on the work sheet by subtracting the Income Statement credit column total from the debit column total; the same difference will result by subtracting one total from the other in the Balance Sheet columns.

PROBLEMS

18-1

Daniel Green
Work Sheet
For Quarter Year Ended June 30, 200-

Account Title	A.N.	Trial Balance Debit	Trial Balance Credit	Adjustments Debit	Adjustments Credit	Income Statement Debit	Income Statement Credit	Balance Sheet Debit	Balance Sheet Credit
Cash		1 200 00						1 200 00	
Accounts Receivable		2 500 00						2 500 00	
Merchandise Inventory		5 000 00		(B) 5 175 00	(A) 5 000 00			5 175 00	
Equipment		6 000 00						6 000 00	
Supplies		400 00			(C) 100 00			300 00	
Accounts Payable			1 800 00						1 800 00
Daniel Green, Capital			14 200 00						14 200 00
Daniel Green, Drawing		1 500 00						1 500 00	
Revenue and Expense Summary				(A) 5 000 00	(B) 5 175 00	5 000 00	5 175 00		
Sales			6 500 00				6 500 00		
Sales Returns & Allowances		250 00				250 00			
Purchases		3 000 00				3 000 00			
Purchases Returns & Allowances			150 00				150 00		
Miscellaneous Expense		100 00				100 00			
Rent Expense		1 200 00				1 200 00			
Salary Expense		1 500 00				1 500 00			
Supplies Expense				(C) 100 00		100 00			
		22 650 00	22 650 00	10 275 00	10 275 00	11 150 00	11 825 00	16 675 00	16 000 00
Net Income						675 00			675 00
						11 825 00	11 825 00	16 675 00	16 675 00

18–2

Timothy Sullivan
Work Sheet
For Month Ended January 31, 200–

Account Title	A.N.	Trial Balance Debit	Credit	Adjustments Debit	Credit	Income Statement Debit	Credit	Balance Sheet Debit	Credit
Cash		3960 00						3960 00	
Accounts Receivable		3515 00						3515 00	
Merchandise Inventory		3800 00		(B) 3950 00	(A) 3800 00			3950 00	
Supplies		385 00			(C) 120 00			205 00	
Prepaid Insurance		300 00			(D) 50 00			250 00	
Accounts Payable			1800 00						1800 00
Timothy Sullivan, Capital			7875 00						7875 00
Timothy Sullivan, Drawing		3000 00						3000 00	
Revenue and Expense Summary				(A) 3800 00	(B) 3950 00	3800 00	3950 00		
Sales			4800 00				4800 00		
Sales Returns & Allowances		35 00				35 00			
Purchases		1700 00				1700 00			
Advertising Expense		100 00				100 00			
Insurance Expense				(D) 50 00		50 00			
Rent Expense		400 00				400 00			
Salary Expense		400 00				400 00			
Supplies Expense				(C) 120 00		120 00			
		13875 00	13875 00	7920 00	7920 00	6245 00	8150 00	11580 00	9675 00
Net Income						1905 00			1905 00
						8150 00	8150 00	11580 00	11580 00

THINK IT OVER

The truck has depreciated $6,000 over a 3-year period. The owner may not have included an expense each fiscal period. Depreciation expense affects the net income or net loss of a business. (In advanced accounting, an adjusting entry for depreciation is included.)

Chapter 19

QUESTIONS

1. An income statement describes how a business operates—its income, costs, and expenses resulting in a net income or a net loss. A capital statement describes the owner's equity. A balance sheet describes the financial condition of a business at the end of a fiscal period—its assets, liabilities, and owner's equity.

2. Cost of goods sold is calculated as beginning inventory + net purchases - ending inventory.

3. A net income results when total income is greater than the cost of goods sold plus total expenses. If cost of goods sold and expenses are greater than net income, the result is a net loss.

4. A report form balance sheet lists assets, liabilities, and owner's equity in a vertical arrangement; the account form lists assets on the left side with liabilities and owner's equity on the right side (similar to a T-account).

PROBLEMS

19-1 (1)

Daniel Green

Income Statement

For Quarter Ended April 30, 200-

Income:				
Sales			6500 00	
Less Sales Returns and Allowances			250 00	
Net Sales				6250 00
Cost of Goods Sold:				
Merchandise Inventory, Apr. 1			5000 00	
Purchases	3000 00			
Less Purchases Ret. & Allow	150 00			
Net Purchases		2850 00		
Merchandise Available for Sale		7850 00		
Less Merchandise Inv., June 30		5175 00		
Cost of Goods Sold				2675 00
Gross Profit on Sales				3575 00
Expenses:				
Miscellaneous Expense			100 00	
Rent Expense			1200 00	
Salary Expense			1500 00	
Supplies Expense			100 00	
Total Expense				2900 00
Net Income				675 00

19-1 (2)

Daniel Green

Capital Statement

For Quarter Ended June 30, 200-

Beginning Balance, April 1			12200 00
Plus: Additional Investment		2000 00	
Net Income		675 00	
		2675 00	
Less: Withdrawals		1500 00	
Net Increase in Capital			1175 00
Ending Balance, June 30			13375 00

19-1 (3)

Daniel Green

Balance Sheet

June 30, 200-

Assets			
Cash		1200 00	
Accounts Receivable		2500 00	
Merchandise Inventory		5175 00	
Equipment		6000 00	
Supplies		300 00	
Total Assets			15175 00
Liabilities			
Accounts Payable			1800 00
Owner's Equity			13375 00
Total Liabilities and Owner's			
Equity			15175 00

19-2 (1)

Timothy Sullivan

Income Statement

For Month Ended January 31, 200-

Income:			
Sales	420 00		
Less Sales Returns & Allow.	35 00		
Net Sales			4165 00
Cost of Goods Sold:			
Merchandise Inv. Jan 1	380 00		
Purchases	170 00		
Merchandise Available			
for Sale	550 00		
Less Merchandise Inv. Jan 31	395 00		
Cost of Goods Sold:			155 00
Gross Profit Profit on Sales			2615 00
Expenses:			
Advertising Expense	100 00		
Insurance Expense	50 00		
Miscellaneous Expense	40 00		
Rent Expense	400 00		
Supplies Expense	120 00		
Total Expenses			710 00
Net Income			1905 00

19-2 (2)

Timothy Sullivan

Capital Statement

For Month Ended January 31, 200-

Beginning Balance, Jan. 1			5375 00
Additional Investment			2500 00
			7875 00
Plus: Net Income		1905 00	
Less Withdrawals		300 00	
Net Increase in Capital			1605 00
Ending Balance, Jan. 31			9480 00

OR

Timothy Sullivan

Capital Statement

For Month Ended January 31, 200-

Beginning Balance, Jan. 1			5375 00
Plus: Additional Investment		2500 00	
Net Income		1905 00	
		4405 00	
Less: Withdrawals		300 00	
Net Increase in Cap.			4105 00
Ending Balance, Jan. 31			9480 00

19–2 (3)

Timothy Sullivan

Balance Sheet

January 31, 200-

Assets		
Cash	3360 00	
Accounts Receivable	3515 00	
Merchandise Inventory	3950 00	
Supplies	205 00	
Prepaid Insurance	250 00	
Total Assets		11280 00
Liabilities		
Accounts Payable		1800 00
Owner's Equity		
Timothy Sullivan, Capital		9480 00
Total Liabilities & Owner's		
Equity		11280 00

19-3 (1)

Abdullah and Pahlevi
Work Sheet
For Year Ended December 31, 200-

Account Title	A.N.	Trial Balance Debit	Trial Balance Credit	Adjustments Debit	Adjustments Credit	Income Statement Debit	Income Statement Credit	Balance Sheet Debit	Balance Sheet Credit
Cash		3625 00						3625 00	
Accounts Receivable		18260 00						18260 00	
Merchandise Inventory, Jan. 1		23320 00		(B) 23195 00	(A) 23320 00			23195 00	
Equipment		7500 00						7500 00	
Prepaid Insurance		500 00			(C) 100 00			400 00	
Supplies		275 00			(D) 96 50			178 50	
Accounts Payable			3105 00						3105 00
T.G. Abdullah, Capital			33802 00						33802 00
T.G. Abdullah, Drawing		10000 00						10000 00	
S.H. Pahlevi, Capital			28404 00						28404 00
S.H. Pahlevi, Drawing		12000 00						12000 00	
Revenue and Expense Summary				(A) 23320 00	(B) 23195 00	23320 00	23195 00		
Sales			51790 00				51790 00		
Sales Returns & Allowances		2570 00				2570 00			
Purchases		31380 00				31380 00			
Purchases Returns & Allowances			1529 00				1529 00		
Advertising Expense		600 00				600 00			
Insurance Expense				(C) 100 00		100 00			
Rent Expense		3600 00				3600 00			
Salary Expense		6000 00				6000 00			
Supplies Expense				(D) 96 50		96 50			
		118630 00	118630 00	45711 50	45711 50	66666 50	76514 00	75158 50	65311 00
Net Income						9847 50			9847 50
						76514 00	76514 00	75158 50	75158 50

19-3 (2)

Abdullah and Pahlevi

Income Statement

For Year Ended December 31, 200-

Income:			
Sales		51790 00	
Less Sales Returns & Allowances		2570 00	
Net Sales			49220 00
Cost of Goods Sold:			
Merchandise Inv. Jan. 1		22320 00	
Purchases	31,380 00		
Less Purchases Returns			
and Allowances	1529 00		
Net Purchases		29851 00	
Merchandise Available for Sale		52171 00	
Less Merchandise Inv. Dec. 31		23195 00	
Cost of Goods Sold			28976 00
Gross Profit on Sales			20244 00
Expenses:			
Advertising Expense		600 00	
Insurance Expense		100 00	
Rent Expense		3600 00	
Salary Expense		6000 00	
Supplies Expense		96 50	
Total Expenses			10396 50
Net Income			9847 50

19-3 (3)

Abdullah and Pahlevi

Capital Statement

For Year Ended December 31, 200-

T.G. Abdullah:			
Beginning Balance, Jan. 1		2 8 8 0 2 00	
Plus Additional Invest.	5000 00		
4/7 of Net Income	5627 14		
	10,627 14		
Less Withdrawals	10,000 00		
Net Increase in Capital		6 2 7 14	
Ending Balance, Dec. 31			2 9 4 2 9 14
S.H. Pahlevi:			
Beginning Balance, Jan. 1		2 8 4 0 4 00	
Plus 3/7 of Net Income	4220 36		
Less Withdrawals	12,000 00		
Net Decrease in Capital		7 7 7 9 64	
Ending Balance, Dec. 31			2 0 6 2 4 36
Total Owner's Equity, Dec. 31			5 0 0 5 3 50

19-3 (4)

Abdullah and Pahlevi
Balance Sheet
December 31, 200-

Assets			
Cash		3625 00	
Accounts Receivable		18260 00	
Merchandise Inventory		23195 00	
Equipment		7500 00	
Prepaid Insurance		400 00	
Supplies		178 50	
Total Assets			53158 50
Liabilities			
Accounts Payable			3105 00
Owner's Equity			
T.G. Abdullah, Capital		29429 14	
S.H. Pahlevi, Capital		20624 36	
Total Owner's Equity			50053 50
Total Liabilities and Owners' Equity			53158 50

THINK IT OVER

An exact amount or an estimated amount of loss on bad debts can be subtracted from the balance of total accounts receivable at the end of the fiscal period. In Garrison's case, a $500 estimate for bad debts will decrease his net income or increase his net loss. (In advanced accounting, an adjusting entry for estimated loss on bad debts is included.)

Chapter 20

QUESTIONS

1. Each adjustment on the work sheet consists of an equal debit and credit in the adjustments columns.

2. Journalizing and posting each adjusting entry brings each of the affected accounts in the ledger up to date; the work sheet does not do this.

3. Closing entries are journalized using the information in the Income Statement columns—all revenue, cost, and expenses—and in the Balance Sheet columns—the drawing account.

4. The first closing entry zeroes out the balance from the Income Statement Cr. column.

5. The second closing entry zeroes out the balance from the Income Statement Dr. column.

6. The third closing entry zeroes out the Revenue and Expense Summary account for either a net income (debit Revenue and Expense Summary, credit Capital) or for a net loss (debit Capital, credit Revenue and Expense Summary).

7. The fourth closing entry zeroes out the drawing account (debit, Capital, credit Drawing).

8. The third closing entry transfers the net income or net loss to owner's equity.

9. The fourth closing entry transfers the drawing account balance to owner's equity.

10. After closing entries have been posted, all income and expense accounts and drawing accounts have been zeroed out.

11. Post-closing trial balance proves the equality of debits and credits in general ledger accounts, which remain open.

PROBLEMS

20-1 (1) and (2)

GENERAL JOURNAL   Page 7

200-June						
		Adjusting Entries				
	30	Revenue and Expense Summary	5 0 0 0 00			
		Merchandise Inventory		5 0 0 0 00		
	30	Merchandise Inventory	5 1 7 5 00			
		Revenue and Expense Summary		5 1 7 5 00		
	30	Supplies Expense	1 0 0 00			
		Supplies		1 0 0 00		
		Closing Entries				
	30	Sales	6 5 0 0 00			
		Purchases Returns and Allowances	1 5 0 00			
		Revenue and Expense Summary		6 6 5 0 00		
	30	Revenue and Expense Summary	6 1 5 0 00			
		Sales Returns and Allowances		2 5 0 00		
		Purchases		3 0 0 0 00		
		Miscellaneous Expense		1 0 0 00		
		Rent Expense		1 2 0 0 00		
		Salary Expense		1 5 0 0 00		
		Supplies Expense		1 0 0 00		
	30	Revenue and Expense Summary	6 7 5 00			
		Daniel Green, Capital		6 7 5 00		
	30	Daniel Green, Capital	1 5 0 0 00			
		Daniel Green, Drawing		1 5 0 0 00		

20–2 (1) and (2)

GENERAL JOURNAL

Date		Account Title	PR	Debit	Credit
200–Jan		*Adjusting Entries*			
	31	Revenue and Expense Summary	33	3 8 0 0 00	
		Merchandise Inventory	13		3 8 0 0 00
	31	Merchandise Inventory	13	3 9 5 0 00	
		Revenue and Expense Summary	33		3 9 5 0 00
	31	Supplies Expense	65	1 2 0 00	
		Supplies	14		1 2 0 00
	31	Insurance Expense	62	5 0 00	
		Prepaid Insurance	15		5 0 00
		Closing Entries			
	31	Sales	41	4 2 0 0 00	
		Revenue and Expense Summary	33		4 2 0 0 00
	31	Revenue and Expense Summary	33	2 4 4 5 00	
		Sales Returns & Allowances	41.1		3 5 00
		Purchases	51		1 7 0 0 00
		Advertising Expense	61		1 0 0 00
		Insurance Expense	62		5 0 00
		Miscellaneous Expense	63		4 0 00
		Rent Expense	64		4 0 0 00
		Supplies Expense	65		1 2 0 00
	31	Revenue and Expense Summary	33	1 9 0 5 00	
		Timothy Sullivan, Capital	31		1 9 0 5 00
	31	Timothy Sullivan, Capital	31	3 0 0 00	
		Timothy Sullivan, Drawing	32		3 0 0 00

20–2 (1) and (2)

Cash   No. *11*

Date			PR	Dr.	Cr.	Balance Dr.	Balance Cr.
200– Jan	1	Balance	✓			1500 00	
	31		CR2	3650 00		5150 00	
	31		CP3		1790 00	3360 00	

Accounts Receivable   No. *12*

Date			PR	Dr.	Cr.	Balance Dr.	Balance Cr.
200– Jan	1	Balance	✓			500 00	
	31		S2	3200 00		3700 00	
	31		CR2		150 00	3550 00	
	31		J1		35 00	3515 00	

Merchandise Inventory   No. *13*

Date			PR	Dr.	Cr.	Balance Dr.	Balance Cr.
200– Jan	1	Balance	✓			3800 00	
	31		6		3800 00		
	31		6	3950 00		3950 00	

Supplies   No. *14*

Date			PR	Dr.	Cr.	Balance Dr.	Balance Cr.
200– Jan	1	Balance	✓			275 00	
	3		CP2	50 00		325 00	
	31		6		120 00	205 00	

Prepaid Insurance   No. *15*

Date			PR	Dr.	Cr.	Balance Dr.	Balance Cr.
200-Jan	1	Balance	✓			300 00	
	31		6		50 00	250 00	

Accounts Payable   No. *21*

Date			PR	Dr.	Cr.	Balance Dr.	Balance Cr.
200-Jan	1	Balance	✓			500 00	1000 00
	31		P2		120 00	370 00	220 00
	31		CP3	40 00		355 00	180 00

Timothy Sullivan, Capital   No. *31*

Date			PR	Dr.	Cr.	Balance Dr.	Balance Cr.
200-Jan	1	Balance	✓				5375 00
	10		CR3		2500 00		7875 00
	31		6		1905 00		9780 00
	31		6	300 00			9480 00

Timothy Sullivan, Drawing   No. *32*

Date			PR	Dr.	Cr.	Balance Dr.	Balance Cr.
200-Jan	15	Balance	CP2	150 00		150 00	
	30		CP2	150 00		300 00	
	31		6		300 00		

Revenue and Expense Summary — No. 33

Date		PR	Dr.	Cr.	Balance Dr.	Balance Cr.
200- Jan 31		6	3800 00		3800 00	
31		6		3950 00		150 00
31		6		4200 00		4350 00
31		6	2445 00			1905 00
31		6	1905 00			

Sales — No. 41

Date		PR	Dr.	Cr.	Balance Dr.	Balance Cr.
200- Jan 31		S2		3200 00		3200 00
31		CR2		1000 00		4200 00
31		6	4200 00			

Sales Returns and Allowances — No. 41.1

Date		PR	Dr.	Cr.	Balance Dr.	Balance Cr.
200- Jan 20		J2	35 00		35 00	
31		6		35 00		

Purchases — No. 51

Date		PR	Dr.	Cr.	Balance Dr.	Balance Cr.
200- Jan 31		P2	1200 00		1200 00	
31		CP3	500 00		1700 00	
31		6		1700 00		

Advertising Expense   No. 61

Date		PR	Dr.	Cr.	Balance Dr.	Balance Cr.
200- Jan 3		CP2	100 00		100 00	
31		6		100 00		

Insurance Expense   No. 62

Date		PR	Dr.	Cr.	Balance Dr.	Balance Cr.
200- Jan 31		6	50 00		50 00	
31		6		50 00		

Miscellaneous Expense   No. 63

Date		PR	Dr.	Cr.	Balance Dr.	Balance Cr.
200- Jan 12		CP2	25 00		25 00	
27		CP2	15 00		40 00	
31		6		40 00		

Rent Expense   No. 64

Date		PR	Dr.	Cr.	Balance Dr.	Balance Cr.
200- Jan 2		CP2	400 00		400 00	
31		6		400 00		

Supplies Expense   No. 65

Date		PR	Dr.	Cr.	Balance Dr.	Balance Cr.
200- Jan 31		6	120 00		120 00	
31		6		120 00		

20-2 (3)

Timothy Sullivan

Post-closing Trial Balance

January 31, 200-

Cash	3360 00	
Accounts Receivable	3515 00	
Merchandise Inventory	3950 00	
Supplies	205 00	
Prepaid Insurance	250 00	
Accounts Payable		1800 00
Timothy Sullivan, Capital		9480 00
Totals	11280 00	11280 00

316 ANSWERS TO SELECTED QUESTIONS AND PROBLEMS

20-3 (1) and (2)

GENERAL JOURNAL   Page 14

Date		Account Title	PR	Debit	Credit
200- Dec		*Adjusting Entries*			
	31	Revenue & Expense Summary		2232000	
		Merchandise Inventory			2232000
	31	Merchandise Inventory		2319500	
		Revenue & Expense Summary			2319500
	31	Insurance Expense		10000	
		Prepaid Insurance			10000
	31	Supplies Expense		9650	
		Supplies			9650
		Closing Entries			
	31	Sales		5179000	
		Purchases Ret. & Allowances		152900	
		Revenue & Expense Summary			5331900
	31	Revenue & Expense Summary		4434650	
		Sales Ret. & Allowances			257000
		Purchases			3138000
		Advertising Expense			60000
		Insurance Expense			10000
		Rent Expense			360000
		Salary Expense			600000
		Supplies Expense			9650
	31	Revenue & Expense Summary		984750	
		T G Abdullah, Capital			562714
		S H Pahlevi, Capital			422036
	31	T G Abdullah, Capital		1000000	
		S H Pahlevi, Capital		1200000	
		T G Abdullah, Drawing			1000000
		S H Pahlevi, Drawing			1200000

20-3 (3)

Abdullah and Pahlevi									

Post-closing Trial Balance

December 31, 200-

Cash		3625 00			
Accounts Receivable		1826 00			
Merchandise Inventory		23195 00			
Equipment		7500 00			
Prepaid Insurance		400 00			
Supplies		178 50			
Accounts Payable				3105 00	
J G Abdullah, Capital				29429 14	
S H Pahlevi, Capital				20624 36	
Totals		53158 50		53158 50	

Chapter 21

QUESTIONS

1. The frequency of use determines which special columns will be used in a combination journal.
2. The opening cash balance and entries in special columns are checkmarked in the PR column.
3. The column totals are used to prove the equality of debits and credits in a combination journal.
4. All special column totals are posted to the account in the column heading.
5. The General Dr. and Cr. column totals are not posted; they are checkmarked.

PROBLEMS

21-1 (1), (2), and (3)

COMBINATION JOURNAL

Date	Explanation	PR	General Dr.	General Cr.	House Exp. Dr.	Auto Exp. Dr.	Cash Dr.	Cash Cr.	
200- May 1	Balance $1,675	✓							
1	Rent	✓			695 00			695 00	
3	Personal Expenses		37 95					37 95	
5	Gas for Car	✓				14 60		14 60	
8	Electric Bill	✓			79 50			79 50	
10	Food Shopping		63 45					63 45	
12	Household Ins.	✓			108 75			108 75	
15	Salary Income			1048 30			1048 30		
21	Automobile Ins.	✓				355 20		355 20	
24	Food Shopping		59 25					59 25	
25	Personal Expenses		48 95					48 95	
26	Auto tune-up	✓				66 50		66 50	
28	Medical Bill		80 00					80 00	
29	Salary Income			1048 30			1048 30	1048 30	*
30	Charge Accts.		91 85					91 85	
31	Telephone Bill	✓			54 30			54 30	
31	Totals		381 45 / 381 45	2096 60 / 2096 60	937 55 / 937 55	436 30 / 436 30	2096 60 / 2096 60	1755 30 / 1755 30	

* Note error correction

21-2 (1) and (2)

COMBINATION JOURNAL

Date	Explanation	PR	General Dr.	General Cr.	House Exp. Dr.	Medical Exp. Dr.	Cash Dr.	Cash Cr.
200- June 1	Balance $1,162.00	✓						
1	Rent	✓			900 00			900 00
2	Food shopping	✓			68 75			68 75
4	Personal Expense		16 50					16 50
5	Gas & Electric Bill	✓			96 25			96 25
8	Dr's visit & medication	✓				67 50		67 50
12	Food Shopping	✓			72 50			72 50
15	Personal Expenses		38 45					38 45
19	Dr's visit & lab. fee	✓				75 00		75 00
22	Telephone Bill	✓			42 92			42 92
25	Food Shopping	✓			61 47			61 47
27	Paid Stern's Charge		52 50					52 50
29	Donation		25 00					25 00
30	Pay check	✓		2400 00			2400 00	
30	Personal Expenses		15 00					15 00
30	Totals		147 45	2400 00	1241 89	142 50	2400 00	1531 84

21–2 (3)

$2,030.16

21–3 (1), (2), and (3)

21-4 (1), (2), (3), and (4)

COMBINATION JOURNAL

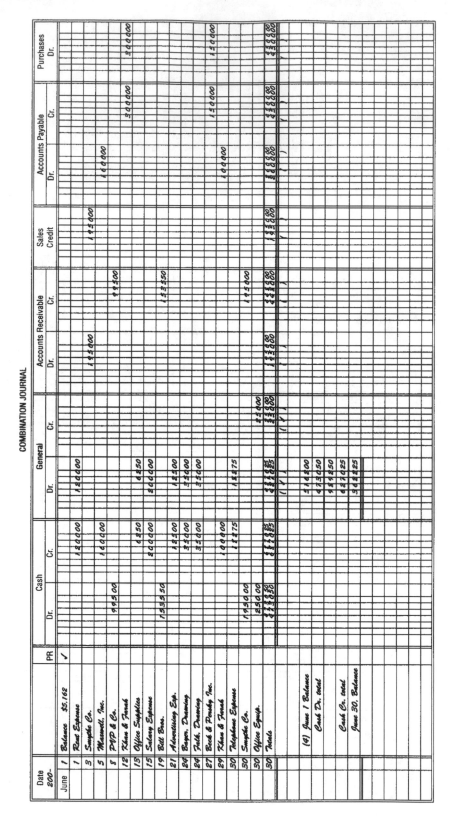

Date 200-		PR	Cash Dr.	Cash Cr.	General Dr.	General Cr.	Accounts Receivable Dr.	Accounts Receivable Cr.	Sales Credit	Accounts Payable Dr.	Accounts Payable Cr.	Purchases Dr.
June 1	Balance $5,162	✓										
1	Rent Expense			120000	120000							
3	Sample Co.											
5	Maxwell, Inc.			100000			112000		112000	100000		
8	PMP & Co.		99500					99500				
12	Khan & Furak										200000	200000
13	Office Supplies			6250	6250							
15	Salary Expense			200000	200000							
19	Bell Bros.		153550					153550				
21	Advertising Exp.			12500	12500							
24	Bayen, Drawing			35000	35000							
24	Falik, Drawing			35000	35000							
27	Best & Pimsley Inc.									100000	150000	150000
29	Khan & Furak			100000	100000							
30	Telephone Expense			18875	18875							
30	Sample Co.		195000					152000				
30	Office Equip.		250			22000						
30	Totals		448300	627885	627885	193000	193000	193000	193000	200000	350000	350000
(4) June 1	Balance				516200							
	Cash Dr. total				473050							
					989250							
	Cash Cr. total				627025							
	June 30. Balance				362225							

Cycle Two Examination

Part I

1.	T	11.	F
2.	T	12.	T
3.	T	13.	F
4.	F	14.	F
5.	F	15.	T
6.	T	16.	F
7.	T	17.	F
8.	F	18.	T
9.	F	19.	T
10.	T	20.	T

Part II

1.	M	6.	F
2.	J	7.	L
3.	N	8.	A
4.	C	9.	B
5.	H	10.	O

Part III (1)

GENERAL JOURNAL   Page 3

Date		PR	General Dr.	General Cr.	Accts. Pay. Dr.	Accts. Rec. Cr.
200- June 8	Jordan Glaser, Drawing		50 00			
	Purchases			50 00		
	Withdraw Merchandise					
18	Sales Returns and Allowances		15 00			
	Dr. George Tyler					15 00
30	Totals		65 00	50 00		15 00
			(✓)	(✓)	⟶	( )

Part III (1)

PURCHASES JOURNAL   Page 3

Date	Account Credited			PR	Purchases Dr. Accts. Pay. Cr.
200- June 3	J.L. Rossini Company				5 0 0 00
29	Fred Pulaski Wholesalers, Inc.				3 0 0 00
30	Total				8 0 0 00
					( ) ( )

Part III (1)

SALES JOURNAL

Page 3

Date		Account Debited		PR	Accts. Rec. Dr. Sales Cr.
200- June	5	Dr. George Tyler			1 6 5 00
	26	Sona Parisian			1 2 5 00
	30	Total			2 9 0 00
					( ) ( )

Part III (1)

CASH RECEIPTS JOURNAL

Page 4

Date			PR	General Cr.	Accts. Rec. Cr.	Sales Cr.	Cash Dr.
200- June	1	Balance on hand $2,500	✓				
	15	Sales	✓			2 9 5 0 00	2 9 5 0 00
	22	Dr. George Tyler			1 5 0 00		1 5 0 00
	30	Sales	✓			3 7 5 0 00	3 7 5 0 00
	30	Totals			1 5 0 00	6 7 0 0 00	6 8 5 0 00
				(✓)	( )	( )	( )

Part III (1)

CASH DISBURSEMENTS JOURNAL

Page 3

Date			Ck. No.	PR	General Dr.	Accts. Pay. Dr.	Purchases Dr.	Salary Exp. Dr.	Cash Cr.
200- June	1	Rent Expense	147		3 7 5 00				3 7 5 00
	10	J.L. Rossini Company	148			5 0 0 00			5 0 0 00
	19	Telephone (Utilities) Expense	149		4 6 00				4 6 00
	30	Totals			4 2 1 00	5 0 0 00			9 2 1 00
					(✓)	( )			( )

Part IV (1)

Fowler's Crystal Palace

Income Statement

For Year Ended December 31, 200-

Income:			
Sales		40590 00	
Less Sales Returns and Allowances		1875 00	
Net Sales			38715 00
Cost of Goods Sold:			
Merchandise Inventory, Jan. 1		10790 00	
Purchases	21,630.00		
Less Purchases Ret. & Allow.	795.00		
Net Purchases		20835 00	
Merchandise Available for Sale		31625 00	
Less Merchandise Inventory, Dec. 31		12080 00	
Cost of Goods Sold			19545 00
Gross Profit on Sales			19170 00
Expenses:			
Advertising Expense		1800 00	
Insurance Expense		500 00	
Miscellaneous Expense		840 00	
Rent Expense		3000 00	
Salary Expense		6000 00	
Supplies Expense		820 00	
Total Expense			11160 00
Net Income			8010 00

Part IV (2)

Fowler's Crystal Palace

Capital Statement

For Year Ended December 31, 200-

Beginning Balance, Jan. 1			25525 00
Additional Investment			1000 00
			26525 00
Less: Withdrawals		12000 00	
Less Net Income		8010 00	
Decrease in Capital			3990 00
Ending Balance, Dec. 31			22535 00

Part IV (3)

Fowler's Crystal Palace

Balance Sheet

December 31, 200-

Assets			
Cash		8400 00	
Accounts Receivable		3850 00	
Merchandise Inventory		12080 00	
Furniture and Fixtures		8500 00	
Prepaid Insurance		100 00	
Supplies		105 00	
Total Assets			27035 00
Liabilities			
Accounts Payable			4500 00
Owner's Equity			
Dina Fowler, Capital			22535 00
Total Liabilities and Owner's Equity			27035 00

Part IV (4)   GENERAL JOURNAL   Page

Date			PR	General Dr.	General Cr.	Accts. Pay. Dr.	Accts. Rec. Cr.
200- Dec.		*Adjusting Entries*					
	31	*Revenue and Expense Summary*		1079 00			
		Merchandise Inventory			1079 00		
	31	*Merchandise Inventory*		1208 00			
		Revenue and Expense Summary			1208 00		
	31	*Insurance Expense*		50 00			
		Prepaid Insurance			50 00		
	31	*Supplies Expense*		220 00			
		Supplies			220 00		
		Closing Entries					
	31	*Sales*		4059 00			
		Purchases Returns and Allowances		795 00			
		Revenue and Expense Summary			4385 00		
	31	*Revenue and Expense Summary*		3465 00			
		Sales Returns and Allowances			1875 00		
		Purchases			8163 00		
		Advertising Expense			1200 00		
		Insurance Expense			50 00		
		Miscellaneous Expense			240 00		
		Rent Expense			3000 00		
		Salary Expense			6000 00		
		Supplies Expense			220 00		
	31	*Revenue and Expense Summary*		8010 00			
		Dina Fowler, Capital			8010 00		
	31	*Dina Fowler, Capital*		12000 00			
		Dina Fowler, Drawing			12000 00		

INDEX

Accounting cycle, 78
Accounts, 9
  adjusting, 197–199
  balances, opening, 24
  balancing, 76–78
  capital, 78
  checking, 91–99
  closed, 76–78
  closing, 199–200
  controlling, 119, 122
  cost, 199
  creditors', posting, 120
  decreasing, 10–11
  drawing, 31–32, 199
  expense, 199
  forms, 15–16, 23
  increasing, 10–11
  number, 45–46
  open, 76–78
  payable, 3–4, 119–120
    schedule, 122, 132
  posting to, 148
  purchasing, 119
  receivable, 3–4
    ledger, 137–138
  revenue, 31, 199
  ruling, 76–78
  sales, 137
  statement, 159, 162
  "T" form, 23
  transactions:
    decreasing, 10–11
    increasing, 10–11
  valuation, 160, 163
Adjusting:
  accounts, 197–199
  entries, 171, 197–199
  general ledger, 197–205
Adjustments, 171–172
Allowances, 159–163
Articles of Partnership, 185
Assets, 3–8, 15, 200
  business, 3–4
  changes in, rules for, 24–25
  claims against, 15
  definition, 3
  family, 4
  personal, 3–4
  total, 16

Balance, 23, 47
  cash, verify, 207, 210–211

check stub, 94–95
credit, 74
debit, 74
post-closing trial, 73, 78, 197, 200–201
sheet, 15–21, 187
  content, 15–16, 66
  form, 15–16, 66
  purpose, 15–16
trial, 45, 47–48, 55–62, 171
Balances:
  opening, 24
  updated, extending, 172
Balancing accounts, 76–78
Bank reconciliation, 91
  statement, 94–95
Book of original entry, 39–40, 123
Bookkeeping cycle, 78
Business:
  assets, 3–4
  liabilities, 4–5
  transactions, 9–13

Canceled checks, 94
Capital, 5, 15, 74, 201
  account, 78
  statement, 63–66, 185–186
Cash:
  balance, verify, 207, 210–211
  disbursements journal, 129–136
    summarizing, 130–131
    source documents, 133
  petty, 101–108
    proving, 103
    replenish, 101, 103–104
  receipts journal, 147–158
    definition, 147
    expanding, 151–152
    posting to accounts, 148
    purpose, 147–148
    source documents, 152
    summarizing, 148–150
  systems, 91–99
Charge purchase, 41
Check stub, 93
  balance, 94
Checking accounts, 91–99
  opening, 91
Checks:
  canceled, 94
  drawing, 93
  endorsing, 91–92
  outstanding, 94

Chronological order, 40, 43
Closing:
    accounts, 199–200
    entry, 73–75, 197, 199
    general ledger, 197–205
    the ledger, 73–89
Columnar journal, 129–130
Combination journal, 207–216
    business use, 208–209
    personal use, 207–208
Compound entry, 39, 41
Controlling account, 119, 122
Correcting entry, 159, 161
Correcting errors in ledger postings, 161–162
Cost:
    accounts, 199
    of goods sold, 185
    of merchandise, 119
Credit, 23
    balance, 74
    memorandum, 160
Creditor, 15
Creditors' accounts, posting, 120
Credits, 199
    and debits, equality of, 25–26
    rules of, 25–26
Cross referencing, 45, 47
Cycle, accounting, 78

Debit, 23, 199
    balance, 74
    and credits, equality of, 25–26
    memorandum, 161
    rules of, 25–26
Decreasing accounts, 10–11
Deposit in transit, 94
Detail audit tape, 147, 152
Direct ledger bookkeeping, 39
Disbursement, petty cash, 101–103
Double-entry bookkeeping, 23, 25–26
Drawee, 91
Drawer, 91
Drawing:
    account, 31–32, 199
    checks, 93

Eight-column work sheet, 171–182
Ending date, 56
Endorsement, 91
    full, 92
    in blank, 91
    qualified, 92
    restrictive, 92
    special, 92
Entry:
    closing, 73–75, 197, 199
    compound, 39, 41
    correcting, 159, 161
    original, book of, 39–40
    simple, 39, 41
Equality of debits and credits, proving, 25–26
Equation, fundamental, 5–13, 16–17
Equity, owner's, 3–8, 31–37, 78, 187
    changes in, 17, 24–25
    definition, 5
    revenue, 32

Errors:
    ledger postings, correcting, 161–162
    locating, 55–56
Expense:
    accounts, 199
    summary, 73–76, 78
Expenses, 31, 33, 63–64
    effect on owner's equity, 32
    prepaid, 171–172
Extending updated balances, 172

Family assets, 4
Financial condition, 16
Financial statements, 63–72, 183–195
Fiscal period, 15, 17
Footing, 45, 47
Forms:
    account, 15–16, 23
    balance sheet, 15–16, 66
    report, 187
    "T," 23
Full endorsement, 92
Fundamental bookkeeping equation, 5–13, 16–17

General journal:
    four-column format, 159–169
    posting, 45–54
    two-column, 39–44
General ledger, 120–122
    adjusting, 197–205
    closing, 197–205
Goods sold, cost of, 185
Gross profit, 185

In balance, 47, 55
Income, 31, 33
    statement, 56, 63, 184–185
Increasing accounts, 10–11
Inventory, merchandise, 172
    cost of goods sold, 185
Investment, 9–10
Invoice, 120

Journal:
    columnar, 129–130
    combination, 207–216
        business use, 208–209
        personal use, 207–208
    definition, 39
    disbursements, 129–136
        source documents, 133
        summarizing, 130–131
    general:
        four-column format, 159–169
        posting, 45–54
        two-column, 39–44
    purchases, 119–122
    receipts, 147–158
        definition, 147
        expanding, 151–152
        posting to accounts, 148
        purpose, 147–148
        source documents, 152
        summarizing, 148–150
    sales, 137–140
Journalizing, 42–43

Late deposit, 94
Ledger, 23–29
 closing, 73–89
Liabilities, 3–8, 15, 201
 business, 4–5
 changes in, rules for, 24–25
 definition, 4
 personal, 4–5
 total, 16

Memorandum, 159
Merchandise:
 inventory, 172
 purchases, 119–128
 sales, 137–146

Net:
 decrease, 65
 income, 31–32, 56–57, 63–64, 74
  determining, 172, 185
 increase, 65
 loss, 31–32, 56, 63–64, 74
  determining, 172, 185
 purchases, 185
 sales, 185
 worth, 5, 15

On account, 119
Open accounts, 76–78
Original entry, book of, 39–40
Out of balance, 55
Outstanding checks, 94
Overdrawn, 95
Owner's equity, 3–8, 31–37, 78, 187
 changes in, 17, 24–25
 definition, 5
 revenue, 32

Partnership, 171, 173–174
 articles of, 185
Payee, 91
Pencil footing, 47
Personal:
 assets, 3–4
 liabilities, 4–5
Petty cash fund, 101–108
 definition, 101
 disbursements, 102–103
 establishing, 101–102
 proving, 103
 purpose, 101
 replenishing, 103–104
Post-closing-trial balance, 73, 78, 197,
 200–201
Posting, 45
 creditors' accounts, 120
 procedure, 45–47
 sales journal, 138–140
Prepaid expenses, 171–172
Profit, 31
Proprietorship, 5
Proving petty cash, 103
Purchases:
 journal, 119–122
  summarizing, 120–122

 merchandise, 119–128
 returns, 159–163
Purchasing, on account, 119

Qualified endorsement, 92

Reconciliation, bank statements, 94–95
Replenish, petty cash, 101, 103–104
Report form, 187
Restrictive endorsement, 92
Returns, 159–163
Revenue, 31, 63–64
 accounts, 31, 199
 effect on owner's equity, 32
 summary, 73–76, 78
Rules of debits and credits, 25–26
Ruling accounts, 76–78

Sales:
 journal, 137–140
  posting, 138–140
  source documents, 138
  summarizing, 138–140
 of merchandise, 137–146
 on accounts, 137
 returns 159–163
  source documents, 160
Schedule of:
 accounts payable, 119, 122, 132
 accounts receivable, 137, 140, 151
Simple entry, 39, 41
Source documents, 40–41, 120
 cash disbursements, 133
 cash receipts, 152
 sales journal, 138
 sales returns, 160
Special:
 columns, 129
 endorsement, 92
Statement of account, 159, 162
Subsidiary ledger, 120
Summarizing, sales journal, 138–140
Supplies, 172

T-Account, 23
Total:
 assets, 16
 liabilities, 16
Transaction, evidence of, 39
Transactions, business, 9–13
Trial balance, 45, 47–48, 55-62, 171
 post-closing, 73, 78

Updated balances, extending, 172

Valuation accounts, 160, 163
Verify cash balance, 207, 210–211
Voucher, 39–40, 101

Withdrawals, 32–33
Work sheet, 55–62
 six-column, 56–57

Zero out, 74, 199